# Blockchain and Cryptocurrencies

# Blockchain and Cryptocurrencies

**Demian Presser**
**Sandra Cutts**

Kruger Brentt
Publishers

2025

Kruger Brentt Publishers UK. LTD.
Company Number 9728962

Regd. Office: 68 St Margarets Road, Edgware, Middlesex HA8 9UU



ISBN: 978-1-78715-369-1

*Disclaimer:*

*Every possible effort has been made to ensure that the information contained in this book is accurate at the time of going to press, and the publisher and author cannot accept responsibility for any errors or omissions, however caused. No responsibility for loss or damage occasioned to any person acting, or refraining from action, as a result of the material in this publication can be accepted by the editor, the publisher or the author. The Publisher is not associated with any product or vendor mentioned in the book. The contents of this work are intended to further general scientific research, understanding and discussion only. Readers should consult with a specialist where appropriate.*

*Every effort has been made to trace the owners of copyright material used in this book, if any. The author and the publisher will be grateful for any omission brought to their notice for acknowledgement in the future editions of the book.*



For information on all our publications visit our website at http://krugerbrentt.com/

# PREFACE

Blockchain technology serves as the foundational framework underpinning cryptocurrencies and various other applications beyond digital currencies. At its core, blockchain is a distributed ledger that records transactions across a network of computers in a secure, transparent, and immutable manner. Each transaction is grouped into a "block," which is cryptographically linked to previous blocks, forming a chronological chain of blocks, hence the term "blockchain." This decentralized architecture ensures data integrity, transparency, and resilience, making it resistant to tampering and fraud.

Cryptocurrencies are digital or virtual currencies that leverage blockchain technology to enable secure peer-to-peer transactions without the need for intermediaries such as banks or governments. Bitcoin, the first and most well-known cryptocurrency, introduced the concept of decentralized digital currency, paving the way for the emergence of thousands of alternative cryptocurrencies, often referred to as "altcoins." These digital assets are typically secured by cryptographic techniques and utilize decentralized consensus mechanisms to validate and record transactions on the blockchain.

Unlike traditional centralized systems, blockchain networks operate in a decentralized manner, with no single point of control or authority. This decentralization ensures greater transparency, censorship resistance, and resilience to single points of failure. Consensus mechanisms such as proof-of-work (PoW), proof-of-stake (PoS), and delegated proof-of-stake (DPoS) are used to achieve agreement on the validity of transactions and the ordering of blocks in the blockchain. These mechanisms ensure network security and integrity without relying on centralized authorities. Cryptography plays a crucial role in securing transactions, protecting user privacy, and ensuring data integrity on the blockchain. Cryptographic techniques such as hashing, digital signatures, and encryption are used to authenticate users, verify transactions, and prevent unauthorized access to data. The blockchain serves as an immutable ledger, meaning that once a transaction is recorded on the blockchain, it cannot be altered or deleted. This immutability ensures the integrity and trustworthiness of the transaction history, making blockchain an ideal solution for applications requiring transparent and tamper-proof record-keeping.

Blockchain technology offers robust security features, including cryptographic encryption, decentralized consensus, and tamper-resistant data storage, making it highly secure against hacking, fraud, and manipulation. The transparent nature of blockchain enables users to trace the entire transaction history of a particular asset, providing greater transparency and accountability in financial transactions and supply chains. By eliminating intermediaries and streamlining processes, blockchain can significantly reduce costs, transaction times, and operational inefficiencies in various industries, such as finance, logistics, and healthcare. Cryptocurrencies have the potential to increase financial inclusion by providing access to financial services for unbanked and underbanked populations worldwide, enabling them to participate in the global economy.

Blockchain networks often struggle to scale to accommodate growing transaction volumes, leading to congestion, high fees, and slow transaction times. The regulatory landscape surrounding blockchain and cryptocurrencies is complex and rapidly evolving, posing challenges for businesses, investors, and policymakers. Cryptocurrency markets are notoriously volatile, with prices subject to rapid fluctuations driven by speculation, market sentiment, and regulatory developments. The energy-intensive process of mining cryptocurrencies, particularly Bitcoin, has raised concerns about its environmental impact and sustainability.

**Demian Presser**
**Sandra Cutts**

# CONTENTS

# CHAPTER 1

# INTRODUCTION TO BLOCKCHAIN TECHNOLOGY

## 1.1 DEFINITION AND CONCEPT OF BLOCKCHAIN

A blockchain is a distributed ledger with growing lists of records (*blocks*) that are securely linked together via cryptographic hashes. Each block contains a cryptographic hash of the previous block, a timestamp, and transaction data (generally represented as a Merkle tree, where data nodes are represented by leaves). Since each block contains information about the previous block, they effectively form a *chain* (compare linked list data structure), with each additional block linking to the ones before it. Consequently, blockchain transactions are irreversible in that, once they are recorded, the data in any given block cannot be altered retroactively without altering all subsequent blocks.

Blockchains are typically managed by a peer-to-peer (P2P) computer network for use as a public distributed ledger, where nodes collectively adhere to a consensus algorithm protocol to add and validate new transaction blocks. Although blockchain records are not unalterable, since blockchain forks are possible, blockchains may be considered secure by design and exemplify a distributed computing system with high Byzantine fault tolerance.

A blockchain was created by a person (or group of people) using the name (or pseudonym) Satoshi Nakamoto in 2008 to serve as the public distributed ledger for bitcoin cryptocurrency transactions, based on previous work by Stuart Haber, W. Scott Stornetta, and Dave Bayer. The implementation of the blockchain within bitcoin made it the first digital currency to solve the double-spending problem without the need for a trusted authority or central server. The bitcoin design has inspired other applications and blockchains that are readable by the public and are widely used by cryptocurrencies. The blockchain may be considered a type of payment rail.

Private blockchains have been proposed for business use. *Computerworld* called the marketing of such privatized blockchains without a proper security model "snake oil"; however, others have argued that permissioned blockchains, if carefully designed, may be more decentralized and therefore more secure in practice than permissionless ones.

### 1.1.1 Structure and Design

A blockchain is a decentralized, distributed, and often public, digital ledger consisting of records called *blocks* that are used to record transactions across many computers so that any involved block cannot be altered retroactively, without the alteration of all subsequent blocks. This allows the participants to verify and audit transactions independently and relatively inexpensively. A blockchain database is managed autonomously using a peer-to-peer network and a distributed timestamping server. They are authenticated by mass collaboration powered by collective self-interests. Such a design facilitates robust workflow where participants' uncertainty regarding data security is marginal. The use of a blockchain removes the characteristic of infinite reproducibility from a digital asset. It confirms that each unit of value was transferred only once, solving the long-standing problem of double-spending. A blockchain has been described as a *value-exchange protocol.* A blockchain can maintain title rights because, when properly set up to detail the exchange agreement, it provides a record that compels offer and acceptance.

Logically, a blockchain can be seen as consisting of several layers:

- infrastructure (hardware);
- networking (node discovery, information propagation and verification);
- consensus (proof of work, proof of stake);
- data (blocks, transactions); and
- application (smart contracts/decentralized applications, if applicable).

#### Blocks

Blocks hold batches of valid transactions that are hashed and encoded into a Merkle tree. Each block includes the cryptographic hash of the prior block in the blockchain, linking the two. The linked blocks form a chain. This iterative process confirms the integrity of the previous block, all the way back to the initial block, which is known as the *genesis block* (Block 0). To assure the integrity of a block and the data contained in it, the block is usually digitally signed.

Sometimes separate blocks can be produced concurrently, creating a temporary fork. In addition to a secure hash-based history, any blockchain has a specified algorithm for scoring different versions of the history so that one with a higher score can be selected over others. Blocks not selected for inclusion in the chain are called orphan blocks. Peers supporting the database have different versions of the history from time to time. They keep only the highest-scoring version of the database known to them. Whenever a peer receives a higher-scoring version (usually the old version with a single new block added) they extend or overwrite their own database and retransmit the improvement to their peers. There is never an absolute guarantee that any particular entry will remain in the best version of history forever. Blockchains are typically built to add the score of new blocks onto old blocks and are given incentives to extend with new blocks rather than overwrite old blocks. Therefore, the probability of an entry becoming superseded decreases exponentially as more blocks are built on top of it, eventually becoming very low. For example, bitcoin uses a proof-of-work system, where the chain with the most cumulative proof-of-work is considered the valid one by the network. There are a number of methods that can be used to demonstrate a sufficient level of computation. Within a blockchain the computation is carried out redundantly rather than in the traditional segregated and parallel manner.

### Block Time

The *block time* is the average time it takes for the network to generate one extra block in the blockchain. By the time of block completion, the included data becomes verifiable. In cryptocurrency, this is practically when the transaction takes place, so a shorter block time means faster transactions. The block time for Ethereum is set to between 14 and 15 seconds, while for bitcoin it is on average 10 minutes.

## Decentralization

By storing data across its peer-to-peer network, the blockchain eliminates some risks that come with data being held centrally. The decentralized blockchain may use ad hoc message passing and distributed networking.

In a so-called "51% attack" a central entity gains control of more than half of a network and can then manipulate that specific blockchain record at will, allowing double-spending.

Blockchain security methods include the use of public-key cryptography. A *public key* (a long, random-looking string of numbers) is an address on the blockchain. Value tokens sent across the network are recorded as belonging to that address. A *private key* is like a password that gives its owner access to their digital assets or the means to otherwise interact with the various capabilities that blockchains now support. Data stored on the blockchain is generally considered incorruptible.

Every node in a decentralized system has a copy of the blockchain. Data quality is maintained by massive database replication and computational trust. No centralized "official" copy exists and no user is "trusted" more than any other. Transactions are broadcast to the network using the software. Messages are delivered on a best-effort basis. Early blockchains rely on energy-intensive mining nodes to validate transactions, add them to the block they are building, and then broadcast the completed block to other nodes. Blockchains use various time-stamping schemes, such as proof-of-work, to serialize changes. Later consensus methods include proof of stake. The growth of a decentralized blockchain is accompanied by the risk of centralization because the computer resources required to process larger amounts of data become more expensive.

### Finality

Finality is the level of confidence that the well-formed block recently appended to the blockchain will not be revoked in the future (is "finalized") and thus can be trusted. Most distributed blockchain protocols, whether proof of work or proof of stake, cannot guarantee the finality of a freshly committed block, and instead rely on "probabilistic finality": as the block goes deeper into a blockchain, it is less likely to be altered or reverted by a newly found consensus.

Byzantine fault tolerance-based proof-of-stake protocols purport to provide so called "absolute finality": a randomly chosen validator proposes a block, the rest of validators vote on it, and, if a supermajority decision approves it, the block is irreversibly committed into the blockchain. A modification of this method, an "economic finality", is used in practical protocols, like the Casper protocol used in Ethereum: validators which sign two different blocks at the same position in the blockchain are subject to "slashing", where their leveraged stake is forfeited.

### Openness

Open blockchains are more user-friendly than some traditional ownership records, which, while open to the public, still require physical access to view. Because all early blockchains were permissionless, controversy has arisen over the blockchain definition. An issue in this ongoing debate is whether a private system with verifiers tasked and authorized (permissioned) by a central authority should be considered a blockchain. Proponents of permissioned or private chains argue that the term "blockchain" may be applied to any data structure that batches data into time-stamped blocks. These blockchains serve as a distributed version of multiversion concurrency control (MVCC) in databases. Just as MVCC prevents two transactions from concurrently modifying a single object in a database, blockchains prevent two transactions from spending the same single output in a blockchain. Opponents say that permissioned systems resemble traditional corporate databases, not supporting decentralized data verification, and that such systems are not hardened against operator tampering and revision. Nikolai Hampton of *Computerworld* said that "many in-house blockchain solutions will be nothing more than cumbersome databases," and "without a clear security model, proprietary blockchains should be eyed with suspicion."

### Permissionless (Public) Blockchain

An advantage to an open, permissionless, or public, blockchain network is that guarding against bad actors is not required and no access control is needed. This means that applications can be added to the network without the approval or trust of others, using the blockchain as a transport layer.

Bitcoin and other cryptocurrencies currently secure their blockchain by requiring new entries to include proof of work. To prolong the blockchain, bitcoin uses Hashcash puzzles. While Hashcash was designed in 1997 by Adam Back, the original idea was first proposed by Cynthia Dwork and Moni Naor and Eli Ponyatovski in their 1992 paper "Pricing via Processing or Combatting Junk Mail".

In 2016, venture capital investment for blockchain-related projects was weakening in the USA but increasing in China. Bitcoin and many other cryptocurrencies use open (public) blockchains. As of April 2018, bitcoin has the highest market capitalization.

### Permissioned (Private) Blockchain

Permissioned blockchains use an access control layer to govern who has access to the network. It has been argued that permissioned blockchains can guarantee a certain level of decentralization, if carefully designed, as opposed to permissionless blockchains, which are often centralized in practice.

### Disadvantages of Permissioned Blockchain

Nikolai Hampton argued in *Computerworld* that "There is also no need for a '51 percent' attack on a private blockchain, as the private blockchain (most likely) already controls 100 percent of all block creation resources. If you could attack or damage the blockchain creation tools on a private corporate server, you could effectively control 100 percent of their network and alter transactions however you wished." This has a set of particularly profound adverse implications during a financial crisis or debt crisis like the financial crisis of 2007–08, where politically powerful actors may make decisions that favor some groups at the expense of others, and "the bitcoin blockchain is protected by the massive group mining effort. It's unlikely that any private blockchain will try to protect records using gigawatts of computing power — it's time-consuming and expensive." He also said, "Within a private blockchain there is also no 'race'; there's no incentive to use more power or discover blocks faster than competitors. This means that many in-house blockchain solutions will be nothing more than cumbersome databases."

### Blockchain Analysis

The analysis of public blockchains has become increasingly important with the popularity of bitcoin, Ethereum, litecoin and other cryptocurrencies. A blockchain, if it is public, provides anyone who wants access to observe and analyse the chain data, given one has the know-how. The process of understanding and accessing the flow of crypto has been an issue for many cryptocurrencies, crypto exchanges and banks. The reason for this is accusations of blockchain-enabled cryptocurrencies enabling illicit dark market trade of drugs, weapons, money laundering, etc. A common belief has been that cryptocurrency is private and untraceable, thus leading many actors to use it for illegal purposes. This is changing and now specialised tech companies provide blockchain tracking services, making crypto exchanges, law-enforcement and banks more aware of what is happening with crypto funds and fiat-crypto exchanges. The development, some argue, has led criminals to prioritise the use of new cryptos such as Monero.

### Standardisation

In April 2016, Standards Australia submitted a proposal to the International Organization for Standardization to consider developing standards to support blockchain technology. This proposal resulted in the creation of ISO Technical Committee 307, Blockchain and Distributed Ledger Technologies. The technical committee has working groups relating to blockchain terminology, reference architecture, security and privacy, identity, smart contracts, governance and interoperability for blockchain and DLT, as well as standards specific to industry sectors and generic government requirements.

More than 50 countries are participating in the standardization process together with external liaisons such as the Society for Worldwide Interbank Financial Telecommunication (SWIFT), the European Commission, the International Federation of Surveyors, the International Telecommunication Union (ITU) and the United Nations Economic Commission for Europe (UNECE).

Many other national standards bodies and open standards bodies are also working on blockchain standards. These include the National Institute of Standards and Technology (NIST), the European Committee for Electrotechnical Standardization (CENELEC), the Institute of Electrical and Electronics Engineers (IEEE), the Organization for the Advancement of Structured Information Standards (OASIS), and some individual participants in the Internet Engineering Task Force (IETF).

### Centralized Blockchain

Although most of blockchain implementation are decentralized and distributed, Oracle launched a centralized blockchain table feature in Oracle 21c database. The Blockchain Table in Oracle 21c database is a centralized blockchain which provide immutable feature. Compared to decentralized blockchains, centralized blockchains normally can provide a higher throughput and lower latency of transactions than consensus-based distributed blockchains.

## 1.1.2 Types

Currently, there are at least four types of blockchain networks — public blockchains, private blockchains, consortium blockchains and hybrid blockchains.

### Public Blockchains

A public blockchain has absolutely no access restrictions. Anyone with an Internet connection can send transactions to it as well as become a validator (i.e., participate in the execution of a consensus protocol). Usually, such networks offer economic incentives for those who secure them and utilize some type of a proof-of-stake or proof-of-work algorithm. Some of the largest, most known public blockchains are the bitcoin blockchain and the Ethereum blockchain.

### Private Blockchains

A private blockchain is permissioned. One cannot join it unless invited by the network administrators. Participant and validator access is restricted. To distinguish between open blockchains and other peer-to-peer decentralized database applications that are not open ad-hoc compute clusters, the terminology Distributed Ledger (DLT) is normally used for private blockchains.

### Hybrid Blockchains

A hybrid blockchain has a combination of centralized and decentralized features. The exact workings of the chain can vary based on which portions of centralization and decentralization are used.

### Sidechains

A sidechain is a designation for a blockchain ledger that runs in parallel to a primary blockchain. Entries from the primary blockchain (where said entries typically represent digital assets) can be linked to and from the sidechain; this allows the sidechain to otherwise operate independently of the primary blockchain (e.g., by using an alternate means of record keeping, alternate consensus algorithm, etc.).

### Consortium Blockchain

A consortium blockchain is a type of blockchain that combines elements of both public and private blockchains. In a consortium blockchain, a group of organizations come together to create and operate the blockchain, rather than a single entity. The consortium members jointly manage the blockchain network and are responsible for validating transactions. Consortium blockchains are permissioned, meaning that only certain individuals or organizations are allowed to participate in the network. This allows for greater control over who can access the blockchain and helps to ensure that sensitive information is kept confidential.

Consortium blockchains are commonly used in industries where multiple organizations need to collaborate on a common goal, such as supply chain management or financial services. One advantage of consortium blockchains is that they can be more efficient and scalable than public blockchains, as the number of nodes required to validate transactions is typically smaller. Additionally, consortium blockchains can provide greater security and reliability than private blockchains, as the consortium members work together to maintain the network. Some examples of consortium blockchains include Quorum and Hyperledger.

### 1.1.3 Uses

Blockchain technology can be integrated into multiple areas. The primary use of blockchains is as a distributed ledger for cryptocurrencies such as bitcoin; there were also a few other operational products that had matured from proof of concept by late 2016. As of 2016, some businesses have been testing the technology and conducting low-level implementation to gauge blockchain's effects on organizational efficiency in their back office.

In 2019, it was estimated that around $2.9 billion were invested in blockchain technology, which represents an 89% increase from the year prior. Additionally, the International Data Corp has estimated that corporate investment into blockchain technology will reach $12.4 billion by 2022. Furthermore, According to PricewaterhouseCoopers (PwC), the second-largest professional services network in the world, blockchain technology has the potential to generate an annual business value of more than $3 trillion by 2030. PwC's estimate is further augmented by a 2018 study that they have conducted, in which PwC surveyed 600 business executives and determined that 84% have at least some exposure to utilizing blockchain technology, which indicates a significant demand and interest in blockchain technology.

In 2019, the BBC World Service radio and podcast series *Fifty Things That Made the Modern Economy* identified blockchain as a technology that would have far-reaching consequences for economics and society. The economist and *Financial Times* journalist and broadcaster Tim Harford discussed why the underlying technology might have much wider applications and the challenges that needed to be overcome. His first broadcast was on June 29, 2019.

The number of blockchain wallets quadrupled to 40 million between 2016 and 2020. A paper published in 2022 discussed the potential use of blockchain technology in sustainable management.

#### Cryptocurrencies

Most cryptocurrencies use blockchain technology to record transactions. For example, the bitcoin network and Ethereum network are both based on blockchain. The criminal enterprise Silk Road, which operated on Tor, utilized cryptocurrency for payments, some of which the US federal government has seized through research on the blockchain and forfeiture. Governments have mixed policies on the legality of their citizens or banks owning cryptocurrencies. China implements blockchain technology in several industries including a national digital currency which launched in 2020. To strengthen their respective currencies, Western governments including the European Union and the United States have initiated similar projects.

## Smart Contracts

Blockchain-based smart contracts are contracts that can be partially or fully executed or enforced without human interaction. One of the main objectives of a smart contract is automated escrow.

A key feature of smart contracts is that they do not need a trusted third party (such as a trustee) to act as an intermediary between contracting entities — the blockchain network executes the contract on its own. This may reduce friction between entities when transferring value and could subsequently open the door to a higher level of transaction automation. An IMF staff discussion from 2018 reported that smart contracts based on blockchain technology might reduce moral hazards and optimize the use of contracts in general. But "no viable smart contract systems have yet emerged." Due to the lack of widespread use, their legal status was unclear.

## Financial Services

According to *Reason*, many banks have expressed interest in implementing distributed ledgers for use in banking and are cooperating with companies creating private blockchains, and according to a September 2016 IBM study, this is occurring faster than expected.

Banks are interested in this technology not least because it has the potential to speed up back office settlement systems. Moreover, as the blockchain industry has reached early maturity institutional appreciation has grown that it is, practically speaking, the infrastructure of a whole new financial industry, with all the implications which that entails.

Banks such as UBS are opening new research labs dedicated to blockchain technology in order to explore how blockchain can be used in financial services to increase efficiency and reduce costs. Berenberg, a German bank, believes that blockchain is an "overhyped technology" that has had a large number of "proofs of concept", but still has major challenges, and very few success stories.

The blockchain has also given rise to initial coin offerings (ICOs) as well as a new category of digital asset called security token offerings (STOs), also sometimes referred to as digital security offerings (DSOs). STO/DSOs may be conducted privately or on public, regulated stock exchange and are used to tokenize traditional assets such as company shares as well as more innovative ones like intellectual property, real estate, art, or individual products. A number of companies are active in this space providing services for compliant tokenization, private STOs, and public STOs.

## Games

Blockchain technology, such as cryptocurrencies and non-fungible tokens (NFTs), has been used in video games for monetization. Many live-service games offer in-game customization options, such as character skins or other in-game items, which the players can earn and trade with other players using in-game currency. Some games also allow for trading of virtual items using real-world currency, but this may be illegal in some countries where video games are seen as akin to gambling, and has led to gray market issues such as skin gambling, and thus publishers typically have shied away from allowing players to earn real-world funds from games. Blockchain games typically allow players to trade these in-game items for cryptocurrency, which can then be exchanged for money.

The first known game to use blockchain technologies was *CryptoKitties*, launched in November 2017, where the player would purchase NFTs with Ethereum cryptocurrency, each NFT consisting of a virtual pet that the player could breed with others to create offspring with combined traits as new NFTs.

The game made headlines in December 2017 when one virtual pet sold for more than US$100,000. *CryptoKitties* also illustrated scalability problems for games on Ethereum when it created significant congestion on the Ethereum network in early 2018 with approximately 30% of all Ethereum transactions being for the game.

By the early 2020s, there had not been a breakout success in video games using blockchain, as these games tend to focus on using blockchain for speculation instead of more traditional forms of gameplay, which offers limited appeal to most players. Such games also represent a high risk to investors as their revenues can be difficult to predict.

However, limited successes of some games, such as *Axie Infinity* during the COVID-19 pandemic, and corporate plans towards metaverse content, refueled interest in the area of GameFi, a term describing the intersection of video games and financing typically backed by blockchain currency, in the second half of 2021. Several major publishers, including Ubisoft, Electronic Arts, and Take Two Interactive, have stated that blockchain and NFT-based games are under serious consideration for their companies in the future.

In October 2021, Valve Corporation banned blockchain games, including those using cryptocurrency and NFTs, from being hosted on its Steam digital storefront service, which is widely used for personal computer gaming, claiming that this was an extension of their policy banning games that offered in-game items with real-world value. Valve's prior history with gambling, specifically skin gambling, was speculated to be a factor in the decision to ban blockchain games. Journalists and players responded positively to Valve's decision as blockchain and NFT games have a reputation for scams and fraud among most PC gamers, and Epic Games, which runs the Epic Games Store in competition to Steam, said that they would be open to accepted blockchain games in the wake of Valve's refusal.

## Supply Chain

There have been several different efforts to employ blockchains in supply chain management.

- **Precious Commodities Mining:** Blockchain technology has been used for tracking the origins of gemstones and other precious commodities. In 2016, *The Wall Street Journal* reported that the blockchain technology company Everledger was partnering with IBM's blockchain-based tracking service to trace the origin of diamonds to ensure that they were ethically mined. As of 2019, the Diamond Trading Company (DTC) has been involved in building a diamond trading supply chain product called Tracer.
- **Food Supply:** As of 2018, Walmart and IBM were running a trial to use a blockchain-backed system for supply chain monitoring for lettuce and spinach – all nodes of the blockchain were administered by Walmart and were located on the IBM cloud.
- **Fashion Industry:** There is an opaque relationship between brands, distributors, and customers in the fashion industry, which prevents the sustainable and stable development of the fashion industry. Blockchain makes up for this shortcoming and makes information transparent, solving the difficulty of sustainable development of the industry.
- **Motor Vehicles:** Mercedes-Benz and partner Icertis developed a blockchain prototype used to facilitate consistent documentation of contracts along the supply chain so that the ethical standards and contractual obligations required of its direct suppliers can be passed on to second tier suppliers and beyond. In another project, the company uses blockchain technology to track the emissions of climate-relevant gases and the amount of secondary material along the supply chain for its battery cell manufacturers.

## Domain Names

There are several different efforts to offer domain name services via the blockchain. These domain names can be controlled by the use of a private key, which purports to allow for uncensorable websites. This would also bypass a registrar's ability to suppress domains used for fraud, abuse, or illegal content. Namecoin is a cryptocurrency that supports the ".bit" top-level domain (TLD). Namecoin was forked from bitcoin in 2011. The .bit TLD is not sanctioned by ICANN, instead requiring an alternative DNS root. As of 2015, .bit was used by 28 websites, out of 120,000 registered names. Namecoin was dropped by OpenNIC in 2019, due to malware and potential other legal issues. Other blockchain alternatives to ICANN include *The Handshake Network*, *EmerDNS*, and *Unstoppable Domains.*

Specific TLDs include ".eth", ".luxe", and ".kred", which are associated with the Ethereum blockchain through the Ethereum Name Service (ENS). The .kred TLD also acts as an alternative to conventional cryptocurrency wallet addresses as a convenience for transferring cryptocurrency.

## Other Uses

Blockchain technology can be used to create a permanent, public, transparent ledger system for compiling data on sales, tracking digital use and payments to content creators, such as wireless users or musicians. The Gartner 2019 CIO Survey reported 2% of higher education respondents had launched blockchain projects and another 18% were planning academic projects in the next 24 months. In 2017, IBM partnered with ASCAP and PRS for Music to adopt blockchain technology in music distribution. Imogen Heap's Mycelia service has also been proposed as a blockchain-based alternative "that gives artists more control over how their songs and associated data circulate among fans and other musicians."

New distribution methods are available for the insurance industry such as peer-to-peer insurance, parametric insurance and microinsurance following the adoption of blockchain. The sharing economy and IoT are also set to benefit from blockchains because they involve many collaborating peers. The use of blockchain in libraries is being studied with a grant from the U.S. Institute of Museum and Library Services.

Other blockchain designs include Hyperledger, a collaborative effort from the Linux Foundation to support blockchain-based distributed ledgers, with projects under this initiative including Hyperledger Burrow (by Monax) and Hyperledger Fabric (spearheaded by IBM). Another is Quorum, a permissioned private blockchain by JPMorgan Chase with private storage, used for contract applications. Oracle introduced a blockchain table feature in its Oracle 21c database. Blockchain is also being used in peer-to-peer energy trading.

Lightweight blockchains, or simplified blockchains, are more suitable for internet of things (IoT) applications than conventional blockchains. One experiment suggested that a lightweight blockchain-based network could accommodate up to 1.34 million authentication processes every second, which could be sufficient for resource-constrained IoT networks.

Blockchain could be used in detecting counterfeits by associating unique identifiers to products, documents and shipments, and storing records associated with transactions that cannot be forged or altered. It is however argued that blockchain technology needs to be supplemented with technologies that provide a strong binding between physical objects and blockchain systems, as well as provisions for content creator verification *ala* KYC standards. The EUIPO established an Anti-Counterfeiting Blockathon Forum, with the objective of "defining, piloting and implementing" an anti-counterfeiting infrastructure at the European level. The Dutch Standardisation organisation NEN uses blockchain together with QR Codes to authenticate certificates.

Beijing and Shanghai are among the cities designated by China to trial blockchain applications as January 30, 2022. In Chinese legal proceedings, blockchain technology was first accepted as a method for authenticating internet evidence by the Hangzhou Internet Court in 2019 and has since been accepted by other Chinese courts.

### 1.1.4 Blockchain Interoperability

With the increasing number of blockchain systems appearing, even only those that support cryptocurrencies, blockchain interoperability is becoming a topic of major importance. The objective is to support transferring assets from one blockchain system to another blockchain system. Wegner stated that "interoperability is the ability of two or more software components to cooperate despite differences in language, interface, and execution platform". The objective of blockchain interoperability is therefore to support such cooperation among blockchain systems, despite those kinds of differences. There are already several blockchain interoperability solutions available. They can be classified into three categories: cryptocurrency interoperability approaches, blockchain engines, and blockchain connectors. Several individual IETF participants produced the draft of a blockchain interoperability architecture.

### 1.1.5 Energy Consumption Concerns

Some cryptocurrencies use blockchain mining—the peer-to-peer computer computations by which transactions are validated and verified. This requires a large amount of energy. In June 2018, the Bank for International Settlements criticized the use of public proof-of-work blockchains for their high energy consumption.

Early concern over the high energy consumption was a factor in later blockchains such as Cardano (2017), Solana (2020) and Polkadot (2020) adopting the less energy-intensive proof-of-stake model. Researchers have estimated that Bitcoin consumes 100,000 times as much energy as proof-of-stake networks.

In 2021, a study by Cambridge University determined that Bitcoin (at 121 terawatt-hours per year) used more electricity than Argentina (at 121TWh) and the Netherlands (109TWh). According to Digiconomist, one bitcoin transaction required 708 kilowatt-hours of electrical energy, the amount an average U.S. household consumed in 24 days.

In February 2021, U.S. Treasury secretary Janet Yellen called Bitcoin "an extremely inefficient way to conduct transactions", saying "the amount of energy consumed in processing those transactions is staggering". In March 2021, Bill Gates stated that "Bitcoin uses more electricity per transaction than any other method known to mankind", adding "It's not a great climate thing."

Nicholas Weaver, of the International Computer Science Institute at the University of California, Berkeley, examined blockchain's online security, and the energy efficiency of proof-of-work public blockchains, and in both cases found it grossly inadequate. The 31TWh-45TWh of electricity used for bitcoin in 2018 produced 17-23 million tonnes of $CO_2$. By 2022, the University of Cambridge and Digiconomist estimated that the two largest proof-of-work blockchains, Bitcoin and Ethereum, together used twice as much electricity in one year as the whole of Sweden, leading to the release of up to 120 million tonnes of $CO_2$ each year. Some cryptocurrency developers are considering moving from the proof-of-work model to the proof-of-stake model.

### 1.1.6 Academic Research

In October 2014, the MIT Bitcoin Club, with funding from MIT alumni, provided undergraduate students at the Massachusetts Institute of Technology access to $100 of bitcoin. The adoption rates, as studied by Catalini and Tucker (2016), revealed that when people who typically adopt technologies early are given delayed access, they tend to reject the technology. Many universities have founded departments focusing on crypto and blockchain, including MIT, in 2017. In the same year, Edinburgh became "one of the first big European universities to launch a blockchain course", according to the *Financial Times*.

#### Adoption Decision

Motivations for adopting blockchain technology (an aspect of innovation adoptation) have been investigated by researchers. For example, Janssen, et al. provided a framework for analysis, and Koens & Poll pointed out that adoption could be heavily driven by non-technical factors. Based on behavioral models, Li has discussed the differences between adoption at the individual level and organizational levels.

#### Collaboration

Scholars in business and management have started studying the role of blockchains to support collaboration. It has been argued that blockchains can foster both cooperation (i.e., prevention of opportunistic behavior) and coordination (i.e., communication and information sharing). Thanks to reliability, transparency, traceability of records, and information immutability, blockchains facilitate collaboration in a way that differs both from the traditional use of contracts and from relational norms. Contrary to contracts, blockchains do not directly rely on the legal system to enforce agreements. In addition, contrary to the use of relational norms, blockchains do not require a trust or direct connections between collaborators.

### Blockchain and Internal Audit

The need for internal audits to provide effective oversight of organizational efficiency will require a change in the way that information is accessed in new formats. Blockchain adoption requires a framework to identify the risk of exposure associated with transactions using blockchain. The Institute of Internal Auditors has identified the need for internal auditors to address this transformational technology. New methods are required to develop audit plans that identify threats and risks. The Internal Audit Foundation study, *Blockchain and Internal Audit,* assesses these factors. The American Institute of Certified Public Accountants has outlined new roles for auditors as a result of blockchain.

### Journals

In September 2015, the first peer-reviewed academic journal dedicated to cryptocurrency and blockchain technology research, *Ledger*, was announced. The inaugural issue was published in December 2016. The journal covers aspects of mathematics, computer science, engineering, law, economics and philosophy that relate to cryptocurrencies. The journal encourages authors to digitally sign a file hash of submitted papers, which are then timestamped into the bitcoin blockchain. Authors are also asked to include a personal bitcoin address on the first page of their papers for non-repudiation purposes.

## 1.2 HISTORICAL EVOLUTION OF BLOCKCHAIN

Cryptographer David Chaum first proposed a blockchain-like protocol in his 1982 dissertation "Computer Systems Established, Maintained, and Trusted by Mutually Suspicious Groups." Further work on a cryptographically secured chain of blocks was described in 1991 by Stuart Haber and W. Scott Stornetta.

They wanted to implement a system wherein document timestamps could not be tampered with. In 1992, Haber, Stornetta, and Dave Bayer incorporated Merkle trees into the design, which improved its efficiency by allowing several document certificates to be collected into one block. Under their company Surety, their document certificate hashes have been published in *The New York Times* every week since 1995.

The first decentralized blockchain was conceptualized by a person (or group of people) known as Satoshi Nakamoto in 2008. Nakamoto improved the design in an important way using a Hashcash-like method to timestamp blocks without requiring them to be signed by a trusted party and introducing a difficulty parameter to stabilize the rate at which blocks are added to the chain. The design was implemented the following year by Nakamoto as a core component of the cryptocurrency bitcoin, where it serves as the public ledger for all transactions on the network. In August 2014, the bitcoin blockchain file size, containing records of all transactions that have occurred on the network, reached 20 GB (gigabytes). In January 2015, the size had grown to almost 30 GB, and from January 2016 to January 2017, the bitcoin blockchain grew from 50 GB to 100 GB in size. The ledger size had exceeded 200 GB by early 2020.

The words *block* and *chain* were used separately in Satoshi Nakamoto's original paper, but were eventually popularized as a single word, *blockchain,* by 2016.

According to Accenture, an application of the diffusion of innovations theory suggests that blockchains attained a 13.5% adoption rate within financial services in 2016, therefore reaching the early adopters' phase. Industry trade groups joined to create the Global Blockchain Forum in 2016, an initiative of the Chamber of Digital Commerce. In May 2018, Gartner found that only 1% of CIOs indicated any kind of blockchain adoption within their organisations, and only 8% of CIOs were in the short-term "planning or [looking at] active experimentation with blockchain". For the year 2019 Gartner reported 5% of CIOs believed blockchain technology was a 'game-changer' for their business.

## 1.3 CORE COMPONENTS: BLOCKS, CHAINS, AND NODES

Blockchain technology, a revolutionary system that underpins cryptocurrencies like Bitcoin, has far-reaching implications beyond digital currencies. At its core, blockchain is a decentralized ledger of all transactions across a network, ensuring transparency, security, and immutability. Understanding the fundamental components of blockchain—blocks, chains, and nodes—is crucial for grasping how this technology operates and why it is so powerful.

The core components of blockchain technology—blocks, chains, and nodes—form the foundation of a system that offers unparalleled security, transparency, and decentralization. By understanding how these components interact and the principles behind consensus mechanisms, we can appreciate the potential of blockchain to revolutionize various industries. As blockchain technology continues to evolve, its applications will expand, offering innovative solutions to complex problems and transforming the way we conduct transactions, manage data, and interact with digital systems.

### 1.3.1 Blocks: The Building Units of Blockchain

Blocks are the fundamental building units of a blockchain. Each block contains a list of transactions and a few critical elements that ensure the integrity and continuity of the blockchain.

- **Transaction Data:** Every block records multiple transactions, which might include cryptocurrency transfers, smart contract interactions, or any other type of data the blockchain is designed to handle.
- **Timestamp:** Each block is time-stamped, providing a chronological order of transactions and ensuring that data is recorded at a specific point in time.
- **Hash:** A block hash is a unique identifier created by running the block's data through a cryptographic hash function. This hash ensures that the data within the block cannot be altered without changing the hash itself, thus guaranteeing data integrity.
- **Previous Block Hash:** This is the hash of the preceding block in the chain. Including this hash links the blocks together in chronological order, forming a continuous and unalterable chain.
- **Nonce:** A nonce (number used once) is a random or pseudo-random number that blockchain miners are solving for in a proof-of-work consensus algorithm. It is an essential part of the mining process and adds variability to the hash output.

### 1.3.2 Chains: Linking Blocks Together

The term "blockchain" literally refers to a chain of blocks. Each block is securely linked to the previous one, forming a chronological chain from the genesis block (the first block) to the current block.

This structure has several critical implications:

- **Immutability:** Once a block is added to the chain, it cannot be altered without changing all subsequent blocks. This immutability is achieved through the cryptographic linking of blocks via their hashes.
- **Security:** The integrity of the entire blockchain depends on the secure linkage of blocks. Altering a single block would require changing the hash of that block and all following blocks, which is computationally infeasible in a decentralized network.
- **Transparency:** Because each block is linked in a sequence, the entire transaction history is visible and verifiable by all participants in the network. This transparency fosters trust and accountability.

### 1.3.3 Nodes: The Backbone of the Blockchain Network

Nodes are the computers that participate in the blockchain network, maintaining copies of the blockchain and validating new transactions and blocks. There are several types of nodes, each serving different functions:

- **Full Nodes:** These nodes store a complete copy of the blockchain and validate all transactions and blocks. Full nodes are crucial for maintaining the integrity and security of the blockchain network. They ensure that all transactions comply with the network's rules and protocols.
- **Light Nodes:** Also known as SPV (Simplified Payment Verification) nodes, light nodes do not store the entire blockchain. Instead, they store only the block headers and verify transactions by requesting information from full nodes. Light nodes require less storage and processing power.
- **Mining Nodes:** These nodes participate in the process of adding new blocks to the blockchain through mining. They use computational power to solve complex mathematical problems (proof of work) or stake their cryptocurrency (proof of stake) to validate transactions and create new blocks.
- **Masternodes:** These are specialized nodes that perform additional tasks beyond standard node operations, such as managing protocol operations and providing services like instant transactions and private transactions. Masternodes typically require a significant investment in the network's cryptocurrency to operate.

### 1.3.4 Consensus Mechanisms: Ensuring Agreement in the Network

For a blockchain to function correctly, all nodes must agree on the state of the blockchain. This agreement is achieved through consensus mechanisms, which are protocols that ensure all nodes reach a common agreement on the blockchain's state. The most common consensus mechanisms include:

- **Proof of Work (PoW):** This mechanism requires nodes (miners) to solve complex mathematical problems to add new blocks to the blockchain. PoW is energy-intensive but provides high security and resistance to attacks.
- **Proof of Stake (PoS):** In PoS, validators are chosen to create new blocks based on the number of coins they hold and are willing to "stake" as collateral. PoS is more energy-efficient than PoW and encourages long-term investment in the network.

- **Delegated Proof of Stake (DPoS):** DPoS involves a voting system where stakeholders elect a small number of delegates to validate transactions and create blocks. This mechanism is faster and more scalable but can be more centralized.
- **Byzantine Fault Tolerance (BFT):** BFT mechanisms, such as Practical Byzantine Fault Tolerance (PBFT), allow nodes to reach consensus even if some nodes act maliciously or fail. BFT is often used in permissioned blockchains where nodes are known and trusted.

### 1.3.5 Real-World Applications and Implications

Blockchain technology has numerous applications beyond cryptocurrencies, leveraging its core components to solve various problems:

- **Supply Chain Management:** Blockchain provides transparency and traceability in supply chains, ensuring the authenticity of products and reducing fraud.
- **Healthcare:** Blockchain secures patient records, ensures data integrity, and facilitates data sharing among healthcare providers while maintaining patient privacy.
- **Finance:** Blockchain enables faster, cheaper, and more secure financial transactions, including cross-border payments and smart contracts for automated financial agreements.
- **Voting Systems:** Blockchain can create secure, transparent, and tamper-proof voting systems, increasing trust in electoral processes.
- **Digital Identity:** Blockchain provides a secure and immutable way to manage digital identities, reducing identity theft and fraud.

## 1.4 DECENTRALIZATION AND DISTRIBUTED LEDGER TECHNOLOGY

### 1.4.1 Decentralization

Decentralization or decentralisation is the process by which the activities of an organization, particularly those regarding planning and decision-making, are distributed or delegated away from a central, authoritative location or group and given to smaller factions within it. Concepts of decentralization have been applied to group dynamics and management science in private businesses and organizations, political science, law and public administration, technology, economics and money.

#### History

The word "*centralisation*" came into use in France in 1794 as the post-Revolution French Directory leadership created a new government structure. The word "*décentralisation*" came into usage in the 1820s. "Centralization" entered written English in the first third of the 1800s; mentions of decentralization also first appear during those years. In the mid-1800s Tocqueville would write that the French Revolution began with "a push towards decentralization ... [but became,] in the end, an extension of centralization." In 1863, retired French bureaucrat Maurice Block wrote an article called "Decentralization" for a French journal that reviewed the dynamics of government and bureaucratic centralization and recent French efforts at decentralization of government functions.

Ideas of liberty and decentralization were carried to their logical conclusions during the 19th and 20th centuries by anti-state political activists calling themselves "anarchists", "libertarians", and even decentralists. Tocqueville was an advocate, writing: "Decentralization has, not only an administrative value but also a civic dimension since it increases the opportunities for citizens to take interest in public affairs; it makes them get accustomed to using freedom. And from the accumulation of these local, active, persnickety freedoms, is born the most efficient counterweight against the claims of the central government, even if it were supported by an impersonal, collective will." Pierre-Joseph Proudhon (1809–1865), influential anarchist theorist wrote: "All my economic ideas as developed over twenty-five years can be summed up in the words: agricultural-industrial federation. All my political ideas boil down to a similar formula: political federation or decentralization."

In the early 20th century, America's response to the centralization of economic wealth and political power was a decentralist movement. It blamed large-scale industrial production for destroying middle-class shop keepers and small manufacturers and promoted increased property ownership and a return to small scale living.

The decentralist movement attracted Southern Agrarians like Robert Penn Warren, as well as journalist Herbert Agar. New Left and libertarian individuals who identified with social, economic, and often political decentralism through the ensuing years included Ralph Borsodi, Wendell Berry, Paul Goodman, Carl Oglesby, Karl Hess, Donald Livingston, Kirkpatrick Sale (author of *Human Scale*), Murray Bookchin, Dorothy Day, Senator Mark O. Hatfield, Mildred J. Loomis and Bill Kauffman.

Leopold Kohr, author of the 1957 book *The Breakdown of Nations* – known for its statement "Whenever something is wrong, something is too big" – was a major influence on E. F. Schumacher, author of the 1973 bestseller *Small Is Beautiful: A Study of Economics As If People Mattered*. In the next few years a number of best-selling books promoted decentralization.

Daniel Bell's *The Coming of Post-Industrial Society* discussed the need for decentralization and a "comprehensive overhaul of government structure to find the appropriate size and scope of units", as well as the need to detach functions from current state boundaries, creating regions based on functions like water, transport, education and economics which might have "different 'overlays' on the map." Alvin Toffler published *Future Shock* (1970) and *The Third Wave* (1980). Discussing the books in a later interview, Toffler said that industrial-style, centralized, top-down bureaucratic planning would be replaced by a more open, democratic, decentralized style which he called "anticipatory democracy". Futurist John Naisbitt's 1982 book "Megatrends" was on The New York Times Best Seller list for more than two years and sold 14 million copies. Naisbitt's book outlines 10 "megatrends", the fifth of which is from centralization to decentralization. In 1996 David Osborne and Ted Gaebler had a best selling book *Reinventing Government* proposing decentralist public administration theories which became labeled the "New Public Management".

Stephen Cummings wrote that decentralization became a "revolutionary megatrend" in the 1980s. In 1983 Diana Conyers asked if decentralization was the "latest fashion" in development administration. Cornell University's project on Restructuring Local Government states that decentralization refers to the "global trend" of devolving responsibilities to regional or local governments. Robert J. Bennett's *Decentralization, Intergovernmental Relations and Markets: Towards a Post-Welfare Agenda* describes how after World War II governments pursued a centralized "welfarist" policy of entitlements which now has become a "post-welfare" policy of intergovernmental and market-based decentralization.

In 1983, "Decentralization" was identified as one of the "Ten Key Values" of the Green Movement in the United States.

A 1999 United Nations Development Programme report stated:

- "A large number of developing and transitional countries have embarked on some form of decentralization programmes. This trend is coupled with a growing interest in the role of civil society and the private sector as partners to governments in seeking new ways of service delivery ... Decentralization of governance and the strengthening of local governing capacity is in part also a function of broader societal trends. These include, for example, the growing distrust of government generally, the spectacular demise of some of the most centralized regimes in the world (especially the Soviet Union) and the emerging separatist demands that seem to routinely pop up in one or another part of the world. The movement toward local accountability and greater control over one's destiny is, however, not solely the result of the negative

> attitude towards central government. Rather, these developments, as we have already noted, are principally being driven by a strong desire for greater participation of citizens and private sector organizations in governance."

## Systems Approach

Those studying the goals and processes of implementing decentralization often use a systems theory approach, which according to the United Nations Development Programme report applies to the topic of decentralization "a whole systems perspective, including levels, spheres, sectors and functions and seeing the community level as the entry point at which holistic definitions of development goals are from the people themselves and where it is most practical to support them. It involves seeing multi-level frameworks and continuous, synergistic processes of interaction and iteration of cycles as critical for achieving wholeness in a decentralized system and for sustaining its development."

However, it has been seen as part of a systems approach. Norman Johnson of Los Alamos National Laboratory wrote in a 1999 paper: "A decentralized system is where some decisions by the agents are made without centralized control or processing. An important property of agent systems is the degree of connectivity or connectedness between the agents, a measure global flow of information or influence. If each agent is connected (exchange states or influence) to all other agents, then the system is highly connected."

University of California, Irvine's Institute for Software Research's "PACE" project is creating an "architectural style for trust management in decentralized applications." It adopted Rohit Khare's definition of decentralization: "A decentralized system is one which requires multiple parties to make their own independent decisions" and applies it to Peer-to-peer software creation, writing:

- In such a decentralized system, there is no single centralized authority that makes decisions on behalf of all the parties. Instead each party, also called a peer, makes local autonomous decisions towards its individual goals which may possibly conflict with those of other peers. Peers directly interact with each other and share information or provide service to other peers. An open decentralized system is one in which the entry of peers is not regulated. Any peer can enter or leave the system at any time ...

## Goals

Decentralization in any area is a response to the problems of centralized systems. Decentralization in government, the topic most studied, has been seen as a solution to problems like economic decline, government inability to fund services and their general decline in performance of overloaded services, the demands of minorities for a greater say in local governance, the general weakening legitimacy of the public sector and global and international pressure on countries with inefficient, undemocratic, overly centralized systems. The following four goals or objectives are frequently stated in various analyses of decentralization.

### Participation

In decentralization, the principle of subsidiarity is often invoked. It holds that the lowest or least centralized authority that is capable of addressing an issue effectively should do so. According to one definition: "Decentralization, or decentralizing governance, refers to the restructuring or reorganization of authority so that there is a system of co-responsibility between institutions of governance at the central, regional and local levels according to the principle of subsidiarity, thus increasing the overall quality and effectiveness of the system of governance while increasing the authority and capacities of sub-national levels."

Decentralization is often linked to concepts of participation in decision-making, democracy, equality and liberty from a higher authority. Decentralization enhances the democratic voice.

Theorists believe that local representative authorities with actual discretionary powers are the basis of decentralization that can lead to local efficiency, equity and development." Columbia University's Earth Institute identified one of three major trends relating to decentralization: "increased involvement of local jurisdictions and civil society in the management of their affairs, with new forms of participation, consultation, and partnerships."

Decentralization has been described as a "counterpoint to globalization [which] removes decisions from the local and national stage to the global sphere of multi-national or non-national interests. Decentralization brings decision-making back to the sub-national levels". Decentralization strategies must account for the interrelations of global, regional, national, sub-national, and local levels.

### Diversity

Norman L. Johnson writes that diversity plays an important role in decentralized systems like ecosystems, social groups, large organizations, political systems. "Diversity is defined to be unique properties of entities, agents, or individuals that are not shared by the larger group, population, structure. Decentralized is defined as a property of a system where the agents have some ability to operate "locally." Both decentralization and diversity are necessary attributes to achieve the self-organizing properties of interest."

Advocates of political decentralization hold that greater participation by better informed diverse interests in society will lead to more relevant decisions than those made only by authorities on the national level. Decentralization has been described as a response to demands for diversity.

### Efficiency

In business, decentralization leads to a management by results philosophy which focuses on definite objectives to be achieved by unit results. Decentralization of government programs is said to increase efficiency – and effectiveness – due to reduction of congestion in communications, quicker reaction to unanticipated problems, improved ability to deliver services, improved information about local conditions, and more support from beneficiaries of programs.

Firms may prefer decentralization because it ensures efficiency by making sure that managers closest to the local information make decisions and in a more timely fashion; that their taking responsibility frees upper management for long term strategics rather than day-to-day decision-making; that managers have hands on training to prepare them to move up the management hierarchy; that managers are motivated by having the freedom to exercise their own initiative and creativity; that managers and divisions are encouraged to prove that they are profitable, instead of allowing their failures to be masked by the overall profitability of the company.

The same principles can be applied to the government. Decentralization promises to enhance efficiency through both inter-governmental competitions with market features and fiscal discipline which assigns tax and expenditure authority to the lowest level of government possible.

It works best where members of the subnational government have strong traditions of democracy, accountability, and professionalism.

### Conflict Resolution

Economic and/or political decentralization can help prevent or reduce conflict because they reduce actual or perceived inequities between various regions or between a region and the central government. Dawn Brancati finds that political decentralization reduces intrastate conflict unless politicians create political parties that mobilize minority and even extremist groups to demand more resources and power within national governments.

However, the likelihood this will be done depends on factors like how democratic transitions happen and features like a regional party's proportion of legislative seats, a country's number of regional legislatures, elector procedures, and the order in which national and regional elections occur. Brancati holds that decentralization can promote peace if it encourages statewide parties to incorporate regional demands and limit the power of regional parties.

## Processes

### Initiation

The processes by which entities move from a more to a less centralized state vary. They can be initiated from the centers of authority ("top-down") or from individuals, localities or regions ("bottom-up"), or from a "mutually desired" combination of authorities and localities working together. Bottom-up decentralization usually stresses political values like local responsiveness and increased participation and tends to increase political stability. Top-down decentralization may be motivated by the desire to "shift deficits downwards" and find more resources to pay for services or pay off government debt. Some hold that decentralization should not be imposed, but done in a respectful manner.

### Appropriate Size

Gauging the appropriate size or scale of decentralized units has been studied in relation to the size of sub-units of hospitals and schools, road networks, administrative units in business and public administration, and especially town and city governmental areas and decision-making bodies.

In creating planned communities ("new towns"), it is important to determine the appropriate population and geographical size. While in earlier years small towns were considered appropriate, by the 1960s, 60,000 inhabitants was considered the size necessary to support a diversified job market and an adequate shopping center and array of services and entertainment. Appropriate size of governmental units for revenue raising also is a consideration.

Even in bioregionalism, which seeks to reorder many functions and even the boundaries of governments according to physical and environmental features, including watershed boundaries and soil and terrain characteristics, appropriate size must be considered. The unit may be larger than many decentralist-bioregionalists prefer.

### Inadvertent or Silent

Decentralization ideally happens as a careful, rational, and orderly process, but it often takes place during times of economic and political crisis, the fall of a regime and the resultant power struggles. Even when it happens slowly, there is a need for experimentation, testing, adjusting, and replicating successful experiments in other contexts. There is no one blueprint for decentralization since it depends on the initial state of a country and the power and views of political interests and whether they support or oppose decentralization.

Decentralization usually is a conscious process based on explicit policies. However, it may occur as "silent decentralization" in the absence of reforms as changes in networks, policy emphasize and resource availability lead inevitably to a more decentralized system.

### Asymmetry

Decentralization may be uneven and "asymmetric" given any one country's population, political, ethnic and other forms of diversity. In many countries, political, economic and administrative responsibilities may be decentralized to the larger urban areas, while rural areas are administered by the central government. Decentralization of responsibilities to provinces may be limited only to those provinces or states which want or are capable of handling responsibility. Some privatization may be more appropriate to an urban than a rural area; some types of privatization may be more appropriate for some states and provinces but not others.

### Determinants

The academic literature frequently mentions the following factors as determinants of decentralization:

- "The number of major ethnic groups".
- "The degree of territorial concentration of those groups".
- "The existence of ethnic networks and communities across the border of the state".
- "The country's dependence on natural resources and the degree to which those resources are concentrated in the region's territory".
- "The country's per capita income relative to that in other regions".
- The presence of self-determination movements.

### In Government Policy

Historians have described the history of governments and empires in terms of centralization and decentralization. In his 1910 *The History of Nations* Henry Cabot Lodge wrote that Persian king Darius I (550–486 BC) was a master of organization and "for the first time in history centralization becomes a political fact." He also noted that this contrasted with the decentralization of Ancient Greece. Since the 1980s a number of scholars have written about cycles of centralization and decentralization. Stephen K. Sanderson wrote that over the last 4000 years chiefdoms and actual states have gone through sequences of centralization and decentralization of economic, political and social power. Yildiz Atasoy writes this process has been going on "since the Stone Age" through not just chiefdoms and states, but empires and today's "hegemonic core states". Christopher K. Chase-Dunn and Thomas D. Hall review other works that detail these cycles, including works which analyze the concept of core elites which compete with state accumulation of wealth and how their "intra-ruling-class competition accounts for the rise and fall of states" and their phases of centralization and decentralization.

Rising government expenditures, poor economic performance and the rise of free market-influenced ideas have convinced governments to decentralize their operations, to induce competition within their services, to contract out to private firms operating in the market, and to privatize some functions and services entirely.

Government decentralization has both political and administrative aspects. Its decentralization may be territorial, moving power from a central city to other localities, and it may be functional, moving decision-making from the top administrator of any branch of government to lower level officials, or divesting of the function entirely through privatization. It has been called the "new public management" which has been described as decentralization, management by objectives, contracting out, competition within government and consumer orientation.

### Political

Political decentralization signifies a reduction in the authority of national governments over policy-making. This process is accomplished by the institution of reforms that either delegate a certain degree of meaningful decision-making autonomy to sub-national tiers of government, or grant citizens the right to elect lower-level officials, like local or regional representatives. Depending on the country, this may require constitutional or statutory reforms, the development of new political parties, increased power for legislatures, the creation of local political units, and encouragement of advocacy groups.

A national government may decide to decentralize its authority and responsibilities for a variety of reasons. Decentralization reforms may occur for administrative reasons, when government officials decide that certain responsibilities and decisions would be handled best at the regional or local level. In democracies, traditionally conservative parties include political decentralization as a directive in their platforms because rightist parties tend to advocate for a decrease in the role of central government. There is also strong evidence to support the idea that government stability increases the probability of political decentralization, since instability brought on by gridlock between opposing parties in legislatures often impedes a government's overall ability to enact sweeping reforms.

The rise of regional ethnic parties in the national politics of parliamentary democracies is also heavily associated with the implementation of decentralization reforms. Ethnic parties may endeavor to transfer more autonomy to their respective regions, and as a partisan strategy, ruling parties within the central government may cooperate by establishing regional assemblies in order to curb the rise of ethnic parties in national elections. This phenomenon famously occurred in 1999, when the United Kingdom's Labour Party appealed to Scottish constituents by creating a semi-autonomous Scottish Parliament in order to neutralize the threat from the increasingly popular Scottish National Party at the national level.

In addition to increasing the administrative efficacy of government and endowing citizens with more power, there are many projected advantages to political decentralization. Individuals who take advantage of their right to elect local and regional authorities have been shown to have more positive attitudes toward politics, and increased opportunities for civic decision-making through participatory democracy mechanisms like public consultations and participatory budgeting are believed to help legitimize government institutions in the eyes of marginalized groups. Moreover, political decentralization is perceived as a valid means of protecting marginalized communities at a local level from the detrimental aspects of development and globalization driven by the state, like the degradation of local customs, codes, and beliefs. In his 2013 book, *Democracy and Political Ignorance*, George Mason University law professor Ilya Somin argued that political decentralization in a federal democracy confronts the widespread issue of political ignorance by allowing citizens to engage in foot voting, or moving to other jurisdictions with more favorable laws. He cites the mass migration of over one million southern-born African Americans to the North or the West to evade discriminatory Jim Crow laws in the late 19th century and early 20th century.

The European Union follows the principle of subsidiarity, which holds that decision-making should be made by the most local competent authority. The EU should decide only on enumerated issues that a local or member state authority cannot address themselves. Furthermore, enforcement is exclusively the domain of member states. In Finland, the Centre Party explicitly supports decentralization. For example, government departments have been moved from the capital Helsinki to the provinces. The centre supports substantial subsidies that limit potential economic and political centralization to Helsinki.

Political decentralization does not come without its drawbacks. A study by Fan concludes that there is an increase in corruption and rent-seeking when there are more vertical tiers in the government, as well as when there are higher levels of subnational government employment. Other studies warn of high-level politicians that may intentionally deprive regional and local authorities of power and resources when conflicts arise. In order to combat these negative forces, experts believe that political decentralization should be supplemented with other conflict management mechanisms like power-sharing, particularly in regions with ethnic tensions.

### Administrative

Four major forms of administrative decentralization have been described.

- Deconcentration, the weakest form of decentralization, shifts responsibility for decision-making, finance and implementation of certain public functions from officials of central governments to those in existing districts or, if necessary, new ones under direct control of the central government.
- Delegation passes down responsibility for decision-making, finance and implementation. It involves the creation of public-private enterprises or corporations, or of "authorities", special projects or service districts. All of them will have a great deal of decision-making discretion and they may be exempt from civil service requirements and may be permitted to charge users for services.
- Devolution transfers responsibility for decision-making, finance and implementation of certain public functions to the sub-national level, such as a regional, local, or state government.
- Divestment, also called privatization, may mean merely contracting out services to private companies. Or it may mean relinquishing totally all responsibility for decision-making, finance and implementation of certain public functions. Facilities will be sold off, workers transferred or fired and private companies or non-for-profit organizations allowed to provide the services. Many of these functions originally were done by private individuals, companies, or associations and later taken over by the government, either directly, or by regulating out of business entities which competed with newly created government programs.

### Fiscal

Fiscal decentralization means decentralizing revenue raising and/or expenditure of moneys to a lower level of government while maintaining financial responsibility. While this process usually is called fiscal federalism, it may be relevant to unitary, federal, or confederal governments. Fiscal federalism also concerns the "vertical imbalances" where the central government gives too much or too little money to the lower levels. It actually can be a way of increasing central government control of lower levels of government, if it is not linked to other kinds of responsibilities and authority.

Fiscal decentralization can be achieved through user fees, user participation through monetary or labor contributions, expansion of local property or sales taxes, intergovernmental transfers of central government tax monies to local governments through transfer payments or grants, and authorization of municipal borrowing with national government loan guarantees. Transfers of money may be given conditionally with instructions or unconditionally without them.

### Market

Market decentralization can be done through privatization of public owned functions and businesses, as described briefly above. But it also is done through deregulation, the abolition of restrictions on businesses competing with government services, for example, postal services, schools, garbage collection. Even as private companies and corporations have worked to have such services contracted out to or privatized by them, others have worked to have these turned over to non-profit organizations or associations.

From the 1970s to the 1990s, there was deregulation of some industries, like banking, trucking, airlines and telecommunications, which resulted generally in more competition and lower prices. According to the Cato Institute, an American libertarian think-tank, in some cases deregulation in some aspects of an industry were offset by increased regulation in other aspects, the electricity industry being a prime example. For example, in banking, Cato Institute believes some deregulation allowed banks to compete across state lines, increasing consumer choice, while an actual increase in regulators and regulations forced banks to make loans to individuals incapable of repaying them, leading eventually to the financial crisis of 2007–2008.

One example of economic decentralization, which is based on a libertarian socialist model, is decentralized economic planning. Decentralized planning is a type of economic system in which decision-making is distributed amongst various economic agents or localized within production agents. An example of this method in practice is in Kerala, India which experimented in 1996 with the People's Plan campaign.

Emmanuelle Auriol and Michel Benaim write about the "comparative benefits" of decentralization versus government regulation in the setting of standards. They find that while there may be a need for public regulation if public safety is at stake, private creation of standards usually is better because "regulators or 'experts' might misrepresent consumers' tastes and needs." As long as companies are averse to incompatible standards, standards will be created that satisfy needs of a modern economy.

### Environmental

Central governments themselves may own large tracts of land and control the forest, water, mineral, wildlife and other resources they contain. They may manage them through government operations or leasing them to private businesses; or they may neglect them to be exploited by individuals or groups who defy nonenforced laws against exploitation. It also may control most private land through land-use, zoning, environmental and other regulations. Selling off or leasing lands can be profitable for governments willing to relinquish control, but such programs can face public scrutiny because of fear of a loss of heritage or of environmental damage. Devolution of control to regional or local governments has been found to be an effective way of dealing with these concerns. Such decentralization has happened in India and other developing nations.

## In Economic Ideology

### Libertarian Socialism

Libertarian socialism is a political philosophy that promotes a non-hierarchical, non-bureaucratic society without private property in the means of production. Libertarian socialists believe in converting present-day private productive property into common or public goods. Libertarian socialism is opposed to coercive forms of social organization. It promotes free association in place of government and opposes the various social relations of capitalism, such as wage slavery. The term *libertarian socialism* is used by some socialists to differentiate their philosophy from state socialism, and by some as a synonym for left anarchism.

Accordingly, libertarian socialists believe that "the exercise of power in any institutionalized form – whether economic, political, religious, or sexual – brutalizes both the wielder of power and the one over whom it is exercised". Libertarian socialists generally place their hopes in decentralized means of direct democracy such as libertarian municipalism, citizens' assemblies, or workers' councils. Libertarian socialists are strongly critical of coercive institutions, which often leads them to reject the legitimacy of the state in favor of anarchism. Adherents propose achieving this through decentralization of political and economic power, usually involving the socialization of most large-scale private property and enterprise (while retaining respect for personal property). Libertarian socialism tends to deny the legitimacy of most forms of economically significant private property, viewing capitalist property relations as forms of domination that are antagonistic to individual freedom.

Political philosophies commonly described as libertarian socialist include most varieties of anarchism (especially anarcho-communism, anarchist collectivism, anarcho-syndicalism, social anarchism and mutualism) as well as autonomism, communalism, participism, libertarian Marxist philosophies such as council communism and Luxemburgism, and some versions of utopian socialism and individualist anarchism. For Murray Bookchin "In the modern world, anarchism first appeared as a movement of the peasantry and yeomanry against declining feudal institutions. In Germany its foremost spokesman during the Peasant Wars was Thomas Muenzer; in England, Gerrard Winstanley, a leading participant in the Digger movement. The concepts held by Muenzer and Winstanley were superbly attuned to the needs of their time – a historical period when the majority of the population lived in the countryside and when the most militant revolutionary forces came from an agrarian world. It would be painfully academic to argue whether Muenzer and Winstanley could have achieved their ideals. What is of real importance is that they spoke to their time; their anarchist concepts followed naturally from the rural society that furnished the bands of the peasant armies in Germany and the New Model in England." The term "anarchist" first entered the English language in 1642, during the English Civil War, as a term of abuse, used by Royalists against their Roundhead opponents. By the time of the French Revolution some, such as the *Enragés*, began to use the term positively, in opposition to Jacobin centralization of power, seeing "revolutionary government" as oxymoronic. By the turn of the 19th century, the English word "anarchism" had lost its initial negative connotation.

For Pierre-Joseph Proudhon, mutualism involved creating "industrial democracy", a system where workplaces would be "handed over to democratically organised workers' associations . . . We want these associations to be models for agriculture, industry and trade, the pioneering core of that vast federation of companies and societies woven into the common cloth of the democratic social Republic." He urged "workers to form themselves into democratic societies, with equal conditions for all members, on pain of a relapse into feudalism." This would result in "Capitalistic and proprietary exploitation, stopped everywhere, the wage system abolished, equal and just exchange guaranteed." Workers would no longer sell their labour to a capitalist but rather work for themselves in co-operatives. Anarcho-communism calls for a confederal form in relationships of mutual aid and free association between communes as an alternative to the centralism of the nation-state. Peter Kropotkin thus suggested that "Representative government has accomplished its historical mission; it has given a mortal blow to court-rule; and by its debates it has awakened public interest in public questions. But to see in it the government of the future socialist society is to commit a gross error. Each economic phase of life implies its own political phase; and it is impossible to touch the very basis of the present economic life-private property – without a corresponding change in the very basis of the political organization. Life already shows in which direction the change will be made. Not in increasing the powers of the State, but in resorting to free organization and free federation in all those branches which are now considered as attributes of the State." When the First Spanish Republic was established in 1873 after the abdication of King Amadeo, the first president, Estanislao Figueras, named Francesc Pi i Margall Minister of the Interior. His acquaintance with Proudhon enabled Pi to warm relations between the Republicans and the socialists in Spain. Pi i Margall became the principal translator of Proudhon's works into Spanish and later briefly became president of Spain in 1873 while being the leader of the Democratic Republican Federal Party. According to George Woodcock "These translations were to have a profound and lasting effect on the development of Spanish anarchism after 1870, but before that time Proudhonian ideas, as interpreted by Pi, already provided much of the inspiration for the federalist movement which sprang up in the early 1860s." According to the *Encyclopædia Britannica* "During the Spanish revolution of 1873, Pi y Margall attempted to establish a decentralized, cantonalist political system on Proudhonian lines."

To date, the best-known examples of an anarchist communist society (i.e., established around the ideas as they exist today and achieving worldwide attention and knowledge in the historical canon), are the anarchist territories during the Spanish Revolution and the Makhnovshchina during the Russian Revolution. Through the efforts and influence of the Spanish anarchists during the Spanish Revolution within the Spanish Civil War, starting in 1936 anarchist communism existed in most of Aragon, parts of the Levante and Andalusia, as well as in the stronghold of Anarchist Catalonia before being crushed by the combined forces of the regime that won the war, Hitler, Mussolini, Spanish Communist Party repression (backed by the USSR) as well as economic and armaments blockades from the capitalist countries and the Second Spanish Republic itself. During the Russian Revolution, anarchists such as Nestor Makhno worked to create and defend – through the Revolutionary Insurgent Army of Ukraine – anarchist communism in Ukraine from 1919 before being conquered by the Bolsheviks in 1921. Several libertarian socialists, notably Noam Chomsky among others, believe that anarchism shares much in common with certain variants of Marxism such as the council communism of Marxist Anton Pannekoek. In Chomsky's *Notes on Anarchism*, he suggests the possibility "that some form of council communism is the natural form of revolutionary socialism in an industrial society. It reflects the belief that democracy is severely limited when the industrial system is controlled by any form of autocratic elite, whether of owners, managers, and technocrats, a 'vanguard' party, or a State bureaucracy."

### Free Market

Free market ideas popular in the 19th century such as those of Adam Smith returned to prominence in the 1970s and 1980s. Austrian School economist Friedrich von Hayek argued that free markets themselves are decentralized systems where outcomes are produced without explicit agreement or coordination by individuals who use prices as their guide. Eleanor Doyle writes that "[e]conomic decision-making in free markets is decentralized across all the individuals dispersed in each market and is synchronized or coordinated by the price system," and holds that an individual right to property is part of this decentralized system. Criticizing central government control, Hayek wrote in *The Road to Serfdom*:

- There would be no difficulty about efficient control or planning were conditions so simple that a single person or board could effectively survey all the relevant facts. It is only as the factors which have to be taken into account become so numerous that it is impossible to gain a synoptic view of them that decentralization becomes imperative.

According to Bruce M. Owen, this does not mean that all firms themselves have to be equally decentralized. He writes: "markets allocate resources through arms-length transactions among decentralized actors. Much of the time, markets work very efficiently, but there is a variety of conditions under which firms do better. Hence, goods and services are produced and sold by firms with various degrees of horizontal and vertical integration." Additionally, he writes that the "economic incentive to expand horizontally or vertically is usually, but not always, compatible with the social interest in maximizing long-run consumer welfare."

It is often claimed that free markets and private property generate centralized monopolies and other ills; free market advocates counter with the argument that government is the source of monopoly. Historian Gabriel Kolko in his book *The Triumph of Conservatism* argued that in the first decade of the 20th century businesses were highly decentralized and competitive, with new businesses constantly entering existing industries. In his view, there was no trend towards concentration and monopolization. While there were a wave of mergers of companies trying to corner markets, they found there was too much competition to do so. According to Kolko, this was also true in banking and finance, which saw decentralization as leading to instability as state and local banks competed with the big New York City firms. He argues that, as a result, the largest firms turned to the power of the state and worked with leaders like United States Presidents Theodore Roosevelt, William H. Taft and Woodrow Wilson to pass as "progressive reforms" centralizing laws like The Federal Reserve Act of 1913 that gave control of the monetary system to the wealthiest bankers; the formation of monopoly "public utilities" that made competition with those monopolies illegal; federal inspection of meat packers biased against small companies; extending Interstate Commerce Commission to regulating telephone companies and keeping rates high to benefit AT&T; and using the Sherman Antitrust Act against companies which might combine to threaten larger or monopoly companies. D. T. Armentano, writing for the Cato Institute, argues that when government licensing, franchises, and other legal restrictions create monopoly and protect companies from open competition, deregulation is the solution.

Author and activist Jane Jacobs's influential 1961 book *The Death and Life of American Cities* criticized large-scale redevelopment projects which were part of government-planned decentralization of population and businesses to suburbs. She believed it destroyed cities' economies and impoverished remaining residents. Her 1980 book *The Question of Separatism: Quebec and the Struggle over Sovereignty* supported secession of Quebec from Canada. Her 1984 book *Cities and the Wealth of Nations* proposed a solution to the problems faced by cities whose economies were being ruined by centralized national governments: decentralization through the "multiplication of sovereignties", meaning an acceptance of the right of cities to secede from the larger nation states that were greatly limiting their ability to produce wealth.

## In the Organizational Structure of a Firm

In managerial economics, the principal-agent problem is a challenge faced by every firm. In response to these incentive and information conflicts, a firm can either centralize their organizational structure by concentrating decision-making to upper management, or decentralize their organizational structure by delegating authority throughout the organization. The delegation of authority comes with a basic trade-off: while it can increase efficiency and information flow, the central authority consequentially suffers a loss of control. However, through creating an environment of trust and allocating authority formally in the firm, coupled with a stronger rule of law in the geographical location of the firm, the negative consequences of the trade-off can be minimized.

In having a decentralized organizational structure, a firm can remain agile to external shocks and competing trends. Decision-making in a centralized organization can face information flow inefficiencies and barriers to effective communication which decreases the speed and accuracy in which decisions are made. A decentralized firm is said to hold greater flexibility given the efficiency in which it can analyze information and implement relevant outcomes. Additionally, having decision-making power spread across different areas allows for local knowledge to inform decisions, increasing their relevancy and implementational effectiveness. In the process of developing new products or services, the decentralization enable the firm gain advantages of closely meet particular division's needs.

Decentralization also impacts human resource management. The high level of individual agency that workers experience within a decentralized firm can create job enrichment. Studies have shown this enhances the development of new ideas and innovations given the sense of involvement that comes from responsibility. The impacts of decentralization on innovation are furthered by the ease of information flow that comes from this organizational structure. With increased knowledge sharing, workers are more able to use relevant information to inform decision-making. These benefits are enhanced in firms with skill-intensive environments. Skilled workers are more able to analyze information, they pose less risk of information duplication given increased communication abilities, and the productivity cost of multi-tasking is lower. These outcomes of decentralizion make it a particularly effective organizational structure for entrepreneurial and competitive firm environments, such as start-up companies. The flexibility, efficiency of information flow and higher worker autonomy complement the rapid growth and innovation seen in successful start up companies.

## In Technology and the Internet

*Technological decentralization* can be defined as a shift from concentrated to distributed modes of production and consumption of goods and services. Generally, such shifts are accompanied by transformations in technology and different technologies are applied for either system. Technology includes tools, materials, skills, techniques and processes by which goals are accomplished in the public and private spheres. Concepts of decentralization of technology are used throughout all types of technology, including especially information technology and appropriate technology.

Technologies often mentioned as best implemented in a decentralized manner, include: water purification, delivery and waste water disposal, agricultural technology and energy technology. Advancing technology may allow decentralized, privatized and free market solutions for what have been public services, such utilities producing and/or delivering power, water, mail, telecommunications and services like consumer product safety, money and banking, medical licensing and detection and metering technologies for highways, parking, and auto emissions. However, in terms of technology, a clear distinction between fully centralized or decentralized technical solutions is often not possible and therefore finding an optimal degree of centralization difficult from an infrastructure planning perspective.

### Information Technology

Information technology encompasses computers and computer networks, as well as information distribution technologies such as television and telephones. The whole computer industry of computer hardware, software, electronics, internet, telecommunications equipment, e-commerce and computer services are included.

Executives and managers face a constant tension between centralizing and decentralizing information technology for their organizations. They must find the right balance of centralizing which lowers costs and allows more control by upper management, and decentralizing which allows sub-units and users more control. This will depend on analysis of the specific situation. Decentralization is particularly applicable to business or management units which have a high level of independence, complicated products and customers, and technology less relevant to other units.

Information technology applied to government communications with citizens, often called e-Government, is supposed to support decentralization and democratization. Various forms have been instituted in most nations worldwide.

The internet is an example of an extremely decentralized network, having no owners at all (although some have argued that this is less the case in recent years). "No one is in charge of internet, and everyone is." As long as they follow a certain minimal number of rules, anyone can be a service provider or a user. Voluntary boards establish protocols, but cannot stop anyone from developing new ones. Other examples of open source or decentralized movements are Wikis which allow users to add, modify, or delete content via the internet. Wikipedia has been described as decentralized (although it is a centralized web site, with a single entity operating the servers). Smartphones have been described as being an important part of the decentralizing effects of smaller and cheaper computers worldwide.

Decentralization continues throughout the industry, for example as the decentralized architecture of wireless routers installed in homes and offices supplement and even replace phone companies' relatively centralized long-range cell towers.

Inspired by system and cybernetics theorists like Norbert Wiener, Marshall McLuhan and Buckminster Fuller, in the 1960s Stewart Brand started the Whole Earth Catalog and later computer networking efforts to bring Silicon Valley computer technologists and entrepreneurs together with countercultural ideas. This resulted in ideas like personal computing, virtual communities and the vision of an "electronic frontier" which would be a more decentralized, egalitarian and free-market libertarian society. Related ideas coming out of Silicon Valley included the free software and creative commons movements which produced visions of a "networked information economy".

Because human interactions in cyberspace transcend physical geography, there is a necessity for new theories in legal and other rule-making systems to deal with decentralized decision-making processes in such systems. For example, what rules should apply to conduct on the global digital network and who should set them? The laws of which nations govern issues of internet transactions (like seller disclosure requirements or definitions of "fraud"), copyright and trademark?

### Decentralized Computing

Decentralized computing is the allocation of resources, both hardware and software, to each individual workstation, or office location. In contrast, centralized computing exists when the majority of functions are carried out, or obtained from a remote centralized location. Decentralized computing is a trend in modern-day business environments. This is the opposite of centralized computing, which was prevalent during the early days of computers. A decentralized computer system has many benefits over a conventional centralized network. Desktop computers have advanced so rapidly, that their potential performance far exceeds the requirements of most business applications. This results in most desktop computers remaining idle (in relation to their full potential). A decentralized system can use the potential of these systems to maximize efficiency. However, it is debatable whether these networks increase overall effectiveness.

All computers have to be updated individually with new software, unlike a centralized computer system. Decentralized systems still enable file sharing and all computers can share peripherals such as printers and scanners as well as modems, allowing all the computers in the network to connect to the internet.

A collection of decentralized computers systems are components of a larger computer network, held together by local stations of equal importance and capability. These systems are capable of running independently of each other.

### Centralization and Re-decentralization of the Internet

The New Yorker reports that although the Internet was originally decentralized, by 2013 it had become less so: "a staggering percentage of communications flow through a small set of corporations – and thus, under the profound influence of those companies and other institutions [...] One solution, espoused by some programmers, is to make the Internet more like it used to be – less centralized and more distributed."

Examples of projects that attempt to contribute to the re-decentralization of the Internet include ArkOS, Diaspora, FreedomBox, IndieWeb, Namecoin, SAFE Network, twtxt and ZeroNet as well as advocacy group Redecentralize.org, which provides support for projects that aim to make the Web less centralized.

In an interview with BBC Radio 5 Live one of the co-founders of Redecentralize.org explained that:

- "As we've gone on there's been more and more internet traffic focused through particular nodes such as Google or Facebook. [...] Centralised services that hold all the user data and host it themselves have become increasingly popular because that business model has worked. As the Internet has become more mass market, people are not necessarily willing or knowledgable to host it themselves, so where that hosting is outsourced it's become the default, which allows a centralization of power and a centralization of data that I think is worrying."

### Blockchain Technology

In blockchain, decentralization refers to the transfer of control and decision-making from a centralized entity (individual, organization, or group thereof) to a distributed network. Decentralized networks strive to reduce the level of trust that participants must place in one another, and deter their ability to exert authority or control over one another in ways that degrade the functionality of the network. Cryptocurrencies use cryptographic proofs such as proof of work (e.g. Bitcoin) or proof of stake (e.g. Cardano) as a means of establishing decentralized consensus. Decentralized protocols, applications, and ledgers (used in Web3) could be more difficult for governments to regulate, similar to difficulties regulating BitTorrent (which is not a blockchain technology).

### Appropriate Technology

"Appropriate technology", originally described as "intermediate technology" by economist E. F. Schumacher in *Small Is Beautiful: A Study of Economics As If People Mattered*, is generally recognized as encompassing technologies that are small-scale, decentralized, labor-intensive, energy-efficient, environmentally sound, and locally controlled.

### Criticism

Factors hindering decentralization include weak local administrative or technical capacity, which may result in inefficient or ineffective services; inadequate financial resources available to perform new local responsibilities, especially in the start-up phase when they are most needed; or inequitable distribution of resources. Decentralization can make national policy coordination too complex; it may allow local elites to capture functions; local cooperation may be undermined by any distrust between private and public sectors; decentralization may result in higher enforcement costs and conflict for resources if there is no higher level of authority. Additionally, decentralization may not be as efficient for standardized, routine, network-based services, as opposed to those that need more complicated inputs. If there is a loss of economies of scale in procurement of labor or resources, the expense of decentralization can rise, even as central governments lose control over financial resources.

Other challenges, and even dangers, include the possibility that corrupt local elites can capture regional or local power centers, while constituents lose representation; patronage politics will become rampant and civil servants feel compromised; further necessary decentralization can be stymied; incomplete information and hidden decision-making can occur up and down the hierarchies; centralized power centers can find reasons to frustrate decentralization and bring power back to themselves.

It has been noted that while decentralization may increase "productive efficiency" it may undermine "allocative efficiency" by making redistribution of wealth more difficult. Decentralization will cause greater disparities between rich and poor regions, especially during times of crisis when the national government may not be able to help regions needing it.

### 1.4.2 Distributed Ledger Technology

A distributed ledger is the consensus of replicated, shared, and synchronized digital data that is geographically spread (distributed) across many sites, countries, or institutions. In contrast to a centralized database, a distributed ledger does not require a central administrator, and consequently does not have a single (central) point-of-failure. In general, a distributed ledger requires a peer-to-peer (P2P) computer network and consensus algorithms so that the ledger is reliably replicated across distributed computer nodes (servers, clients, etc.). The most common form of distributed ledger technology is the blockchain (commonly associated with the Bitcoin cryptocurrency), which can either be on a public or private network. Infrastructure for data management is a common barrier to implementing DLT.

#### Characteristics

Distributed ledger data is typically spread across multiple nodes (computational devices) on a P2P network, where each replicates and saves an identical copy of the ledger data and updates itself independently of other nodes. The primary advantage of this distributed processing pattern is the lack of a central authority, which would constitute a single point of failure. When a ledger update transaction is broadcast to the P2P network, each distributed node processes a new update transaction independently, and then collectively all working nodes use a consensus algorithm to determine the correct copy of the updated ledger. Once a consensus has been determined, all the other nodes update themselves with the latest, correct copy of the updated ledger. Security is enforced through cryptographic keys and signatures.

#### Applications

In 2016, some banks tested distributed ledger systems for payments to determine their usefulness. In 2020, Axoni launched Veris, a distributed ledger platform that manages equity swap transactions. The platform, which matches and reconciles post-trade data on stock swaps, is used by BlackRock Inc., Goldman Sachs Group Inc., and Citigroup, Inc. A pilot scheme by the Monetary Authority of Singapore completed its first live trades using DLT in 2022. The pilot by Singapore's central bank involved DBS and JP Morgan. The banks traded using smart contracts against liquidity pools of tokenized Singapore government bonds, Japanese government bonds, yen, and Singapore dollars. Singapore has set up two more pilots. Standard

Chartered Bank is exploring tokens for trade finance; and HSBC and United Overseas Bank are working with Marketnode, a digital markets infrastructure provider, on products for wealth management.

## Types

In the context of cryptocurrencies, distributed ledger technologies can be categorized in terms of their data structures, consensus algorithms, permissions, and whether they are mined. DLT data structure types include linear data structures (blockchains) to more complex directed acyclic graph (DAG) and hybrid data structures. DLT consensus algorithm types include proof-of-work (PoW) and proof-of-stake (PoS) algorithms and DAG consensus-building and voting algorithms. DLTs are generally either permissioned (private) or permissionless (public). PoW cryptocurrencies are generally either 'mined' or 'non-mined', where the latter typically indicates 'pre-mined' cryptocurrencies, such as XRP or IOTA. PoS cryptocurrencies do not use miners, instead usually relying on validation among owners of the cryptocurrency, such as Cardano or Solana. Blockchains are the most common DLT type, with a 256-bit secure hash algorithm (SHA). DLTs based on DAG data structures or hybrid blockchain-DAG decrease transaction data size and transaction costs, while increasing transaction speeds compared with Bitcoin, the first cryptocurrency. Examples of DAG DLT cryptocurrencies include MIOTA (IOTA Tangle DLT) and HBAR (Hedera Hashgraph, a patented DLT).

# CHAPTER 2
# CRYPTOCURRENCIES: A PRIMER

## 2.1 OVERVIEW OF CRYPTOCURRENCIES

A cryptocurrency, crypto-currency, or crypto is a digital currency designed to work as a medium of exchange through a computer network that is not reliant on any central authority, such as a government or bank, to uphold or maintain it.

Individual coin ownership records are stored in a digital ledger, which is a computerized database using strong cryptography to secure transaction records, control the creation of additional coins, and verify the transfer of coin ownership. Despite the term that has come to describe many of the fungible blockchain tokens that have been created, cryptocurrencies are not considered to be currencies in the traditional sense, and varying legal treatments have been applied to them in various jurisdicitons, including classification as commodities, securities, and currencies. Cryptocurrencies are generally viewed as a distinct asset class in practice. Some crypto schemes use validators to maintain the cryptocurrency. In a proof-of-stake model, owners put up their tokens as collateral. In return, they get authority over the token in proportion to the amount they stake. Generally, these token stakers get additional ownership in the token over time via network fees, newly minted tokens, or other such reward mechanisms.

Cryptocurrency does not exist in physical form (like paper money) and is typically not issued by a central authority. Cryptocurrencies typically use decentralized control as opposed to a central bank digital currency (CBDC). When a cryptocurrency is minted, created prior to issuance, or issued by a single issuer, it is generally considered centralized. When implemented with decentralized control, each cryptocurrency works through distributed ledger technology, typically a blockchain, that serves as a public financial transaction database.

The first cryptocurrency was Bitcoin, which was first released as open-source software in 2009. As of June 2023, there were more than 25,000 other cryptocurrencies in the marketplace, of which more than 40 had a market capitalization exceeding $1 billion.

### 2.1.1 History

In 1983, American cryptographer David Chaum conceived of a type of cryptographic electronic money called ecash. Later, in 1995, he implemented it through Digicash, an early form of cryptographic electronic payments. Digicash required user software in order to withdraw notes from a bank and designate specific encrypted keys before they could be sent to a recipient. This allowed the digital currency to be untraceable by a third party.

In 1996, the National Security Agency published a paper entitled *How to Make a Mint: The Cryptography of Anonymous Electronic Cash*, describing a cryptocurrency system. The paper was first published in an MIT mailing list and later in 1997 in *The American Law Review.*

In 1998, Wei Dai described "b-money," an anonymous, distributed electronic cash system. Shortly thereafter, Nick Szabo described bit gold. Like Bitcoin and other cryptocurrencies that would follow it, BitGold (not to be confused with the later gold-based exchange BitGold) was described as an electronic currency system that required users to complete a proof of work function with solutions being cryptographically put together and published.

In January 2009, Bitcoin was created by pseudonymous developer Satoshi Nakamoto. It used SHA-256, a cryptographic hash function, in its proof-of-work scheme. In April 2011, Namecoin was created as an attempt at forming a decentralized DNS. In October 2011, Litecoin, was released which used scrypt as its hash function instead of SHA-256. Peercoin, created in August 2012, used a hybrid of proof-of-work and proof-of-stake.

Cryptocurrency has undergone several periods of growth and retraction, including several bubbles and market crashes, such as in 2011, 2013–2014/15, 2017–2018 and 2021–2023.

On 6 August 2014, the UK announced its Treasury had commissioned a study of cryptocurrencies, and what role, if any, they could play in the UK economy. The study was also to report on whether regulation should be considered. Its final report was published in 2018, and it issued a consultation on cryptoassets and stablecoins in January 2021.

In June 2021, El Salvador became the first country to accept Bitcoin as legal tender, after the Legislative Assembly had voted 62–22 to pass a bill submitted by President Nayib Bukele classifying the cryptocurrency as such.

In August 2021, Cuba followed with Resolution 215 to recognize and regulate cryptocurrencies such as Bitcoin.

In September 2021, the government of China, the single largest market for cryptocurrency, declared all cryptocurrency transactions illegal. This completed a crackdown on cryptocurrency that had previously banned the operation of intermediaries and miners within China.

On 15 September 2022, the world's second largest cryptocurrency at that time, Ethereum transitioned its consensus mechanism from proof-of-work (PoW) to proof-of-stake (PoS) in an upgrade process known as "the Merge". According to the Ethereum Founder, the upgrade can cut both Ethereum's energy use and carbon-dioxide emissions by 99.9%.

On 11 November 2022, FTX Trading Ltd., a cryptocurrency exchange, which also operated a crypto hedge fund, and had been valued at $18 billion, filed for bankruptcy. The financial impact of the collapse extended beyond the immediate FTX customer base, as reported, while, at a Reuters conference, financial industry executives said that "regulators must step in to protect crypto investors." Technology analyst Avivah Litan commented on the cryptocurrency ecosystem that "everything...needs to improve dramatically in terms of user experience, controls, safety, customer service."

## 2.1.2 Formal Definition

According to Jan Lansky, a cryptocurrency is a system that meets six conditions:

- The system does not require a central authority; its state is maintained through distributed consensus.
- The system keeps an overview of cryptocurrency units and their ownership.
- The system defines whether new cryptocurrency units can be created. If new cryptocurrency units can be created, the system defines the circumstances of their origin and how to determine the ownership of these new units.
- Ownership of cryptocurrency units can be proved exclusively cryptographically.
- The system allows transactions to be performed in which ownership of the cryptographic units is changed. A transaction statement can only be issued by an entity proving the current ownership of these units.
- If two different instructions for changing the ownership of the same cryptographic units are simultaneously entered, the system performs at most one of them.

In March 2018, the word *cryptocurrency* was added to the *Merriam-Webster Dictionary*.

### Altcoins

After the early innovation of Bitcoin in 2008, and the early network effect gained by Bitcoin, tokens, cryptocurrencies, and other digital assets that were not Bitcoin became collectively known during the 2010s as alternative cryptocurrencies, or "altcoins." Sometimes the term "alt coins" was used, or disparagingly, "shitcoins". Paul Vigna of *The Wall Street Journal* described altcoins in 2020 as "alternative versions of Bitcoin" given its role as the model protocol for cryptocurrency designers. A Polytechnic University of Catalonia thesis in 2021 used a broader description including not only alternative versions of Bitcoin, but every cryptocurrency other than bitcoin. "As of early 2020, there were more than 5,000 cryptocurrencies. Altcoin is the combination of two words "alt" and "coin" and includes all alternatives to Bitcoin."

Altcoins often have underlying differences when compared to Bitcoin. For example, Litecoin aims to process a block every 2.5 minutes, rather than Bitcoin's 10 minutes, which allows Litecoin to confirm transactions faster than Bitcoin. Another example is Ethereum, which has smart contract functionality that allows decentralized applications to be run on its blockchain. Ethereum was the most used blockchain in 2020, according to Bloomberg News. In 2016, it had the largest "following" of any altcoin, according to the *New York Times.*

Significant market price rallies across multiple altcoin markets are often referred to as an "altseason".

#### Stablecoins

Stablecoins are cryptocurrencies designed to maintain a stable level of purchasing power. Notably, these designs are not foolproof, as a number of stablecoins have crashed or lost their peg. For example, on 11 May 2022, Terra's stablecoin UST fell from $1 to 26 cents. The subsequent failure of Terraform Labs resulted in the loss of nearly $40B invested in the Terra and Luna coins. In September 2022, South Korean prosecutors requested the issuance of an Interpol Red Notice against the company's founder, Do Kwon. In Hong Kong, the expected regulatory framework for stablecoins in 2023/24 is being shaped and includes a few considerations.

### 2.1.3 Architecture

Cryptocurrency is produced by an entire cryptocurrency system collectively, at a rate which is defined when the system is created and which is publicly stated. In centralized banking and economic systems such as the US Federal Reserve System, corporate boards or governments control the supply of currency. In the case of cryptocurrency, companies or governments cannot produce new units, and have not so far provided backing for other firms, banks or corporate entities which hold asset value measured in it. The underlying technical system upon which cryptocurrencies are based was created by Satoshi Nakamoto.

Within a proof-of-work system such as Bitcoin, the safety, integrity and balance of ledgers is maintained by a community of mutually distrustful parties referred to as miners. Miners use their computers to help validate and timestamp transactions, adding them to the ledger in accordance with a particular timestamping scheme. In a proof-of-stake blockchain, transactions are validated by holders of the associated cryptocurrency, sometimes grouped together in stake pools.

Most cryptocurrencies are designed to gradually decrease the production of that currency, placing a cap on the total amount of that currency that will ever be in circulation. Compared with ordinary currencies held by financial institutions or kept as cash on hand, cryptocurrencies can be more difficult for seizure by law enforcement.

### Blockchain

The validity of each cryptocurrency's coins is provided by a blockchain. A blockchain is a continuously growing list of records, called *blocks*, which are linked and secured using cryptography. Each block typically contains a hash pointer as a link to a previous block, a timestamp and transaction data. By design, blockchains are inherently resistant to modification of the data. It is "an open, distributed ledger that can record transactions between two parties efficiently and in a verifiable and permanent way". For use as a distributed ledger, a blockchain is typically managed by a peer-to-peer network collectively adhering to a protocol for validating new blocks. Once recorded, the data in any given block cannot be altered retroactively without the alteration of all subsequent blocks, which requires collusion of the network majority. Blockchains are secure by design and are an example of a distributed computing system with high Byzantine fault tolerance. Decentralized consensus has therefore been achieved with a blockchain.

### Nodes

A *node* is a computer that connects to a cryptocurrency network. The node supports the cryptocurrency's network through either relaying transactions, validation, or hosting a copy of the blockchain. In terms of relaying transactions, each network computer (node) has a copy of the blockchain of the cryptocurrency it supports. When a transaction is made, the node creating the transaction broadcasts details of the transaction using encryption to other nodes throughout the node network so that the transaction (and every other transaction) is known. Node owners are either volunteers, those hosted by the organization or body responsible for developing the cryptocurrency blockchain network technology, or those who are enticed to host a node to receive rewards from hosting the node network.

### Timestamping

Cryptocurrencies use various timestamping schemes to "prove" the validity of transactions added to the blockchain ledger without the need for a trusted third party. The first timestamping scheme invented was the proof-of-work scheme. The most widely used proof-of-work schemes are based on SHA-256 and scrypt. Some other hashing algorithms that are used for proof-of-work include CryptoNote, Blake, SHA-3, and X11. Another method is called the proof-of-stake scheme. Proof-of-stake is a method of securing a cryptocurrency network and achieving distributed consensus through requesting users to show ownership of a certain amount of currency.

It is different from proof-of-work systems that run difficult hashing algorithms to validate electronic transactions. The scheme is largely dependent on the coin, and there is currently no standard form of it. Some cryptocurrencies use a combined proof-of-work and proof-of-stake scheme.

## Mining

On a blockchain, *mining* is the validation of transactions. For this effort, successful miners obtain new cryptocurrency as a reward. The reward decreases transaction fees by creating a complementary incentive to contribute to the processing power of the network. The rate of generating hashes, which validate any transaction, has been increased by the use of specialized machines such as FPGAs and ASICs running complex hashing algorithms like SHA-256 and scrypt. This arms race for cheaper-yet-efficient machines has existed since Bitcoin was introduced in 2009. Mining is measured by hash rate typically in TH/s.

With more people entering the world of virtual currency, generating hashes for validation has become more complex over time, forcing miners to invest increasingly large sums of money to improve computing performance. Consequently, the reward for finding a hash has diminished and often does not justify the investment in equipment and cooling facilities (to mitigate the heat the equipment produces), and the electricity required to run them. Popular regions for mining include those with inexpensive electricity, a cold climate, and jurisdictions with clear and conducive regulations. By July 2019, Bitcoin's electricity consumption was estimated to be approximately 7 gigawatts, around 0.2% of the global total, or equivalent to the energy consumed nationally by Switzerland.

Some miners pool resources, sharing their processing power over a network to split the reward equally, according to the amount of work they contributed to the probability of finding a block. A "share" is awarded to members of the mining pool who present a valid partial proof-of-work.

The Chinese Government has halted trading of virtual currency, banned initial coin offerings and shut down mining. Many Chinese miners have since relocated to Canada and Texas. One company is operating data centers for mining operations at Canadian oil and gas field sites, due to low gas prices. In June 2018, Hydro Quebec proposed to the provincial government to allocate 500 megawatts of power to crypto companies for mining. According to a February 2018 report from *Fortune*,

Iceland has become a haven for cryptocurrency miners in part because of its cheap electricity.

In March 2018, the city of Plattsburgh, New York put an 18-month moratorium on all cryptocurrency mining in an effort to preserve natural resources and the "character and direction" of the city. In 2021, Kazakhstan became the second-biggest crypto-currency mining country, producing 18.1% of the global exahash rate. The country built a compound containing 50,000 computers near Ekibastuz.

### GPU Price Rise

An increase in cryptocurrency mining increased the demand for graphics cards (GPU) in 2017. The computing power of GPUs makes them well-suited to generating hashes. Popular favorites of cryptocurrency miners such as Nvidia's GTX 1060 and GTX 1070 graphics cards, as well as AMD's RX 570 and RX 580 GPUs, doubled or tripled in price – or were out of stock. A GTX 1070 Ti which was released at a price of $450 sold for as much as $1,100. Another popular card, the GTX 1060 (6 GB model) was released at an MSRP of $250, and sold for almost $500. RX 570 and RX 580 cards from AMD were out of stock for almost a year. Miners regularly buy up the entire stock of new GPU's as soon as they are available. Nvidia has asked retailers to do what they can when it comes to selling GPUs to gamers instead of miners. Boris Böhles, PR manager for Nvidia in the German region, said: "Gamers come first for Nvidia."

### Mining Accelerator Chips

Numerous companies developed dedicated crypto-mining accelerator chips, capable of price-performance far higher than that of CPU or GPU mining. At one point Intel markeA cryptocurrency wallet is a means of storing the public and private "keys" (address) or seed which can be used to receive or spend the cryptocurrency. With the private key, it is possible to write in the public ledger, effectively spending the associated cryptocurrency. With the public key, it is possible for others to send currency to the wallet. There exist multiple methods of storing keys or seed in a wallet. These methods range from using paper wallets (which are public, private or seed keys written on paper), to using hardware wallets (which are hardware to store your wallet information), to a digital wallet (which is a computer with a software hosting your wallet information), to hosting your wallet using an exchange where cryptocurrency is traded, or by storing your wallet information on a digital medium such as plaintext.

### Anonymity

Bitcoin is pseudonymous, rather than anonymous; the cryptocurrency in a wallet is not tied to a person, but rather to one or more specific keys (or "addresses"). Thereby, Bitcoin owners are not immediately identifiable, but all transactions are publicly available in the blockchain. Still, cryptocurrency exchanges are often required by law to collect the personal information of their users. Some cryptocurrencies, such as Monero, Zerocoin, Zerocash, and CryptoNote, implement additional measures to increase privacy, such as by using zero-knowledge proofs. A recent 2020 study presented different attacks on privacy in cryptocurrencies. The attacks demonstrated how the anonymity techniques are not sufficient safeguards. In order to improve privacy, researchers suggested several different ideas including new cryptographic schemes and mechanisms for hiding the IP address of the source.

### 2.1.4 Economics

Cryptocurrencies are used primarily outside banking and governmental institutions and are exchanged over the Internet.

#### Block Rewards

Proof-of-work cryptocurrencies, such as Bitcoin, offer block rewards incentives for miners. There has been an implicit belief that whether miners are paid by block rewards or transaction fees does not affect the security of the blockchain, but a study suggests that this may not be the case under certain circumstances.

The rewards paid to miners increase the supply of the cryptocurrency. By making sure that verifying transactions is a costly business, the integrity of the network can be preserved as long as benevolent nodes control a majority of computing power. The verification algorithm requires a lot of processing power, and thus electricity in order to make verification costly enough to accurately validate public blockchain. Not only do miners have to factor in the costs associated with expensive equipment necessary to stand a chance of solving a hash problem, they must further consider the significant amount of electrical power in search of the solution. Generally, the block rewards outweigh electricity and equipment costs, but this may not always be the case.

The current value, not the long-term value, of the cryptocurrency supports the reward scheme to incentivize miners to engage in costly mining activities. In 2018, Bitcoin's design caused a 1.4% welfare loss compared to an efficient cash system, while a cash system with 2% money growth has a minor 0.003% welfare cost. The main source for this inefficiency is the large mining cost, which is estimated to be US$360 million per year. This translates into users being willing to accept a cash system with an inflation rate of 230% before being better off using Bitcoin as a means of payment. However, the efficiency of the Bitcoin system can be significantly improved by optimizing the rate of coin creation and minimizing transaction fees. Another potential improvement is to eliminate inefficient mining activities by changing the consensus protocol altogether.

## Transaction Fees

Transaction fees for cryptocurrency depend mainly on the supply of network capacity at the time, versus the demand from the currency holder for a faster transaction. The currency holder can choose a specific transaction fee, while network entities process transactions in order of highest offered fee to lowest. Cryptocurrency exchanges can simplify the process for currency holders by offering priority alternatives and thereby determine which fee will likely cause the transaction to be processed in the requested time.

For Ethereum, transaction fees differ by computational complexity, bandwidth use, and storage needs, while Bitcoin transaction fees differ by transaction size and whether the transaction uses SegWit. In February 2023, the median transaction fee for Ether corresponded to $2.2845, while for Bitcoin it corresponded to $0.659. Some cryptocurrencies have no transaction fees, and instead rely on client-side proof-of-work as the transaction prioritization and anti-spam mechanism.

## Exchanges

Cryptocurrency exchanges allow customers to trade cryptocurrencies for other assets, such as conventional fiat money, or to trade between different digital currencies. Crypto marketplaces do not guarantee that an investor is completing a purchase or trade at the optimal price. As a result, as of 2020 it was possible to arbitrage to find the difference in price across several markets.

## Atomic Swaps

Atomic swaps are a mechanism where one cryptocurrency can be exchanged directly for another cryptocurrency, without the need for a trusted third party such as an exchange.

## ATMs

Jordan Kelley, founder of Robocoin, launched the first Bitcoin ATM in the United States on 20 February 2014. The kiosk installed in Austin, Texas, is similar to bank ATMs but has scanners to read government-issued identification such as a driver's license or a passport to confirm users' identities.

## Initial Coin Offerings

An initial coin offering (ICO) is a controversial means of raising funds for a new cryptocurrency venture. An ICO may be used by startups with the intention of avoiding regulation. However, securities regulators in many jurisdictions, including in the U.S., and Canada, have indicated that if a coin or token is an "investment contract" (e.g., under the Howey test, i.e., an investment of money with a reasonable expectation of profit based significantly on the entrepreneurial or managerial efforts of others), it is a security and is subject to securities regulation.

In an ICO campaign, a percentage of the cryptocurrency (usually in the form of "tokens") is sold to early backers of the project in exchange for legal tender or other cryptocurrencies, often Bitcoin or Ether.

According to PricewaterhouseCoopers, four of the 10 biggest proposed initial coin offerings have used Switzerland as a base, where they are frequently registered as non-profit foundations. The Swiss regulatory agency FINMA stated that it would take a "balanced approach" to ICO projects and would allow "legitimate innovators to navigate the regulatory landscape and so launch their projects in a way consistent with national laws protecting investors and the integrity of the financial system." In response to numerous requests by industry representatives, a legislative ICO working group began to issue legal guidelines in 2018, which are intended to remove uncertainty from cryptocurrency offerings and to establish sustainable business practices.

## Price Trends

The market capitalization of a cryptocurrency is calculated by multiplying the price by the number of coins in circulation. The total cryptocurrency market cap has historically been dominated by Bitcoin accounting for at least 50% of the market cap value where altcoins have increased and decreased in market cap value in relation to Bitcoin. Bitcoin's value is largely determined by speculation among other technological limiting factors known as blockchain rewards coded into the architecture technology of Bitcoin itself. The cryptocurrency market cap follows a trend known as the "halving", which is when the block rewards received from Bitcoin are halved due to technological mandated limited factors instilled into Bitcoin which in turn limits the supply of Bitcoin. As the date reaches near of a halving (twice thus far historically) the cryptocurrency market cap increases, followed by a downtrend. By June 2021, cryptocurrency had begun to be offered by some wealth managers in the US for 401(k)s.

## Volatility

Cryptocurrency prices are much more volatile than established financial assets such as stocks. For example, over one week in May 2022, Bitcoin lost 20% of its value and Ethereum lost 26%, while Solana and Cardano lost 41% and 35% respectively. The falls were attributed to warnings about inflation. By comparison, in the same week, the Nasdaq tech stock index fell 7.6 per cent and the FTSE 100 was 3.6 per cent down. In the longer term, of the 10 leading cryptocurrencies identified by the total value of coins in circulation in January 2018, only four (Bitcoin, Ethereum, Cardano and Ripple (XRP)) were still in that position in early 2022. The total value of all cryptocurrencies was $2 trillion at the end of 2021, but had halved nine months later. The Wall Street Journal has commented that the crypto sector has become "intertwined" with the rest of the capital markets and "sensitive to the same forces that drive tech stocks and other risk assets", such as inflation forecasts.

### Databases

There are also *centralized* databases, outside of blockchains, that store crypto market data. Compared to the blockchain, databases perform fast as there is no verification process. Four of the most popular cryptocurrency market databases are CoinMarketCap, CoinGecko, BraveNewCoin, and Cryptocompare.

## 2.1.5 Social and Political Aspects

According to Alan Feuer of *The New York Times*, libertarians and anarcho-capitalists were attracted to the philosophical idea behind Bitcoin. Early Bitcoin supporter Roger Ver said: "At first, almost everyone who got involved did so for philosophical reasons. We saw Bitcoin as a great idea, as a way to separate money from the state." Economist Paul Krugman argues that cryptocurrencies like Bitcoin are "something of a cult" based in "paranoid fantasies" of government power.

David Golumbia says that the ideas influencing Bitcoin advocates emerge from right-wing extremist movements such as the Liberty Lobby and the John Birch Society and their anti-Central Bank rhetoric, or, more recently, Ron Paul and Tea Party-style libertarianism. Steve Bannon, who owns a "good stake" in Bitcoin, sees cryptocurrency as a form of disruptive populism, taking control back from central authorities.

Bitcoin's founder, Satoshi Nakamoto, has supported the idea that cryptocurrencies go well with libertarianism. "It's very attractive to the libertarian viewpoint if we can explain it properly," Nakamoto said in 2008.

According to the European Central Bank, the decentralization of money offered by Bitcoin has its theoretical roots in the Austrian school of economics, especially with Friedrich von Hayek in his book *Denationalisation of Money: The Argument Refined*, in which Hayek advocates a complete free market in the production, distribution and management of money to end the monopoly of central banks.

## 2.1.6 Increasing Regulation

The rise in the popularity of cryptocurrencies and their adoption by financial institutions has led some governments to assess whether regulation is needed to protect users. The Financial Action Task Force (FATF) has defined cryptocurrency-related services as "virtual asset service providers" (VASPs) and recommended that they be regulated with the same money laundering (AML) and know your customer (KYC) requirements as financial institutions.

In May 2020, the Joint Working Group on interVASP Messaging Standards published "IVMS 101", a universal common language for communication of required originator and beneficiary information between VASPs. The FATF and financial regulators were informed as the data model was developed.

In June 2020, FATF updated its guidance to include the "Travel Rule" for cryptocurrencies, a measure which mandates that VASPs obtain, hold, and exchange information about the originators and beneficiaries of virtual asset transfers. Subsequent standardized protocol specifications recommended using JSON for relaying data between VASPs and identity services. As of December 2020, the IVMS 101 data model has yet to be finalized and ratified by the three global standard setting bodies that created it.

The European Commission published a digital finance strategy in September 2020. This included a draft regulation on Markets in Crypto-Assets (MiCA), which aimed to provide a comprehensive regulatory framework for digital assets in the EU.

On 10 June 2021, the Basel Committee on Banking Supervision proposed that banks that held cryptocurrency assets must set aside capital to cover all potential losses. For instance, if a bank were to hold Bitcoin worth $2 billion, it would be required to set aside enough capital to cover the entire $2 billion. This is a more extreme standard than banks are usually held to when it comes to other assets. However, this is a proposal and not a regulation.

The IMF is seeking a coordinated, consistent and comprehensive approach to supervising cryptocurrencies. Tobias Adrian, the IMF's financial counsellor and head of its monetary and capital markets department said in a January 2022 interview that "Agreeing global regulations is never quick. But if we start now, we can achieve the goal of maintaining financial stability while also enjoying the benefits which the underlying technological innovations bring,"

In May 2024, 15 years after the advent of the first blockchain, Bitcoin, the US Congress advanced a bill to the full House of Representatives to provide regulatory clarity for digital assets. The Financial Innovation and Technology for the 21st Century Act, which defines responsibilities between various US agencies, notably between the Commodity Futures Trading Commission (CFTC) for decentralized blockchains and the Securities and Exchange Commission (SEC) for blockchains that are functional but not decentralized. Stablecoins are excluded from both CFTC and SEC regulation in this bill, "except for fraud and certain activities by registered firms."

## China

In September 2017, China banned ICOs to cause abnormal return from cryptocurrency decreasing during announcement window. The liquidity changes by banning ICOs in China was temporarily negative while the liquidity effect became positive after news. On 18 May 2021, China banned financial institutions and payment companies from being able to provide cryptocurrency transaction related services. This led to a sharp fall in the price of the biggest proof of work cryptocurrencies. For instance, Bitcoin fell 31%, Ethereum fell 44%, Binance Coin fell 32% and Dogecoin fell 30%. Proof of work mining was the next focus, with regulators in popular mining regions citing the use of electricity generated from highly polluting sources such as coal to create Bitcoin and Ethereum. In September 2021, the Chinese government declared all cryptocurrency transactions of any kind illegal, completing its crackdown on cryptocurrency.

### Cook Islands

In April 2024, TVNZ's 1 News reported that the Cook Islands government was proposing legislation that would allow "recovery agents" to use various means including hacking to investigate or find cryptocurrency that may have been used for illegal means or is the "proceeds of crime." The Tainted Cryptocurrency Recovery Bill was drafted by two lawyers hired by US-based debt collection company Drumcliffe. The proposed legislation was criticised by Cook Islands Crown Law's deputy solicitor general David Greig, who described it as "flawed" and said that some provisions were "clearly unconstitutional". The Cook Islands Financial Services Development Authority described Drumcliffe's involvement as a conflict of interest.

Similar criticism was echoed by Auckland University of Technology cryptocurrency specialist and senior lecturer Jeff Nijsse and University of Otago political scientist Professor Robert Patman, who described it as government overreach and described it as inconsistent with international law. Since the Cook Islands is an associated state that is part of the Realm of New Zealand, Patman said that the law would have "implications for New Zealand's governance arrangements." A spokesperson for New Zealand Foreign Minister Winston Peters confirmed that New Zealand officials were discussing the legislation with their Cook Islands counterparts. Cook Islands Prime Minister Mark Brown defended the legislation as part of the territory's fight against international cybercrime.

### El Salvador

On 9 June 2021, El Salvador announced that it will adopt Bitcoin as legal tender, becoming the first country to do so.

### South Africa

South Africa, which has seen a large number of scams related to cryptocurrency, is said to be putting a regulatory timeline in place that will produce a regulatory framework. The largest scam occurred in April 2021, where the two founders of an African-based cryptocurrency exchange called Africrypt, Raees Cajee and Ameer Cajee, disappeared with $3.8 billion worth of Bitcoin. Additionally, Mirror Trading

International disappeared with $170 million worth of cryptocurrency in January 2021.

### South Korea

In March 2021, South Korea implemented new legislation to strengthen their oversight of digital assets. This legislation requires all digital asset managers, providers and exchanges to be registered with the Korea Financial Intelligence Unit in order to operate in South Korea. Registering with this unit requires that all exchanges are certified by the Information Security Management System and that they ensure all customers have real name bank accounts. It also requires that the CEO and board members of the exchanges have not been convicted of any crimes and that the exchange holds sufficient levels of deposit insurance to cover losses arising from hacks.

### Switzerland

Switzerland was one of the first countries to implement the FATF's Travel Rule. FINMA, the Swiss regulator, issued its own guidance to VASPs in 2019. The guidance followed the FATF's Recommendation 16, however with stricter requirements. According to FINMA's requirements, VASPs need to verify the identity of the beneficiary of the transfer.

### Turkey

On 30 April 2021, the Central Bank of the Republic of Turkey banned the use of cryptocurrencies and cryptoassets for making purchases on the grounds that the use of cryptocurrencies for such payments poses significant transaction risks.

### United Kingdom

In the United Kingdom, as of 10 January 2021, all cryptocurrency firms, such as exchanges, advisors and professionals that have either a presence, market product or provide services within the UK market must register with the Financial Conduct Authority. Additionally, on 27 June 2021, the financial watchdog demanded that Binance, the world's largest cryptocurrency exchange, cease all regulated activities in the UK.

### United States

In 2021, 17 states passed laws and resolutions concerning cryptocurrency regulation. The U.S. Securities and Exchange Commission (SEC) is considering what steps to take. On 8 July 2021, Senator Elizabeth Warren, part of the Senate Banking Committee, wrote to the chairman of the SEC and demanded answers on cryptocurrency regulation due to the increase in cryptocurrency exchange use and the danger this posed to consumers. On 5 August 2021, SEC Chairman Gary

Gensler responded to Senator Elizabeth Warren's letter regarding cryptocurrency regulation and called for legislation focused on "crypto trading, lending and DeFi platforms," because of how vulnerable the investors could be when they traded on crypto trading platforms without a broker. He also argued that many tokens in the crypto market may be unregistered securities without required disclosures or market oversight. Additionally, Gensler did not hold back in his criticism of stablecoins. These tokens, which are pegged to the value of fiat currencies, may allow individuals to bypass important public policy goals related to traditional banking and financial systems, such as anti-money laundering, tax compliance, and sanctions.

On 19 October 2021, the first bitcoin-linked exchange-traded fund (ETF) from ProShares started trading on the NYSE under the ticker "BITO." ProShares CEO Michael L. Sapir said the ETF would expose Bitcoin to a wider range of investors without the hassle of setting up accounts with cryptocurrency providers. Ian Balina, the CEO of Token Metrics, stated that the approval of the "BITO" ETF by the SEC was a significant endorsement for the crypto industry because many regulators globally were not in favor of crypto as well as the hesitance to accept crypto from retail investors. This event would eventually open more opportunities for new capital and new people in this space.

The United States Department of the Treasury, on 20 May 2021, announced that it would require any transfer worth $10,000 or more to be reported to the Internal Revenue Service since cryptocurrency already posed a problem where illegal activity like tax evasion was facilitated broadly. This release from the IRS was a part of efforts to promote better compliance and consider more severe penalties for tax evaders.

On 17 February 2022, the Justice department named Eun Young Choi as the first director of a National Cryptocurrency Enforcement Team to aid in identification of and dealing with misuse of cryptocurrencies and other digital assets.

The Biden administration faced a dilemma as it tried to develop regulations for the cryptocurrency industry. On one hand, officials were hesitant to restrict the growing and profitable industry. On the other hand, they were committed to preventing illegal cryptocurrency transactions. To reconcile these conflicting goals, on 9 March 2022, President Biden issued an executive order.

Followed by the executive order, on 16 September 2022, the Comprehensive Framework for Responsible Development of Digital Assets document was released to support development of cryptocurrencies and restrict their illegal use.

The executive order included all digital assets, but cryptocurrencies posed both the greatest security risks and potential economic benefits. Though this might not address all of the challenges in crypto industry, it was a significant milestone in the U.S. cryptocurrency regulation history.

In February 2023, the Securities and Exchange Commission (SEC) ruled that cryptocurrency exchange Kraken's estimated $42 billion in staked assets globally operated as an illegal securities seller. The company agreed to a $30 million settlement with the SEC and to cease selling its staking service in the U.S. The case would impact other major crypto exchanges operating staking programs.

On 23 March 2023, the U.S. Securities and Exchange Commission (SEC) issued an alert to investors stating that firms offering crypto asset securities may not be complying with U.S. laws. The SEC stated that unregistered offerings of crypto asset securities may not include important information.

### 2.1.7 Legality

The legal status of cryptocurrencies varies substantially from country to country and is still undefined or changing in many of them. At least one study has shown that broad generalizations about the use of Bitcoin in illicit finance are significantly overstated and that blockchain analysis is an effective crime fighting and intelligence gathering tool. While some countries have explicitly allowed their use and trade, others have banned or restricted it. According to the Library of Congress in 2021, an «absolute ban» on trading or using cryptocurrencies applies in 9 countries: Algeria, Bangladesh, Bolivia, China, Egypt, Iraq, Morocco, Nepal, and the United Arab Emirates. An «implicit ban» applies in another 39 countries or regions, which include: Bahrain, Benin, Burkina Faso, Burundi, Cameroon, Chad, Cote d'Ivoire, the Dominican Republic, Ecuador, Gabon, Georgia, Guyana, Indonesia, Iran, Jordan, Kazakhstan, Kuwait, Lebanon, Lesotho, Macau, Maldives, Mali, Moldova, Namibia, Niger, Nigeria, Oman, Pakistan, Palau, Republic of Congo, Saudi Arabia, Sengeal, Tajikistan, Tanzania, Togo, Turkey, Turkmenistan, Qatar and Vietnam. In the United States and Canada, state and provincial securities regulators, coordinated through the North American Securities Administrators Association, are investigating "Bitcoin scams" and ICOs in 40 jurisdictions.

Various government agencies, departments, and courts have classified Bitcoin differently. China Central Bank banned the handling of Bitcoins by financial institutions in China in early 2014. In Russia, though owning cryptocurrency is legal, its residents are only allowed to purchase goods from other residents using the Russian ruble while nonresidents are allowed to use foreign currency. Regulations and bans that apply to Bitcoin probably extend to similar cryptocurrency systems. In August 2018, the Bank of Thailand announced its plans to create its own cryptocurrency, the Central Bank Digital Currency (CBDC).

## Advertising Bans

Cryptocurrency advertisements have been banned on the following platforms:

- Google - Ended August 2021
- Twitter
- Facebook - Ended December 2021
- Bing - Ended June 2022
- Snapchat
- LinkedIn
- MailChimp
- Baidu
- Tencent
- Weibo
- Line
- Yandex

## U.S. Tax Status

On 25 March 2014, the United States Internal Revenue Service (IRS) ruled that Bitcoin will be treated as property for tax purposes. Therefore, virtual currencies are considered commodities subject to capital gains tax.

## Legal Concerns Relating to an Unregulated Global Economy

As the popularity and demand for online currencies has increased since the inception of Bitcoin in 2009, so have concerns that such an unregulated person to person global economy that cryptocurrencies offer may become a threat to society. Concerns abound that altcoins may become tools for anonymous web criminals.

Cryptocurrency networks display a lack of regulation that has been criticized as enabling criminals who seek to evade taxes and launder money. Money laundering issues are also present in regular bank transfers, however with bank-to-bank wire transfers for instance, the account holder must at least provide a proven identity.

Transactions that occur through the use and exchange of these altcoins are independent from formal banking systems, and therefore can make tax evasion simpler for individuals. Since charting taxable income is based upon what a recipient reports to the revenue service, it becomes extremely difficult to account for transactions made using existing cryptocurrencies, a mode of exchange that is complex and difficult to track.

Systems of anonymity that most cryptocurrencies offer can also serve as a simpler means to launder money. Rather than laundering money through an intricate net of financial actors and offshore bank accounts, laundering money through altcoins can be achieved through anonymous transactions. Cryptocurrency makes legal enforcement against extremist groups more complicated, which consequently strengthens them. White supremacist Richard Spencer went as far as to declare Bitcoin the "currency of the alt-right".

## Loss, Theft, and Fraud

In February 2014, the world's largest Bitcoin exchange, Mt. Gox, declared bankruptcy. Likely due to theft, the company claimed that it had lost nearly 750,000 Bitcoins belonging to their clients. This added up to approximately 7% of all Bitcoins in existence, worth a total of $473 million. Mt. Gox blamed hackers, who had exploited the transaction malleability problems in the network. The price of a Bitcoin fell from a high of about $1,160 in December to under $400 in February.

On 21 November 2017, Tether announced that it had been hacked, losing $31 million in USDT from its core treasury wallet. On 7 December 2017, Slovenian cryptocurrency exchange Nicehash reported that hackers had stolen over $70M using a hijacked company computer. On 19 December 2017, Yapian, the owner of South Korean exchange Youbit, filed for bankruptcy after suffering two hacks that year. Customers were still granted access to 75% of their assets.

In May 2018, Bitcoin Gold had its transactions hijacked and abused by unknown hackers. Exchanges lost an estimated $18m and Bitcoin Gold was delisted from Bittrex after it refused to pay its share of the damages. On 13 September 2018, Homero Josh Garza was sentenced to 21 months of imprisonment, followed by three years of supervised release. Garza had founded the cryptocurrency startups GAW Miners and ZenMiner in 2014, acknowledged in a plea agreement that the companies were part of a pyramid scheme, and pleaded guilty to wire fraud in 2015. The U.S. Securities and Exchange Commission separately brought a civil enforcement action against Garza, who was eventually ordered to pay a judgment of $9.1 million plus $700,000 in interest. The SEC's complaint stated that Garza, through his companies, had fraudulently sold "investment contracts representing shares in the profits they claimed would be generated" from mining.

In January 2018, Japanese exchange Coincheck reported that hackers had stolen $530M worth of cryptocurrencies. In June 2018, South Korean exchange Coinrail was hacked, losing over $37M worth of cryptos. The hack worsened an already ongoing cryptocurrency selloff by an additional $42 billion. On 9 July 2018, the exchange Bancor, whose code and fundraising had been subjects of controversy, had $23.5 million in cryptocurrency stolen.

A 2020 EU report found that users had lost crypto-assets worth hundreds of millions of US dollars in security breaches at exchanges and storage providers. Between 2011 and 2019, reported breaches ranged from four to twelve a year. In 2019, more than a billion dollars worth of cryptoassets was reported stolen. Stolen assets "typically find their way to illegal markets and are used to fund further criminal activity".

According to a 2020 report produced by the United States Attorney General's Cyber-Digital Task Force, the following three categories make up the majority of illicit cryptocurrency uses:

- financial transactions associated with the commission of crimes;
- money laundering and the shielding of legitimate activity from tax, reporting, or other legal requirements; or
- crimes, such as theft, directly implicating the cryptocurrency marketplace itself."

The report concludes that "for cryptocurrency to realize its truly transformative potential, it is imperative that these risks be addressed" and that "the government has legal and regulatory tools available at its disposal to confront the threats posed by cryptocurrency's illicit uses".

According to the UK 2020 national risk assessment—a comprehensive assessment of money laundering and terrorist financing risk in the UK—the risk of using cryptoassets such as Bitcoin for money laundering and terrorism financing is assessed as "medium" (from "low" in the previous 2017 report). Legal scholars suggested that the money laundering opportunities may be more perceived than real. Blockchain analysis company Chainalysis concluded that illicit activities like cybercrime, money laundering and terrorism financing made up only 0.15% of all crypto transactions conducted in 2021, representing a total of $14 billion.

In December 2021, Monkey Kingdom, a NFT project based in Hong Kong, lost US$1.3 million worth of cryptocurrencies via a phishing link used by the hacker. On November 2, 2023, Sam Bankman-Fried was pronounced guilty on seven counts of fraud related to FTX. Federal criminal court sentencing experts speculated on the potential amount of prison time likely to be meted out. On March 28, 2024, the court sentenced Bankman-Fried to 25 years in prison.

## Money Laundering

According to blockchain data company Chainalysis, criminals laundered US$8,600,000,000 worth of cryptocurrency in 2021, up by 30% from the previous year. The data suggests that rather than managing numerous illicit havens, cybercriminals make use of a small group of purpose built centralized exchanges for sending and receiving illicit cryptocurrency. In 2021, those exchanges received 47% of funds sent by crime linked addresses. Almost $2.2bn worth of cryptocurrencies was embezzled from DeFi protocols in 2021, which represents 72% of all cryptocurrency theft in 2021. According to *Bloomberg* and the *New York Times*, Federation Tower, a two skyscraper complex in the heart of Moscow City, is home to many cryptocurrency businesses under suspicion of facilitating extensive money laundering, including accepting illicit cryptocurrency funds obtained through scams, darknet markets, and ransomware. Notable businesses include Garantex, Eggchange, Cashbank, Buy-Bitcoin, Tetchange, Bitzlato, and Suex, which was sanctioned by the U.S. in 2021. Bitzlato founder and owner Anatoly Legkodymov was arrested following money-laundering charges by the United States Department of Justice.

Dark money has also been flowing into Russia through a dark web marketplace called Hydra, which is powered by cryptocurrency, and enjoyed more than $1 billion in sales in 2020, according to Chainalysis. The platform demands that sellers liquidate cryptocurrency only through certain regional exchanges, which has made it difficult for investigators to trace the money.

Almost 74% of ransomware revenue in 2021 — over $400 million worth of cryptocurrency — went to software strains likely affiliated with Russia, where oversight is notoriously limited. However, Russians are also leaders in the benign adoption of cryptocurrencies, as the ruble is unreliable, and President Putin favours the idea of "overcoming the excessive domination of the limited number of reserve currencies."

In 2022, RenBridge - an unregulated alternative to exchanges for transferring value between blockchains - was found to be responsible for the laundering of at least $540 million since 2020. It is especially popular with people attempting to launder money from theft. This includes a cyberattack on Japanese crypto exchange Liquid that has been linked to North Korea.

## Darknet Markets

Properties of cryptocurrencies gave them popularity in applications such as a safe haven in banking crises and means of payment, which also led to the cryptocurrency use in controversial settings in the form of online black markets, such as Silk Road. The original Silk Road was shut down in October 2013 and there have been two more versions in use since then. In the year following the initial shutdown of Silk Road, the number of prominent dark markets increased from four to twelve, while the amount of drug listings increased from 18,000 to 32,000. Darknet markets present challenges in regard to legality. Cryptocurrency used in dark markets are not clearly or legally classified in almost all parts of the world. In the U.S., Bitcoins are labelled as "virtual assets". This type of ambiguous classification puts pressure on law enforcement agencies around the world to adapt to the shifting drug trade of dark markets.

### Wash Trades

Various studies have found that crypto-trading is rife with wash trading. Wash trading is a process, illegal in some jurisdictions, involving buyers and sellers being the same person or group, and may be used to manipulate the price of a cryptocurrency or inflate volume artificially. Exchanges with higher volumes can demand higher premiums from token issuers. A study from 2019 concluded that up to 80% of trades on unregulated cryptocurrency exchanges could be wash trades. A 2019 report by Bitwise Asset Management claimed that 95% of all Bitcoin trading volume reported on major website CoinMarketCap had been artificially generated, and of 81 exchanges studied, only 10 provided legitimate volume figures.

### As a Tool to Evade Sanctions

In 2022, cryptocurrencies attracted attention when Western nations imposed severe economic sanctions on Russia in the aftermath of its invasion of Ukraine in February. However, American sources warned in March that some crypto-transactions could potentially be used to evade economic sanctions against Russia and Belarus. In April 2022, the computer programmer Virgil Griffith received a five-year prison sentence in the US for attending a Pyongyang cryptocurrency conference, where he gave a presentation on blockchains which might be used for sanctions evasion.

## 2.1.8 Impacts and Analysis

The Bank for International Settlements summarized several criticisms of cryptocurrencies in Chapter V of their 2018 annual report. The criticisms include the lack of stability in their price, the high energy consumption, high and variable transactions costs, the poor security and fraud at cryptocurrency exchanges, vulnerability to debasement (from forking), and the influence of miners.

### Speculation, Fraud, and Adoption

Cryptocurrencies have been compared to Ponzi schemes, pyramid schemes and economic bubbles, such as housing market bubbles. Howard Marks of Oaktree Capital Management stated in 2017 that digital currencies were "nothing but an unfounded fad (or perhaps even a pyramid scheme), based on a willingness to ascribe value to something that has little or none beyond what people will pay for it", and compared them to the tulip mania (1637), South Sea Bubble (1720), and dot-com bubble (1999), which all experienced profound price booms and busts.

Regulators in several countries have warned against cryptocurrency and some have taken measures to dissuade users. However, research in 2021 by the UK's financial regulator suggests such warnings either went unheard, or were ignored. Fewer than one in 10 potential cryptocurrency buyers were aware of consumer warnings on the FCA website, and 12% of crypto users were not aware that their holdings were not protected by statutory compensation. Of 1,000 respondents between the ages of eighteen and forty, almost 70% wrongly assumed cryptocurrencies were regulated, 75% of younger crypto investors claimed to be driven by competition with friends and family, 58% said that social media enticed them to make high risk investments. The FCA recommends making use of its warning list, which flags unauthorized financial firms.

Many banks do not offer virtual currency services themselves and can refuse to do business with virtual currency companies. In 2014, Gareth Murphy, a senior banking officer, suggested that the widespread adoption of cryptocurrencies may lead to too much money being obfuscated, blinding economists who would use such information to better steer the economy. While traditional financial products have strong consumer protections in place, there is no intermediary with the power to limit consumer losses if Bitcoins are lost or stolen. One of the features cryptocurrency lacks in comparison to credit cards, for example, is consumer protection against fraud, such as chargebacks.

The French regulator Autorité des marchés financiers (AMF) lists 16 websites of companies that solicit investment in cryptocurrency without being authorized to do so in France. An October 2021 paper by the National Bureau of Economic Research found that Bitcoin suffers from systemic risk as the top 10,000 addresses control about one-third of all Bitcoin in circulation. It is even worse for Bitcoin miners, with 0.01% controlling 50% of the capacity. According to researcher Flipside Crypto, less than 2% of anonymous accounts control 95% of all available Bitcoin supply. This is considered risky as a great deal of the market is in the hands of a few entities.

A paper by John Griffin, a finance professor at the University of Texas, and Amin Shams, a graduate student found that in 2017 the price of Bitcoin had been substantially inflated using another cryptocurrency, Tether. Roger Lowenstein, author of "*Bank of America: The Epic Struggle to Create the Federal Reserve,*" says in a New York Times story that FTX will face over $8 billion in claims.

## Non-Fungible Tokens

Non-fungible tokens (NFTs) are digital assets that represent art, collectibles, gaming, etc. Like crypto, their data is stored on the blockchain. NFTs are bought and traded using cryptocurrency. The Ethereum blockchain was the first place where NFTs were implemented, but now many other blockchains have created their own versions of NFTs.

## Banks

As the first big Wall Street bank to embrace cryptocurrencies, Morgan Stanley announced on 17 March 2021 that they will be offering access to Bitcoin funds for their wealthy clients through three funds which enable Bitcoin ownership for investors with an aggressive risk tolerance. BNY Mellon on 11 February 2021 announced that it would begin offering cryptocurrency services to its clients. On 20 April 2021, Venmo added support to its platform to enable customers to buy, hold and sell cryptocurrencies. In October 2021, financial services company Mastercard announced it is working with digital asset manager Bakkt on a platform that would allow any bank or merchant on the Mastercard network to offer cryptocurrency services.

## Environmental Effects

Mining for proof-of-work cryptocurrencies requires enormous amounts of electricity and consequently comes with a large carbon footprint due to causing greenhouse gas emissions. Proof-of-work blockchains such as Bitcoin, Ethereum, Litecoin, and Monero were estimated to have added between 3 million and 15 million tons of carbon dioxide ($CO_2$) to the atmosphere in the period from 1 January 2016 to 30 June 2017. By November 2018, Bitcoin was estimated to have an annual energy consumption of 45.8TWh, generating 22.0 to 22.9 million tons of $CO_2$, rivalling nations like Jordan and Sri Lanka. By the end of 2021, Bitcoin was estimated to produce 65.4 million tons of $CO_2$, as much as Greece, and consume between 91 and 177 terawatt-hours annually.

Critics have also identified a large electronic waste problem in disposing of mining rigs. Mining hardware is improving at a fast rate, quickly resulting in older generations of hardware. Bitcoin is the least energy-efficient cryptocurrency, using 707.6 kilowatt-hours of electricity per transaction. Before June 2021, China was the primary location for Bitcoin mining. However, due to concerns over power usage and other factors, China forced out Bitcoin operations, at least temporarily. As a result, the United States promptly emerged as the top global leader in the industry. An example of a gross amount of electronic waste associated with Bitcoin mining operations in the US is a facility that located in Dalton, Georgia which is consuming nearly the same amount of electricity as the combined power usage of 97,000 households in its vicinity. Another example is that Riot Platforms operates a Bitcoin mining facility in Rockdale, Texas, which consumes approximately as much electricity as the nearby 300,000 households. This makes it the most energy-intensive Bitcoin mining operation in the United States.

The world's second-largest cryptocurrency, Ethereum, uses 62.56 kilowatt-hours of electricity per transaction. XRP is the world's most energy efficient cryptocurrency, using 0.0079 kilowatt-hours of electricity per transaction. Although the biggest PoW blockchains consume energy on the scale of medium-sized countries, the annual power demand from proof-of-stake (PoS) blockchains is on a scale equivalent to a housing estate. *The Times* identified six "environmentally friendly" cryptocurrencies: Chia, IOTA, Cardano, Nano, Solarcoin and Bitgreen. Academics and researchers have used various methods for estimating the energy use and energy efficiency of blockchains. A study of the six largest proof-of-stake networks in May 2021 concluded:

- Cardano has the lowest electricity use per node;
- Polkadot has the lowest electricity use overall; and
- Solana has the lowest electricity use per transaction.

In terms of annual consumption (kWh/yr), the figures were: Polkadot (70,237), Tezos (113,249), Avalanche (489,311), Algorand (512,671), Cardano (598,755) and Solana (1,967,930). This equates to Polkadot consuming 7 times the electricity of an average U.S. home, Cardano 57 homes and Solana 200 times as much. The research concluded that PoS networks consumed 0.001% the electricity of the Bitcoin network. University College London researchers reached a similar conclusion. Variable renewable energy power stations could invest in Bitcoin mining to reduce curtailment, hedge electricity price risk, stabilize the grid, increase the profitability of renewable energy power stations and therefore accelerate transition to sustainable energy.

## Technological Limitations

There are also purely technical elements to consider. For example, technological advancement in cryptocurrencies such as Bitcoin result in high up-front costs to miners in the form of specialized hardware and software. Cryptocurrency transactions are normally irreversible after a number of blocks confirm the transaction. Additionally, cryptocurrency private keys can be permanently lost from local storage due to malware, data loss or the destruction of the physical media. This precludes the cryptocurrency from being spent, resulting in its effective removal from the markets.

## Academic Studies

In September 2015, the establishment of the peer-reviewed academic journal *Ledger* (ISSN 2379-5980) was announced. It covers studies of cryptocurrencies and related technologies, and is published by the University of Pittsburgh. The journal encourages authors to digitally sign a file hash of submitted papers, which will then be timestamped into the Bitcoin blockchain. Authors are also asked to include a personal Bitcoin address in the first page of their papers.

## Aid Agencies

A number of aid agencies have started accepting donations in cryptocurrencies, including UNICEF. Christopher Fabian, principal adviser at UNICEF Innovation, said the children's fund would uphold donor protocols, meaning that people making donations online would have to pass checks before they were allowed to deposit funds. However, in 2021, there was a backlash against donations in Bitcoin because of the environmental emissions it caused. Some agencies stopped accepting Bitcoin and others turned to "greener" cryptocurrencies. The U.S., arm of Greenpeace stopped accepting bitcoin donations after seven years. It said: "As the amount of energy needed to run Bitcoin became clearer, this policy became no longer tenable." In 2022, the Ukrainian government raised over US$10,000,000 worth of aid through cryptocurrency following the 2022 Russian invasion of Ukraine.

## Criticism

Bitcoin has been characterized as a speculative bubble by eight winners of the Nobel Memorial Prize in Economic Sciences: Paul Krugman, Robert J. Shiller, Joseph Stiglitz, Richard Thaler, James Heckman, Thomas Sargent, Angus Deaton, and Oliver Hart; and by central bank officials including Alan Greenspan, Agustín Carstens, Vítor Constâncio, and Nout Wellink.

Investors Warren Buffett and George Soros have respectively characterized it as a "mirage" and a "bubble"; while business executives Jack Ma and JP Morgan Chase CEO Jamie Dimon have called it a "bubble" and a "fraud", respectively, although Jamie Dimon later said he regretted dubbing Bitcoin a fraud. BlackRock CEO Laurence D. Fink called Bitcoin an "index of money laundering". In June 2022, business magnate Bill Gates said that cryptocurrencies are "100% based on greater fool theory".

Legal scholars criticize the lack of regulation, which hinders conflict resolution when crypto assets are at the center of a legal dispute, for example a divorce or an inheritance. In Switzerland, jurists generally deny that cryptocurrencies are objects that fall under property law, as cryptocurrencies do not belong to any class of legally defined objects (*Typenzwang*, the legal numerus clausus). Therefore, it is debated whether anybody could even be sued for embezzlement of cryptocurrency if he/she had access to someone's wallet. However, in the law of obligations and contract law, any kind of object would be legally valid, but the object would have to be tied to an identified counterparty. However, as the more popular cryptocurrencies can be freely and quickly exchanged into legal tender, they are financial assets and have to be taxed and accounted for as such.

In 2018, an increase in crypto-related suicides was noticed after the cryptocurrency market crashed in August. The situation was particularly critical in Korea as crypto traders were on "suicide watch". A cryptocurrency forum on Reddit even started providing suicide prevention support to affected investors. The May 2022 collapse of the Luna currency operated by Terra also led to reports of suicidal investors in crypto-related subreddits.

## 2.2 BIRTH OF BITCOIN AND THE SATOSHI NAKAMOTO WHITEPAPER

### 2.2.1 Birth of Bitcoin

Bitcoin, the first and most well-known cryptocurrency, was born out of a desire to create a decentralized, secure, and transparent financial system. Its inception marks a significant milestone in the history of digital currency and blockchain technology.

The birth of Bitcoin represents a landmark in the evolution of digital currency and decentralized technology. From its conceptualization by Satoshi Nakamoto to its growing adoption and impact on the financial world, Bitcoin has challenged traditional notions of money and governance. Its underlying blockchain technology has opened up new possibilities for secure and transparent record-keeping across various industries. Despite the challenges and controversies it faces, Bitcoin continues to be a driving force in the ongoing transformation of the global financial landscape.

#### The Precursor to Bitcoin: Digital Cash

Before Bitcoin, various attempts were made to create digital currencies. These early projects aimed to address the limitations of traditional financial systems, such as centralization, lack of privacy, and inefficiencies in transaction processing. Notable examples include:

- **DigiCash (1989):** Founded by cryptographer David Chaum, DigiCash was an early form of digital currency that used cryptographic protocols to ensure transaction privacy. However, it relied on a centralized entity, which eventually led to its downfall due to financial difficulties.
- **Hashcash (1997):** Developed by Adam Back, Hashcash was a proof-of-work system designed to combat email spam and denial-of-service attacks. Its concept of using computational puzzles to validate transactions would later influence Bitcoin's mining mechanism.
- **Bit Gold (1998):** Proposed by Nick Szabo, Bit Gold was a decentralized digital currency that used a proof-of-work system to generate and verify

transactions. Although it was never implemented, Bit Gold introduced many concepts that would later be incorporated into Bitcoin.

## The Birth of Bitcoin: Satoshi Nakamoto

Bitcoin's creation is attributed to the pseudonymous figure Satoshi Nakamoto, whose true identity remains unknown. On October 31, 2008, Nakamoto published a white paper titled "Bitcoin: A Peer-to-Peer Electronic Cash System," outlining the principles and mechanics of a decentralized digital currency. This white paper described a system where transactions could be conducted directly between parties without the need for intermediaries, such as banks or payment processors.

### Key Concepts Introduced in the White Paper

- **Decentralization:** Bitcoin operates on a decentralized network, where no single entity has control over the entire system. This decentralization ensures that the network remains resilient and resistant to censorship.
- **Blockchain:** Bitcoin transactions are recorded on a public ledger known as the blockchain. Each block in the blockchain contains a list of transactions, and blocks are linked together in a chronological chain, ensuring the integrity and immutability of the transaction history.
- **Proof-of-Work:** To add a new block to the blockchain, miners must solve complex mathematical puzzles, a process known as proof-of-work. This mechanism ensures that transactions are validated and prevents double-spending.
- **Cryptographic Security:** Bitcoin uses cryptographic techniques to secure transactions and control the creation of new units. Public and private keys are used to facilitate transactions, ensuring that only the rightful owner can spend their bitcoins.

## The Genesis Block and Early Development

On January 3, 2009, Satoshi Nakamoto mined the first block of the Bitcoin blockchain, known as the Genesis Block (Block 0). Embedded within the coinbase of the Genesis Block was the message: "The Times 03/Jan/2009 Chancellor on brink of second bailout for banks." This message is widely interpreted as a commentary on the instability of the traditional financial system and a motivation for creating an alternative. Nakamoto released the first version of the Bitcoin software on January 9, 2009, and the Bitcoin network officially went live. Early adopters, including cryptographers and enthusiasts from the cypherpunk community, began mining and transacting with Bitcoin, testing the system's robustness and security.

## The First Bitcoin Transaction

The first recorded Bitcoin transaction occurred on January 12, 2009, when Satoshi Nakamoto sent 10 bitcoins to Hal Finney, a prominent cryptographer and early Bitcoin supporter. This transaction demonstrated the functionality of the Bitcoin network and set the stage for its future growth.

## Bitcoin's Early Reception and Growth

In its early years, Bitcoin was primarily used by a niche community of enthusiasts and technologists. Its value was initially negligible, and it was mostly exchanged for experimental purposes or as a novelty. However, as more people began to recognize its potential, Bitcoin's adoption and value started to grow.

### Notable Milestones

- **The Pizza Purchase (May 22, 2010):** One of the most famous early transactions was when programmer Laszlo Hanyecz paid 10,000 bitcoins for two pizzas. This event, known as "Bitcoin Pizza Day," is often cited as the first real-world transaction using Bitcoin and highlighted its potential as a medium of exchange.
- **Bitcoin Exchanges:** The establishment of Bitcoin exchanges, such as Mt. Gox in 2010, allowed users to buy and sell bitcoins for traditional currencies. These exchanges provided liquidity and helped establish a market value for Bitcoin.
- **Increased Adoption:** Over time, more merchants and businesses began to accept Bitcoin as a form of payment. This increased adoption helped legitimize Bitcoin and attract a broader user base.

## The Rise of Bitcoin and Blockchain Technology

As Bitcoin gained popularity, its underlying technology, blockchain, attracted attention for its potential applications beyond digital currency. Blockchain technology offered a decentralized and secure way to record transactions, leading to innovations in various fields, including finance, supply chain management, healthcare, and more.

### Challenges and Controversies

Despite its growth, Bitcoin has faced several challenges and controversies:

- **Regulatory Concerns:** Governments and regulatory bodies have struggled to define and regulate Bitcoin, leading to varying degrees of acceptance and legal status worldwide.
- **Security Issues:** While Bitcoin's blockchain is secure, exchanges and wallets have been targeted by hackers, resulting in significant losses for users.

- **Scalability:** As Bitcoin's popularity grew, so did concerns about its ability to handle a large number of transactions efficiently. This led to debates and proposals for scaling solutions, such as the Lightning Network and Segregated Witness (SegWit).
- **Environmental Impact:** The proof-of-work consensus mechanism requires substantial computational power, raising concerns about the environmental impact of Bitcoin mining.

## 2.2.2 The Satoshi Nakamoto Whitepaper

The birth of the Satoshi Nakamoto whitepaper is a landmark event in the history of digital finance and cryptography. This document, titled "Bitcoin: A Peer-to-Peer Electronic Cash System," laid the foundation for Bitcoin and has had a profound impact on the world of finance and technology.

The birth of the Satoshi Nakamoto whitepaper marks a pivotal moment in the history of digital finance. By introducing Bitcoin, Nakamoto provided a solution to many of the challenges faced by previous digital currencies and laid the groundwork for a new era of decentralized finance. The whitepaper's concepts of decentralization, peer-to-peer networking, blockchain technology, proof-of-work, and cryptographic security have not only created a new form of currency but also sparked innovations across various industries. The impact of Bitcoin and the principles outlined in the whitepaper continue to reverberate, challenging traditional systems and inspiring new technological advancements.

### Background Leading to the Whitepaper

The idea of digital money is not new; many attempts were made before Bitcoin to create an effective digital cash system. However, these efforts often failed due to reliance on centralized systems, which made them vulnerable to shutdown and fraud. Notable early attempts include:

- **DigiCash (1989):** Founded by David Chaum, DigiCash was an electronic currency system that aimed to secure privacy through cryptographic protocols. It was an early precursor but failed due to financial troubles and reliance on a central authority.
- **Hashcash (1997):** Created by Adam Back, Hashcash introduced the concept of proof-of-work to prevent email spam and denial-of-service attacks. This concept later became crucial in Bitcoin's mining mechanism.
- **Bit Gold (1998):** Proposed by Nick Szabo, Bit Gold envisioned a decentralized digital currency system using proof-of-work. Though it was never implemented, many of its concepts influenced Bitcoin.

### The Emergence of Satoshi Nakamoto

On October 31, 2008, a person or group of people using the pseudonym Satoshi Nakamoto published the whitepaper "Bitcoin: A Peer-to-Peer Electronic Cash System" on a cryptography mailing list. The whitepaper proposed a new type of digital currency that solved many of the problems faced by previous digital cash systems, especially the double-spending problem, without relying on a central authority.

### Key Concepts in the Whitepaper

The whitepaper is a concise nine-page document that introduces several groundbreaking concepts:

- **Decentralization:** Bitcoin operates on a decentralized network where no single entity has control. This decentralization is key to its security and resistance to censorship.
- **Peer-to-Peer Network:** Transactions are conducted directly between users without intermediaries. The network itself verifies and records transactions on a public ledger, known as the blockchain.
- **Blockchain Technology:** The blockchain is a public ledger of all transactions that have ever taken place on the Bitcoin network. Each block contains a list of transactions and a reference to the previous block, forming a chain.
- **Proof-of-Work:** To add a new block to the blockchain, miners must solve a computationally intensive puzzle, which is the proof-of-work. This mechanism prevents double-spending and secures the network against attacks.
- **Cryptographic Security:** Bitcoin uses public-key cryptography for transaction security. Each user has a public key (an address) and a private key. Transactions are signed with the private key, ensuring that only the owner of the bitcoins can spend them.

### Immediate Reception and Impact

The initial reaction to the whitepaper was mixed. While some members of the cryptography community recognized its potential, others were skeptical. However, a small group of enthusiasts, including Hal Finney, Nick Szabo, and Wei Dai, began corresponding with Nakamoto and contributing to the development of the Bitcoin software.

#### Genesis Block

On January 3, 2009, Satoshi Nakamoto mined the first block of the Bitcoin blockchain, known as the Genesis Block. Embedded in the coinbase of this block was the message: "The Times 03/Jan/2009 Chancellor on brink of second bailout for banks." This message is widely interpreted as a critique of the traditional financial system and a motivation for creating an alternative.

### Development and Early Adoption

The first version of the Bitcoin software was released on January 9, 2009. Nakamoto continued to work on the project, collaborating with other developers via online forums and email. The first Bitcoin transaction took place on January 12, 2009, when Nakamoto sent 10 bitcoins to Hal Finney, a prominent cryptographer and early Bitcoin supporter.

### Long-term Effects

Bitcoin and the whitepaper that introduced it have had profound and far-reaching impacts:

- **Cryptocurrencies:** Bitcoin paved the way for thousands of other cryptocurrencies, each with unique features and applications. The cryptocurrency market has grown into a multi-billion dollar industry.
- **Blockchain Technology:** Beyond cryptocurrencies, blockchain technology has found applications in various fields, including supply chain management, healthcare, finance, and voting systems. Its principles of transparency, security, and decentralization are being leveraged to solve real-world problems.
- **Decentralized Finance (DeFi):** DeFi represents a growing sector within the cryptocurrency space that aims to recreate traditional financial systems using decentralized blockchain technology. This includes lending, borrowing, trading, and earning interest without intermediaries.
- **Economic and Social Impact:** Bitcoin has influenced economic theories and discussions around money, value, and trust. It has provided financial services to unbanked populations and challenged traditional financial institutions to innovate.
- **Regulation and Legal Status:** The rise of Bitcoin has prompted governments and regulatory bodies to grapple with how to regulate digital currencies. While some countries have embraced it, others have imposed strict regulations or outright bans.

## 2.3 ALTCOINS AND CRYPTOCURRENCY ECOSYSTEM

### 2.3.1 Altcoins

Altcoins, or alternative coins, refer to all cryptocurrencies other than Bitcoin.

The term encompasses a vast array of digital currencies and tokens, each with unique features, use cases, and technological innovations. Altcoins represent a diverse and dynamic segment of the cryptocurrency market, offering a wide range of functionalities and use cases beyond what Bitcoin provides. From transaction efficiency and privacy to smart contracts and decentralized finance, altcoins continue to push the boundaries of what is possible with blockchain technology. However, they also face significant challenges and risks that must be addressed to ensure their long-term success and adoption. As the cryptocurrency landscape continues to evolve, altcoins will undoubtedly play a critical role in shaping the future of digital finance and decentralized systems.

## Origins of Altcoins

The first altcoin, Namecoin, was introduced in April 2011. Like Bitcoin, Namecoin is based on a proof-of-work algorithm and uses the same SHA-256 hash function. However, it was designed to provide decentralized DNS (Domain Name System) services, aiming to make internet censorship more difficult. Following Namecoin, many other altcoins were created to improve upon Bitcoin's perceived limitations, such as transaction speed, energy efficiency, and governance models. Each new altcoin aimed to address specific issues or provide novel functionalities that Bitcoin could not offer.

## Types of Altcoins

Altcoins can be categorized based on their underlying technology, purpose, and unique features. Here are some common types of altcoins:

- **Mining-based Coins:** These altcoins use a proof-of-work (PoW) consensus mechanism similar to Bitcoin. Examples include Litecoin and Dogecoin.
- **Stablecoins:** Stablecoins are designed to minimize price volatility by being pegged to a reserve asset, such as fiat currency or commodities. Examples include Tether (USDT) and USD Coin (USDC).
- **Security Tokens:** These tokens represent ownership in an external asset, such as real estate or stocks, and are subject to federal securities regulations. Examples include Polymath and tZERO.
- **Utility Tokens:** Utility tokens provide access to a product or service within a blockchain ecosystem. They are not intended as investments. Examples include Basic Attention Token (BAT) and Chainlink (LINK).
- **Governance Tokens:** These tokens grant holders voting rights to influence the development and decision-making process of a blockchain project. Examples include Uniswap (UNI) and Compound (COMP).

- **Privacy Coins:** Privacy coins focus on enhancing transaction anonymity and user privacy. Examples include Monero (XMR) and Zcash (ZEC).

## Prominent Examples of Altcoins

### Ethereum (ETH)

Launched in 2015 by Vitalik Buterin, Ethereum is the second-largest cryptocurrency by market capitalization. Unlike Bitcoin, Ethereum is a programmable blockchain that supports smart contracts and decentralized applications (dApps). Smart contracts are self-executing contracts with the terms directly written into code, enabling trustless and automated transactions. Ethereum's native currency, Ether (ETH), is used to pay for transaction fees and computational services on the network. The Ethereum platform has spurred the development of numerous other altcoins and tokens through its ERC-20 and ERC-721 token standards.

### Litecoin (LTC)

Created by Charlie Lee in 2011, Litecoin is often referred to as the "silver to Bitcoin's gold." It was designed to provide faster transaction times and lower fees compared to Bitcoin. Litecoin achieves this by using a different hashing algorithm (Scrypt) and a shorter block generation time (2.5 minutes compared to Bitcoin's 10 minutes).

### Ripple (XRP)

Ripple, launched in 2012, focuses on enabling fast and low-cost international money transfers. Unlike most cryptocurrencies, Ripple does not use a blockchain. Instead, it relies on a distributed ledger protocol and a consensus algorithm called the Ripple Protocol Consensus Algorithm (RPCA). Ripple's native currency, XRP, is used as a bridge currency for cross-border transactions between different fiat currencies.

### Cardano (ADA)

Cardano, founded by Charles Hoskinson in 2017, is a third-generation blockchain platform that aims to address scalability, interoperability, and sustainability issues faced by earlier blockchains. Cardano uses a proof-of-stake (PoS) consensus mechanism called Ouroboros, which is designed to be more energy-efficient than proof-of-work systems. The native cryptocurrency, ADA, is used for transactions and staking within the Cardano network.

### Binance Coin (BNB)

Binance Coin was launched in 2017 by the cryptocurrency exchange Binance. Initially created as an ERC-20 token on the Ethereum blockchain, BNB has since migrated to Binance's own blockchain, Binance Chain. BNB is used to pay for transaction fees on the Binance exchange, participate in token sales on Binance Launchpad, and as a means of payment within the Binance ecosystem.

### Roles and Functions of Altcoins

Altcoins serve a variety of roles within the broader cryptocurrency ecosystem, including:

- **Transaction Efficiency:** Many altcoins aim to improve upon Bitcoin's transaction speed and cost. For instance, Litecoin offers faster block generation times, resulting in quicker transactions.
- **Smart Contracts and dApps:** Platforms like Ethereum enable the creation and execution of smart contracts and decentralized applications, expanding the use cases of blockchain technology beyond simple transactions.
- **Privacy and Security:** Privacy-focused altcoins such as Monero and Zcash provide enhanced anonymity for users who prioritize transaction privacy.
- **Decentralized Finance (DeFi):** Altcoins play a crucial role in the DeFi sector, offering decentralized financial services like lending, borrowing, and trading without intermediaries. Examples include Compound, Aave, and Uniswap.
- **Stable Value:** Stablecoins like USDT and USDC provide stability by pegging their value to fiat currencies, making them useful for transactions, remittances, and as a store of value.
- **Governance:** Governance tokens allow holders to vote on important decisions regarding the development and management of blockchain projects. This decentralized governance model empowers the community to shape the future of the project.

### Challenges and Risks of Altcoins

While altcoins offer numerous benefits and innovations, they also face several challenges and risks:

- **Market Volatility:** Many altcoins experience significant price volatility, which can deter adoption and usage as a stable medium of exchange.
- **Regulatory Uncertainty:** The regulatory environment for altcoins is still evolving, with different jurisdictions adopting varying approaches to regulation. This uncertainty can impact the development and adoption of altcoins.

- **Security Risks:** Altcoins can be susceptible to security vulnerabilities, such as hacking, 51% attacks, and smart contract bugs, which can result in financial losses for users.
- **Liquidity Issues:** Some altcoins suffer from low liquidity, making it difficult for users to buy, sell, or trade them without significant price slippage.
- **Scams and Fraud:** The proliferation of altcoins has also led to the emergence of scams and fraudulent projects, where unscrupulous developers create and promote worthless or malicious tokens to deceive investors.

### 2.3.2 Cryptocurrency Ecosystem

The cryptocurrency ecosystem is a complex and rapidly evolving space encompassing various digital currencies, technologies, platforms, and participants. It extends beyond the use of cryptocurrencies like Bitcoin and Ethereum to include a wide range of applications, from decentralized finance (DeFi) and smart contracts to non-fungible tokens (NFTs) and blockchain-based governance.

The cryptocurrency ecosystem is a vibrant and multifaceted landscape that continues to evolve at a rapid pace. It encompasses a wide range of technologies, participants, and applications, each contributing to the overall development and maturation of the space.

While challenges such as regulatory uncertainty, scalability, and security remain, the opportunities for innovation, financial inclusion, and decentralized governance present a promising future for cryptocurrencies and blockchain technology.

As the ecosystem continues to grow and adapt, its impact on the global financial system and various industries is likely to be profound and far-reaching.

#### Key Components of the Cryptocurrency Ecosystem

**Cryptocurrencies:**

- **Bitcoin (BTC):** The first and most widely known cryptocurrency, created by Satoshi Nakamoto. It serves as a store of value and a medium of exchange.
- **Altcoins:** All other cryptocurrencies besides Bitcoin, including major ones like Ethereum (ETH), Ripple (XRP), Litecoin (LTC), and thousands of others. Each has unique features and use cases.

**Blockchain Technology:**

- **Public Blockchains:** Decentralized and transparent ledgers where anyone can participate, like Bitcoin and Ethereum.

- **Private Blockchains:** Permissioned networks where only selected entities can participate, often used in enterprise settings.

**Smart Contracts:**

- Self-executing contracts with the terms directly written into code, running on blockchain platforms like Ethereum. They enable trustless and automated transactions.

**Decentralized Finance (DeFi):**

- Financial services built on blockchain technology that operate without intermediaries. Examples include lending platforms like Aave, decentralized exchanges (DEXs) like Uniswap, and stablecoins like DAI.

**Non-Fungible Tokens (NFTs):**

- Unique digital assets representing ownership of specific items or content, such as art, music, and virtual real estate, often traded on platforms like OpenSea.

**Wallets:**

- Digital tools that allow users to store, send, and receive cryptocurrencies. They can be software-based (like MetaMask) or hardware-based (like Ledger and Trezor).

**Exchanges:**

- Platforms where users can buy, sell, and trade cryptocurrencies. These include centralized exchanges (CEXs) like Coinbase and Binance, and decentralized exchanges (DEXs) like Uniswap and SushiSwap.

**Miners and Validators:**

- Participants who secure blockchain networks by validating and processing transactions. In proof-of-work (PoW) systems, these are miners (e.g., Bitcoin miners). In proof-of-stake (PoS) systems, they are validators (e.g., Ethereum 2.0 validators).

## Major Players in the Cryptocurrency Ecosystem

- **Developers:** Individuals and teams who create and maintain blockchain protocols, smart contracts, DApps, and other cryptocurrency-related technologies.
- **Investors and Traders:** People and institutions who invest in or trade cryptocurrencies for profit. This includes retail investors, hedge funds, and venture capital firms.

- **Regulators and Governments:** Entities that develop and enforce laws and regulations governing the use, trading, and taxation of cryptocurrencies. Regulatory approaches vary widely by country and can significantly impact the ecosystem.
- **Financial Institutions:** Banks, payment processors, and fintech companies that are increasingly integrating cryptocurrencies into their services, such as offering custody solutions or facilitating crypto payments.
- **Enterprise and Businesses:** Companies that leverage blockchain technology for various applications, from supply chain management to digital identity verification.

## Dynamics and Trends in the Cryptocurrency Ecosystem

- **Adoption and Integration:** Cryptocurrencies are increasingly being adopted for various purposes, including payments, investments, and as a hedge against inflation. Major companies like Tesla and PayPal have started accepting or integrating cryptocurrencies.
- **Regulatory Developments:** Governments worldwide are working on developing frameworks for regulating cryptocurrencies. While some countries embrace them (e.g., El Salvador adopting Bitcoin as legal tender), others impose strict regulations or bans (e.g., China's crackdown on crypto mining and trading).
- **Technological Innovations:** Continuous advancements in blockchain technology, such as the development of Ethereum 2.0, which aims to transition from PoW to PoS, improving scalability, security, and sustainability.
- **Market Volatility:** Cryptocurrencies are known for their high price volatility, influenced by factors like market sentiment, regulatory news, technological developments, and macroeconomic trends.
- **Security and Risk Management:** Security remains a critical concern, with issues like hacking, fraud, and phishing attacks. The ecosystem is developing better security practices, such as multi-signature wallets and decentralized insurance platforms.
- **Interoperability:** Efforts to improve interoperability between different blockchain networks are underway, with projects like Polkadot and Cosmos enabling seamless communication and transactions across multiple blockchains.

### Challenges and Opportunities

**Challenges:**

- **Regulatory Uncertainty:** The lack of clear and consistent regulations creates uncertainty for businesses and investors, potentially hindering adoption and innovation.
- **Scalability Issues:** Many blockchain networks, including Bitcoin and Ethereum, face scalability challenges, leading to high transaction fees and slow processing times during peak usage.
- **Environmental Concerns:** The energy consumption of PoW-based cryptocurrencies like Bitcoin has raised environmental concerns, prompting the search for more sustainable consensus mechanisms.
- **Security Risks:** The ecosystem is susceptible to various security risks, including hacking, smart contract vulnerabilities, and phishing attacks, which can result in significant financial losses.

**Opportunities:**

- **Financial Inclusion:** Cryptocurrencies and DeFi platforms offer financial services to unbanked and underbanked populations, providing access to banking, lending, and investment opportunities.
- **Innovation and New Use Cases:** The flexibility and programmability of blockchain technology enable the development of innovative applications across various industries, including finance, healthcare, and supply chain management.
- **Decentralized Governance:** Decentralized governance models empower communities to make decisions collectively, fostering more democratic and transparent project management.
- **Institutional Adoption:** Increasing interest and involvement from institutional investors and corporations are driving mainstream adoption and legitimacy, leading to greater market stability and growth.

## 2.4 TOKENS AND INITIAL COIN OFFERINGS (ICOS)

### 2.4.1 Tokens

Tokens in the cryptocurrency world represent a wide range of digital assets and have a crucial role within the blockchain ecosystem. They are distinct from cryptocurrencies like Bitcoin and Ethereum, which serve as digital currencies, in that tokens can represent various types of assets or utilities on blockchain platforms. Tokens play a pivotal role in the cryptocurrency and blockchain ecosystem, facilitating a wide range of applications and innovations.

From providing utility within specific platforms to enabling decentralized finance and representing unique digital assets, tokens have transformed how value is created, transferred, and managed in the digital age.

As the ecosystem continues to evolve, tokens will likely become even more integral to the functioning and expansion of blockchain technologies, driving forward new business models, governance structures, and financial services.

## What Are Tokens?

Tokens are digital assets created on existing blockchain platforms, primarily Ethereum, but also others like Binance Smart Chain, Solana, and more. Unlike cryptocurrencies, which operate on their own blockchains, tokens leverage the infrastructure of an existing blockchain. They can be used to represent a variety of assets and functions, ranging from utility within a specific application to actual financial assets.

## Types of Tokens

**Utility Tokens:**

- **Definition:** These tokens provide access to a product or service within a specific blockchain ecosystem.
- **Examples:** Basic Attention Token (BAT) is used within the Brave browser to reward users and content creators. Filecoin (FIL) is used to buy and sell storage on the Filecoin network.

**Security Tokens:**

- **Definition:** These represent ownership in an external asset, such as equity in a company, real estate, or other investments, and are subject to federal securities regulations.
- **Examples:** Polymath (POLY) facilitates the creation and issuance of security tokens. tZERO is a platform for trading tokenized securities.

**Stablecoins:**

- **Definition:** Tokens that are pegged to a stable asset, such as fiat currency or commodities, to minimize price volatility.
- **Examples:** Tether (USDT) is pegged to the US dollar, DAI is a decentralized stablecoin pegged to the US dollar but backed by cryptocurrency collateral.

**Governance Tokens:**

- **Definition:** Tokens that grant holders voting rights to influence the development and decision-making process of a blockchain project or decentralized application (dApp).

- **Examples:** Uniswap (UNI) allows holders to vote on protocol changes and updates. MakerDAO (MKR) token holders can vote on proposals affecting the MakerDAO ecosystem.

**Non-Fungible Tokens (NFTs):**

- **Definition:** Unique digital assets representing ownership of specific items or content, such as art, music, virtual real estate, and collectibles.
- **Examples:** Cryptokitties are collectible digital cats, each with unique attributes. Beeple's digital artwork "Everydays: The First 5000 Days" sold as an NFT for millions of dollars.

## How Tokens Work

Tokens operate on top of blockchain networks using smart contracts, which are self-executing contracts with the terms directly written into code. Here's a breakdown of how they function:

- **Creation:** Tokens are created through a process called an Initial Coin Offering (ICO) or a Token Generation Event (TGE). During this process, developers write a smart contract on a blockchain platform that defines the token's characteristics, such as its total supply, issuance, and other properties.
- **Distribution:** Once created, tokens can be distributed through various methods, including public sales (ICOs), airdrops (free distribution to wallet holders), or private sales to institutional investors.
- **Usage:** Tokens can be used within the ecosystem for various purposes depending on their type. For instance, utility tokens can be used to access services, governance tokens for voting on proposals, and NFTs for buying and selling digital art.
- **Storage and Transfer:** Tokens are stored in digital wallets that support the underlying blockchain. They can be transferred between users through transactions that are recorded on the blockchain.

## Significance of Tokens

- **Ecosystem Development:** Tokens are integral to the development and operation of blockchain ecosystems. They provide the means to fund projects, incentivize participation, and facilitate decentralized governance.
- **Decentralized Finance (DeFi):** Tokens are at the heart of the DeFi movement, enabling decentralized lending, borrowing, trading, and earning interest without intermediaries. Examples include lending

protocols like Aave and Compound, which use tokens for interest-bearing assets.

- **Innovation and New Business Models:** Tokens enable innovative business models and applications. For instance, NFTs have revolutionized the art world by providing artists with a new way to monetize their work and engage with collectors.
- **Regulatory Challenges:** The diverse nature of tokens presents regulatory challenges. Security tokens, in particular, must comply with securities laws, which vary by jurisdiction. This complexity necessitates careful legal and regulatory considerations for projects issuing tokens.
- **Economic Incentives:** Tokens align economic incentives for participants within a network. For example, governance tokens incentivize active participation in the decision-making process, while utility tokens encourage usage of a platform.

### Examples of Token Platforms

- **Ethereum:** The most popular platform for token creation, thanks to its robust smart contract capabilities. The ERC-20 standard is widely used for fungible tokens, while ERC-721 and ERC-1155 standards are used for NFTs.
- **Binance Smart Chain (BSC):** Offers lower transaction fees and faster processing times compared to Ethereum, making it a popular alternative for token projects.
- **Solana:** Known for its high throughput and low fees, Solana is becoming a favored platform for DeFi and NFT projects.
- **Polkadot:** Enables interoperability between different blockchains, allowing tokens to be transferred across multiple networks seamlessly.

## 2.4.2 Initial Coin Offerings (ICOs)

An initial coin offering (ICO) or initial currency offering is a type of funding using cryptocurrencies. It is often a form of crowdfunding, although a private ICO which does not seek public investment is also possible. In an ICO, a quantity of cryptocurrency is sold in the form of "tokens" ("coins") to speculators or investors, in exchange for legal tender or other (generally established and more stable) cryptocurrencies such as Bitcoin or Ether. The tokens are promoted as future functional units of currency if or when the ICO's funding goal is met and the project successfully launches.

An ICO can be a source of capital for startup companies. ICOs can allow startups to avoid regulations that prevent them from seeking investment directly from the public, and intermediaries such as venture capitalists, banks, and stock exchanges, which may demand greater scrutiny and some percentage of future profits or joint ownership. ICOs may fall outside existing regulations, depending on the nature of the project, or be banned altogether in some jurisdictions, such as China and South Korea.

Due to the lack of regulation and enforcement of securities law, ICOs have been the vehicle for scams and fraud. Fewer than half of all ICOs survive four months after the offering, while almost half of ICOs sold in 2017 failed by February 2018. Despite their record of failure and the falling prices of cryptocurrencies, a record $7 billion was raised via ICO from January–June 2018.

## History

The first token sale (also known as an ICO) was held by Mastercoin in July 2013. Ethereum raised money with a token sale in 2014, raising around 31,000 BTC in July, equal to approximately $18.3 million at the time.

ICOs and token sales became popular in 2017. There were at least 18 websites tracking ICOs before mid-year. In May, the ICO for a new web browser called Brave generated about $35 million in under 30 seconds. Messaging app developer Kik's September 2017 ICO raised nearly $100 million. At the start of October 2017, ICO coin sales worth $2.3 billion had been conducted during the year, more than ten times as much as in all of 2016. As of November 2017, there were around 50 offerings a month, with the highest-grossing ICO as of January 2018, being Filecoin raising $257 million (and $200 million of that within the first hour of their token sale).

By the end of 2017, ICOs had raised almost 40 times as much capital as they had raised in 2016, although still amounting to less than two percent of the capital raised by IPOs. ICOs are sometimes called "token sales". Amy Wan, a crowdfunding and syndication lawyer, described the coin in an ICO as "a symbol of ownership interest in an enterprise—a digital stock certificate" stating that they are likely subject to regulation as securities in the U.S. under the Howey test.

Ethereum is (as of February 2018) the leading blockchain platform for ICOs with more than 80% market share. Tokens are generally based on the Ethereum ERC-20 standard. On January 30, 2018, Facebook banned advertisements for ICOs as well as for cryptocurrencies and binary options. By April 2018, ICO advertising has been banned not only by Facebook, but by Twitter, Google, and MailChimp. Facebook changed their mind and June 26, 2018 announced to reopen for approved advertisers.

Efforts are under way to deploy ICO technology to represent regulated securities, referred to as Security Token Offerings (STOs), Digital Security Offerings (DSOs), and when listed on a regulated stock exchange, tokenized IPOs.

An initial stake-pool offering (ISPO), also known as an ISO, is a novel variation of an ICO for funding cryptocurrency projects. In an ISPO, users stake their cryptocurrency holdings (mostly notably ADA) through a stake-pool operated by the cryptocurrency project.

The first formal ISPO, and so far most successful, was launched on July, 1st, 2021. By October 2021 more than 35,000 participants across the world contributed more than 600 million ADA (worth more than $1 billion USD in October 2021). Participants received 0.065 $MELD / $ADA staked / epoch while keeping full ownership of their ADA.

## Criticisms

### As a Mechanism for Scams

Although ICOs can be used for fraud, they are also used for legal activities such as corporate finance and charitable fundraising. The Securities and Exchange Commission (SEC) has warned investors to beware of scammers using ICOs to execute "pump and dump" schemes, in which the scammer talks up the value of an ICO in order to generate interest and drive up the value of the coins, and then quickly "dumps" the coins for a profit.

Snapchat, LinkedIn and MailChimp all have limited companies from marketing ICOs via their platforms. Jimmy Wales, founder of Wikipedia, stated in 2017 that "there are a lot of these initial coin offerings which in my opinion are absolute scams and people should be very wary of things that are going on in that area."

Chinese internet platforms Baidu, Tencent, and Weibo have also prohibited ICO advertisements. The Japanese platform Line and the Russian platform Yandex have similar prohibitions. The UK Financial Conduct Authority has warned that ICOs are very high risk and speculative investments, are scams in some cases, and often offer no protections for investors. Even in cases of legitimate ICOs, funded projects are typically in an early and therefore high-risk stage of development. The European Securities and Markets Authority (ESMA) notes high risks associated with ICOs and the risk that investors may lose all of their cash.

### As a Bubble

A 2017 *Wired* article predicted in 2017 that the bubble was about to burst. In 2017, some investors flooded into ICOs in hopes of participating in the financial gains of similar size to those enjoyed by early Bitcoin or Ethereum speculators.

## Regulation

Following a speculative boom in cryptocurrency prices that peaked in December 2017, regulation of cryptocurrencies has been rapidly changing. The pace of change has been driven in part by incidents of cybertheft, trading halts, and possible market manipulation.

Cryptocurrencies are based on distributed ledger technologies which enable anyone to purchase or transfer their cryptocurrency holdings to any other person without the need for an intermediary (such as an exchange) or to update a central record of ownership. Cryptocurrencies can be transferred easily across national and jurisdictional boundaries. This makes it difficult for central authorities to control and monitor the ownership and movement of holdings of cryptocurrencies.

Countries have different approaches to how they regulate cryptocurrencies. This can depend on the nature of the cryptocurrency itself. There are two main types of cryptocurrencies from a regulatory perspective: utility tokens and asset-backed tokens. Utility tokens may have value because they enable the holder to exchange the token for a good or service in the future, such as Bitcoin. Asset-backed tokens may have value because there is an underlying asset which the holder of the token can attribute value to. In many countries it is uncertain whether utility tokens require regulation, while it is more likely that asset-backed tokens do require regulation.

This makes it complex for the issuers of cryptocurrencies to analyze which countries their tokens (or coins) can be sold into, and for the prospective purchasers of cryptocurrencies to understand which regulations, if any, should apply.

The Gibraltar British Overseas Territory Financial Services Commission announced in early February 2018 that regulations are being developed to qualify “authorized sponsors” of ICOs, who are supposed to be “responsible for assuring compliance with disclosure” and compliance with “financial crimes rules”.

# CHAPTER 3
# BLOCKCHAIN ARCHITECTURE

## 3.1 CONSENSUS MECHANISM: PROOF OF WORK VS. PROOF OF STAKE

### 3.1.1 Proof of Work

Proof of work (PoW) is a form of cryptographic proof in which one party (the *prover*) proves to others (the *verifiers*) that a certain amount of a specific computational effort has been expended. Verifiers can subsequently confirm this expenditure with minimal effort on their part. The concept was invented by Moni Naor and Cynthia Dwork in 1993 as a way to deter denial-of-service attacks and other service abuses such as spam on a network by requiring some work from a service requester, usually meaning processing time by a computer. The term "proof of work" was first coined and formalized in a 1999 paper by Markus Jakobsson and Ari Juels. The concept was adapted to digital tokens by Hal Finney in 2004 through the idea of "reusable proof of work" using the 160-bit secure hash algorithm 1 (SHA-1).

Proof of work was later popularized by Bitcoin as a foundation for consensus in a permissionless decentralized network, in which miners compete to append blocks and mine new currency, each miner experiencing a success probability proportional to the computational effort expended. PoW and PoS (proof of stake) remain the two best known Sybil deterrence mechanisms. In the context of cryptocurrencies they are the most common mechanisms.

A key feature of proof-of-work schemes is their asymmetry: the *work* – the computation – must be moderately hard (yet feasible) on the prover or requester side but easy to check for the verifier or service provider. This idea is also known as a CPU cost function, client puzzle, computational puzzle, or CPU pricing function. Another common feature is built-in incentive-structures that reward allocating computational capacity to the network with value in the form of cryptocurrency.

The purpose of proof-of-work algorithms is not proving that certain work was carried out or that a computational puzzle was "solved", but deterring manipulation of data by establishing large energy and hardware-control requirements to be able to do so. Proof-of-work systems have been criticized by environmentalists for their energy consumption.

## Background

One popular system, used in Hashcash, uses partial hash inversions to prove that computation was done, as a goodwill token to send an e-mail. For instance, the following header represents about 2 hash computations to send a message to `calvin@comics.net` on January 19, 2038:

**X-Hashcash: 1:52:380119:calvin@comics.net:::9B760005E92F0DAE**

It is verified with a single computation by checking that the SHA-1 hash of the stamp (omit the header name `X-Hashcash:` including the colon and any amount of whitespace following it up to the digit '1') begins with 52 binary zeros, that is 13 hexadecimal zeros:

**0000000000000756af69e2ffbdb930261873cd71**

Whether PoW systems can actually solve a particular denial-of-service issue such as the spam problem is subject to debate; the system must make sending spam emails obtrusively unproductive for the spammer, but should also not prevent legitimate users from sending their messages. In other words, a genuine user should not encounter any difficulties when sending an email, but an email spammer would have to expend a considerable amount of computing power to send out many emails at once. Proof-of-work systems are being used by other, more complex cryptographic systems such as bitcoin, which uses a system similar to Hashcash.

## Variants

There are two classes of proof-of-work protocols.

- **Challenge**–response protocols assume a direct interactive link between the requester (client) and the provider (server). The provider chooses a challenge, say an item in a set with a property, the requester finds the relevant response in the set, which is sent back and checked by the provider. As the challenge is chosen on the spot by the provider, its difficulty can be adapted to its current load. The work on the requester side may be bounded if the challenge-response protocol has a known solution (chosen by the provider), or is known to exist within a bounded search space.

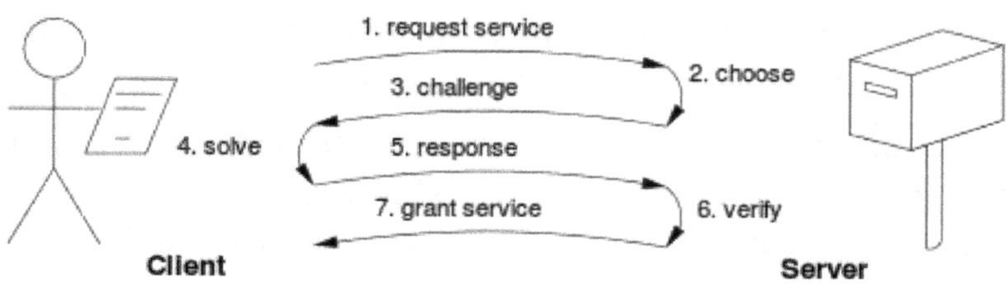


- **Solution**–verification protocols do not assume such a link: as a result, the problem must be self-imposed before a solution is sought by the requester, and the provider must check both the problem choice and the found solution. Most such schemes are unbounded probabilistic iterative procedures such as Hashcash.

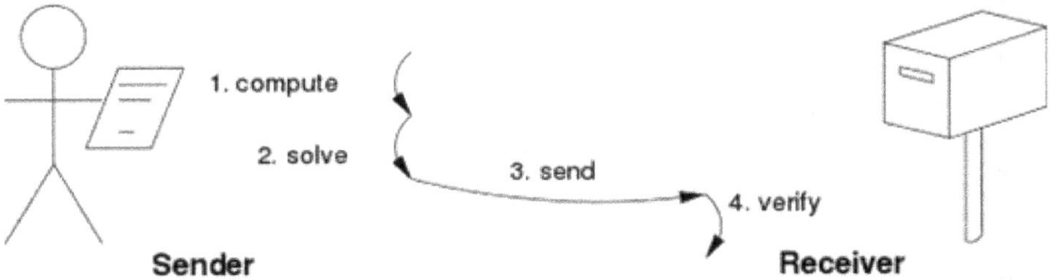


- **Known**-solution protocols tend to have slightly lower variance than unbounded probabilistic protocols because the variance of a rectangular distribution is lower than the variance of a Poisson distribution (with the same mean). A generic technique for reducing variance is to use multiple independent sub-challenges, as the average of multiple samples will have a lower variance.

There are also fixed-cost functions such as the time-lock puzzle. Moreover, the underlying functions used by these schemes may be:

- CPU-bound where the computation runs at the speed of the processor, which greatly varies in time, as well as from high-end server to low-end portable devices.
- Memory-bound where the computation speed is bound by main memory accesses (either latency or bandwidth), the performance of which is expected to be less sensitive to hardware evolution.
- Network-bound if the client must perform few computations, but must collect some tokens from remote servers before querying the final service provider. In this sense, the work is not actually performed by the requester, but it incurs delays anyway because of the latency to get the required tokens.

Finally, some PoW systems offer shortcut computations that allow participants who know a secret, typically a private key, to generate cheap PoWs. The rationale is that mailing-list holders may generate stamps for every recipient without incurring a high cost. Whether such a feature is desirable depends on the usage scenario.

## List of Proof-of-Work Functions

- Integer square root modulo a large prime
- Weaken Fiat–Shamir signatures
- Ong–Schnorr–Shamir signature broken by Pollard

- Partial hash inversion This paper formalizes the idea of a proof of work and introduces "the dependent idea of a bread pudding protocol", a "re-usable proof-of-work" (RPoW) system.
- Hash sequences
- Puzzles
- Diffie-Hellman–based puzzle
- Moderate
- Mbound
- Hokkaido
- Cuckoo Cycle
- Merkle tree–based
- Guided tour puzzle protocol

## Proof of Useful Work (PoUW)

At the IACR conference Crypto 2022 researchers presented a paper describing Ofelimos, a blockchain protocol with a consensus mechanism based on "proof of useful work" (PoUW). Rather than miners consuming energy in solving complex, but essentially useless, puzzles to validate transactions, Ofelimos achieves consensus while simultaneously providing a decentralized optimization problem solver. The protocol is built around Doubly Parallel Local Search (DPLS), a local search algorithm that is used as the PoUW component. The paper gives an example that implements a variant of WalkSAT, a local search algorithm to solve Boolean problems.

## Bitcoin-Type Proof of Work

In 2009, the Bitcoin network went online. Bitcoin is a proof-of-work digital currency that, like Finney's RPoW, is also based on the Hashcash PoW. But in Bitcoin, double-spend protection is provided by a decentralized P2P protocol for tracking transfers of coins, rather than the hardware trusted computing function used by RPoW. Bitcoin has better trustworthiness because it is protected by computation. Bitcoins are "mined" using the Hashcash proof-of-work function by individual miners and verified by the decentralized nodes in the P2P bitcoin network. The difficulty is periodically adjusted to keep the block time around a target time.

### Energy Consumption

Since the creation of Bitcoin, proof-of-work has been the predominant design of Peer-to-peer cryptocurrency. Studies have estimated the total energy consumption of cryptocurrency mining. The PoW mechanism requires a vast amount of computing resources, which consume a significant amount of electricity. 2018 estimates from the University of Cambridge equate Bitcoin's energy consumption to that of Switzerland.

### History Modification

Each block that is added to the blockchain, starting with the block containing a given transaction, is called a confirmation of that transaction. Ideally, merchants and services that receive payment in the cryptocurrency should wait for at least one confirmation to be distributed over the network, before assuming that the payment was done. The more confirmations that the merchant waits for, the more difficult it is for an attacker to successfully reverse the transaction in a blockchain—unless the attacker controls more than half the total network power, in which case it is called a 51% attack.

### ASICs and Mining Pools

Within the Bitcoin community there are groups working together in mining pools. Some miners use application-specific integrated circuits (ASICs) for PoW. This trend toward mining pools and specialized ASICs has made mining some cryptocurrencies economically infeasible for most players without access to the latest ASICs, nearby sources of inexpensive energy, or other special advantages. Some PoWs claim to be ASIC-resistant, i.e., to limit the efficiency gain that an ASIC can have over commodity hardware, like a GPU, to be well under an order of magnitude. ASIC resistance has the advantage of keeping mining economically feasible on commodity hardware, but also contributes to the corresponding risk that an attacker can briefly rent access to a large amount of unspecialized commodity processing power to launch a 51% attack against a cryptocurrency.

## Environmental Concerns

These miners compete to solve crypto challenges on the Bitcoin blockchain, and their solutions must be agreed upon by all nodes and reach consensus. The solutions are then used to validate transactions, add blocks and generate new bitcoins. Miners are rewarded for solving these puzzles and successfully adding new blocks. However, the Bitcoin-style mining process is very energy intensive because the proof of work shaped like a lottery mechanism.

The underlying computational work has no other use but to provide security to the network that provides open access and has to work in adversarial conditions. Miners have to use a lot of energy to add a new block containing a transaction to the blockchain. The energy used in this competition is what fundamentally gives bitcoin its level of security and resistance to attacks. Also, miners have to invest computer hardwares that need large spaces as fixed cost.

In January 2022 Vice-Chair of the European Securities and Markets Authority Erik Thedéen called on the EU to ban the proof of work model in favor of the proof of stake model due its lower energy emissions. In November 2022 the state of New York enacted a two-year moratorium on cryptocurrency mining that does not completely use renewable energy as a power source for two years. Existing mining companies will be grandfathered in to continue mining without the use of renewable energy but they will not be allowed to expand or renew permits with the state, no new mining companies that do not completely use renewable energy will not also not be allowed to begin mining.

### 3.1.2 Proof of Stake

Proof-of-stake (PoS) protocols are a class of consensus mechanisms for blockchains that work by selecting validators in proportion to their quantity of holdings in the associated cryptocurrency. This is done to avoid the computational cost of proof-of-work (POW) schemes. The first functioning use of PoS for cryptocurrency was Peercoin in 2012, although the scheme, on the surface, still resembled a POW.

#### Description

For a blockchain transaction to be recognized, it must be appended to the blockchain. In the proof of stake blockchain the appending entities are named *minters* or validators (in the proof of work blockchains this task is carried out by the miners); in most protocols, the validators receive a reward for doing so. For the blockchain to remain secure, it must have a mechanism to prevent a malicious user or group from taking over a majority of validation. PoS accomplishes this by requiring that validators have some quantity of blockchain tokens, requiring potential attackers to acquire a large fraction of the tokens on the blockchain to mount an attack.

Proof of work (PoW), another commonly used consensus mechanism, uses a validation of computational prowess to verify transactions, requiring a potential attacker to acquire a large fraction of the computational power of the validator network. This incentivizes consuming huge quantities of energy. PoS is more energy-efficient.

Early PoS implementations were plagued by a number of new attacks that exploited the unique vulnerabilities of the PoS protocols. Eventually two dominant designs emerged: so called *Byzantine Fault Tolerance-based* and *chain-based* approaches. Bashir identifies three more types of PoS:

- committee-based PoS (a.k.a. nominated PoS, NPoS);
- delegated proof of stake (DPoS); and
- liquid proof of stake (LPoS).

## Attacks

The additional vulnerabilities of PoS schemes are directly related to their advantage: a relatively low amount of calculations required when constructing a blockchain.

### Long-Range Attacks

The low amount of computing power involved allows a class of attacks that replace a non-negligible portion of the main blockchain with a hijacked version. These attacks are called in literature by different names, *Long-Range*, *Alternative History*, *Alternate History*, *History Revision*, and are unfeasible in the PoW schemes due to the sheer volume of calculations required. The early stages of a blockchain are much more malleable for rewriting, as they likely have much smaller group of stakeholders involved, simplifying the collusion. If the per-block and per-transaction rewards are offered, the malicious group can, for example, redo the entire history and collect these rewards. The classic "Short-Range" attack (bribery attack) that rewrites just a small tail portion of the chain is also possible.

### Nothing at Stake

Since validators do not need to spend a considerable amount of computing power (and thus money) on the process, they are prone to the *Nothing-at-Stake* attack: the participation in a successful validation increases the validator's earnings, so there is a built-in incentive for the validators to accept all chain forks submitted to them, thus increasing the chances of earning the validation fee. The PoS schemes enable low-cost creation of blockchain alternatives starting at any point in history (*costless simulation*), submitting these forks to eager validators endangers the stability of the system. If this situation persists, it can allow double-spending, where a digital token can be spent more than once. This can be mitigated through penalizing validators who validate conflicting chains ("economic finality") or by structuring the rewards so that there is no economic incentive to create conflicts. Byzantine Fault Tolerance based PoS are generally considered robust against this threat.

### Bribery Attack

Bribery attack, where the attackers financially induce some validators to approve their fork of blockchain, is enhanced in PoS, as rewriting a large portion of history might enable the collusion of once-rich stakeholders that no longer hold significant amounts at stake to claim a necessary majority at some point back in time, and grow the alternative blockchain from there, an operation made possible by the low computing cost of adding blocks in the PoS scheme.

## Variants

### Chain-based PoS

This is essentially a modification of the PoW scheme, where the competition is based not on applying brute force to solving the identical puzzle in the smallest amount of time, but instead on varying the difficulty of the puzzle depending on the stake of the participant; the puzzle is solved if on a tick of the clock (|| is concatenation):

$$Hash(ProposedNewBlock \,||\, ClockTime) < target * StakeValue$$

The smaller amount of calculations required for solving the puzzle for high-value stakeholders helps to avoid excessive hardware.

### Nominated PoS (NPoS)

Also known as "committee-based", this scheme involves an election of a committee of validators using a verifiable random function with probabilities of being elected higher with higher stake. Validators then randomly take turns producing blocks. NPoS is utilized by Ouroboros Praos and BABE.

### BFT-based PoS

The outline of the BFT PoS "epoch" (adding a block to the chain) is as follows:

- A "proposer" with a "proposed block" is randomly selected by adding it to the temporary pool used to select just one consensual block;
- The other participants, validators, obtain the pool, validate, and vote for one;
- The BFT consensus is used to finalize the most-voted block.

The scheme works as long as no more than a third of validators are dishonest. BFT schemes are used in Tendermint and Casper FFG.

### Delegated Proof of Stake (DPoS)

Proof of stake delegated systems use a two-stage process: first, the stakeholders elect a validation committee, a.k.a. *witnesses*, by voting proportionally to their stakes, then the witnesses take turns in a round-robin fashion to propose new blocks that are then voted upon by the witnesses, usually in the BFT-like fashion. Since there are fewer validators in the DPoS than in many other PoS schemes, the consensus can be established faster. The scheme is used in many chains, including EOS, Lisk, Tron.

### Liquid Proof of Stake (LPoS)

In the liquid PoS anyone with a stake can declare themselves a validator, but for the small holders is makes sense to delegate their voting rights instead to larger players in exchange for some benefits (like periodic payouts). A market is established where the validators compete on the fees, reputation, and other factors. Token holders are free to switch their support to another validator at any time. LPoS is used in Tezos.

### 'Stake' Definition

The exact definition of "stake" varies from implementation to implementation. For instance, some cryptocurrencies use the concept of "coin age", the product of the number of tokens with the amount of time that a single user has held them, rather than merely the number of tokens, to define a validator's stake.

## Implementations

The first functioning implementation of a proof-of-stake cryptocurrency was Peercoin, introduced in 2012. Other cryptocurrencies, such as Blackcoin, Nxt, Cardano, and Algorand followed. However, as of 2017, PoS cryptocurrencies were still not as widely used as proof-of-work cryptocurrencies. In September 2022, Ethereum, the world second largest cryptocurrency in 2022, switched from proof of work to a proof of stake consensus mechanism system, after several proposals and some delays.

## Concerns

### Security

Critics have argued that the proof of stake model is less secure compared to the proof of work model.

### Centralization

Critics have argued that the proof of stake will likely lead cryptocurrency blockchains being more centralized in comparison to proof of work as the system favors users who have a large amount of cryptocurrency, which in turn could lead to users who have a large amount of cryptocurrency having major influence on the management and direction for a crypto blockchain.

## Energy Consumption

- In 2021, a study by the University of London found that in general the energy consumption of the proof-of-work based Bitcoin was about a thousand times higher than that of the highest consuming proof-of-stake system that was studied even under the most favorable conditions and that most proof of stake systems cause less energy consumption in most configurations.
- In January 2022, Vice-Chair of the European Securities and Markets Authority Erik Thedéen called on the EU to ban the proof of work model in favor of the proof of stake model due to its lower energy consumption.
- On 15 September 2022, Ethereum transitioned its consensus mechanism from proof-of-work to proof-of-stake in an upgrade process known as "the Merge". This has cut Ethereum's energy usage by 99%.

## 3.2 SMART CONTRACTS AND DECENTRALIZED APPLICATIONS (DAPPS)

### 3.2.1 Smart Contracts

A smart contract is a computer program or a transaction protocol that is intended to automatically execute, control or document events and actions according to the terms of a contract or an agreement. The objectives of smart contracts are the reduction of need for trusted intermediators, arbitration costs, and fraud losses, as well as the reduction of malicious and accidental exceptions. Smart contracts are commonly associated with cryptocurrencies, and the smart contracts introduced by Ethereum are generally considered a fundamental building block for decentralized finance (DeFi) and NFT applications.

The original Ethereum white paper by Vitalik Buterin in 2014 describes the Bitcoin protocol as a weak version of the smart contract concept as originally defined by Nick Szabo, and proposed a stronger version based on the Solidity language, which is Turing complete. Since Bitcoin, various cryptocurrencies have supported programming languages which allow for more advanced smart contracts between untrusted parties.

A smart contract should not be confused with a smart legal contract, which refers to a traditional, natural-language, legally-binding agreement that has selected terms expressed and implemented in machine-readable code.

#### Legal Status of Smart Contracts

A *smart contract* does not typically constitute a valid binding agreement at law. Proposals exist to regulate smart contracts. Smart contracts are not legal agreements, but instead transactions which are executed automatically by a computer program or a transaction protocol, such as technological means for the automation of payment obligations such as by transferring cryptocurrencies or other tokens. Some scholars have argued that the imperative or declarative nature of programming languages would impact the legal validity of smart contracts.

Since the 2015 launch of the Ethereum blockchain, the term "smart contract" has been applied to general purpose computation that takes place on a blockchain. The US National Institute of Standards and Technology describes a "smart contract" as a "collection of code and data (sometimes referred to as functions and state) that is deployed using cryptographically signed transactions on the blockchain network". In this interpretation a smart contract is any kind of computer program which uses a blockchain.

A smart contract also can be regarded as a secured stored procedure, as its execution and codified effects (like the transfer of tokens between parties) cannot be manipulated without modifying the blockchain itself. In this interpretation, the execution of contracts is controlled and audited by the platform, not by arbitrary server-side programs connecting to the platform.

In 2018, a US Senate report said: "While smart contracts might sound new, the concept is rooted in basic contract law. Usually, the judicial system adjudicates contractual disputes and enforces terms, but it is also common to have another arbitration method, especially for international transactions. With smart contracts, a program enforces the contract built into the code." States in the US which have passed legislation on the use of smart contracts include Arizona, Iowa, Nevada, Tennessee, and Wyoming. In April 2020,

In April 2021, the UK Jurisdiction Taskforce (UKJT) published the Digital Dispute Resolution Rules (the Digital DR Rules) which was intended to enable the rapid resolution of blockchain and crypto legal disputes in Britain.

## Workings

Similar to a transfer of value on a blockchain, deployment of a smart contract on a blockchain occurs by sending a transaction from a wallet for the blockchain. The transaction includes the compiled code for the smart contract as well as a special receiver address. That transaction must then be included in a block that is added to the blockchain, at which point the smart contract's code will execute to establish the initial state of the smart contract. Byzantine fault-tolerant algorithms secure the smart contract in a decentralized way from attempts to tamper with it. Once a smart contract is deployed, it cannot be updated. Smart contracts on a blockchain can store arbitrary state and execute arbitrary computations. End clients interact with a smart contract through transactions. Such transactions with a smart contract can invoke other smart contracts. These transactions might result in changing the state and sending coins from one smart contract to another or from one account to another.

The most popular blockchain for running smart contracts is Ethereum. On Ethereum, smart contracts are typically written in a Turing-complete programming language called Solidity, and compiled into low-level bytecode to be executed by the Ethereum Virtual Machine. Due to the halting problem and other security problems, Turing-completeness is considered to be a risk and is deliberately avoided by languages like Vyper. Some of the other smart contract programming languages missing Turing-completeness are Simplicity, Scilla, Ivy and Bitcoin Script. However, measurements in 2020 using regular expressions showed that only 35.3% of 53,757 Ethereum smart contracts at that time included recursions and loops — constructs connected to the halting problem. Several languages are designed to enable formal verification: Bamboo, IELE, Simplicity, Michelson (can be verified with Coq), Liquidity (compiles to Michelson), Scilla, DAML and Pact.

Notable examples of blockchain platforms supporting smart contracts include the following:

- **Ethereum:** Implements a Turing-complete language on its blockchain, a prominent smart contract framework
- **Bitcoin:** Provides a Turing-incomplete script language that allows the creation of custom smart contracts on top of Bitcoin like multisignature accounts, payment channels, escrows, time locks, atomic cross-chain trading, oracles, or multi-party lottery with no operator.
- **Binance Smart Chain:** A blockchain platform for smart contracts
- **Cardano:** A blockchain platform for smart contracts, using proof of stake
- **Solana:** A blockchain platform for smart contracts
- **Avalanche:** A blockchain platform for smart contracts
- **Tron:** A blockchain platform for smart contracts
- **EOS.IO:** A blockchain platform for smart contracts
- **Tezos:** A blockchain platform modifying its own set of rules with minimal disruption to the network through an on-chain governance model

Processes on a blockchain are generally deterministic in order to ensure Byzantine fault-tolerance. Nevertheless, real world application of smart contracts, such as lotteries and casinos, require secure randomness. In fact, blockchain technology reduces the costs for conducting of a lottery and is therefore beneficial for the participants. Randomness on blockchain can be implemented by using block hashes or timestamps, oracles, commitment schemes, special smart contracts like RANDAO and Quanta, as well as sequences from mixed strategy Nash equilibria.

## Applications

In 1998, Szabo proposed that smart contract infrastructure can be implemented by replicated asset registries and contract execution using cryptographic hash chains and Byzantine fault-tolerant replication. Askemos implemented this approach in 2002 using Scheme (later adding SQLite) as the contract script language. One proposal for using bitcoin for replicated asset registration and contract execution is called "colored coins". Replicated titles for potentially arbitrary forms of property, along with replicated contract execution, are implemented in different projects.

As of 2015, UBS was experimenting with "smart bonds" that use the bitcoin blockchain in which payment streams could hypothetically be fully automated, creating a self-paying instrument. Inheritance wishes could hypothetically be implemented automatically upon registration of a death certificate by means of smart contracts. Birth certificates can also work together with smart contracts.

Chris Snook of *Inc.com* suggests smart contracts could also be used to handle real estate transactions and could be used in the field of title records and in the public register. Seth Oranburg and Liya Palagashvili argue that smart contracts could also be used in employment contracts, especially temporary employment contracts, which according to them would benefit the employer. Smart contract on block chain technology for smart villages

### Security Issues

The transactions data from a blockchain-based smart contract is visible to all users in the blockchain. The data provides cryptographic view of the transactions, however, this leads to a situation where bugs, including security holes, are visible to all yet may not be quickly fixed. Such an attack, difficult to fix quickly, was successfully executed on The DAO in June 2016, draining approximately US$50 million worth of Ether at the time, while developers attempted to come to a solution that would gain consensus. The DAO program had a time delay in place before the hacker could remove the funds; a hard fork of the Ethereum software was done to claw back the funds from the attacker before the time limit expired. Other high-profile attacks include the Parity multisignature wallet attacks, and an integer underflow/overflow attack (2018), totaling over US$184 million.

Issues in Ethereum smart contracts, in particular, include ambiguities and easy-but-insecure constructs in its contract language Solidity, compiler bugs, Ethereum Virtual Machine bugs, attacks on the blockchain network, the immutability of bugs and that there is no central source documenting known vulnerabilities, attacks and problematic constructs.

### Difference from Smart Legal Contracts

Smart legal contracts are distinct from smart contracts. As mentioned above, a smart contract is not necessarily legally enforceable as a contract. On the other hand, a smart legal contract has all the elements of a legally enforceable contract in the jurisdiction in which it can be enforced and it can be enforced by a court or tribunal. Therefore, while every smart legal contract will contain some elements of a smart contract, not every smart contract will be a smart legal contract. There is no formal definition of a smart legal contract in the legal industry. A Ricardian contract is a type of smart legal contract.

## 3.2.2 Decentralized Applications (DApps)

A decentralised application (DApp, dApp, Dapp, or dapp) is an application that can operate autonomously, typically through the use of smart contracts, that run on a decentralized computing, blockchain or other distributed ledger system. Like traditional applications, DApps provide some function or utility to its users. However, unlike traditional applications, DApps operate without human intervention and are not owned by any one entity, rather DApps distribute tokens that represent ownership. These tokens are distributed according to a programmed algorithm to the users of the system, diluting ownership and control of the DApp. Without any one entity controlling the system, the application is therefore decentralised. Decentralised applications have been popularised by distributed ledger technologies (DLT), such as the Ethereum or Cardano blockchain, on which DApps are built, amongst other public blockchains. DApps are divided into numerous categories: exchanges, businesses, gambling, games, finance, development, storage, wallet, governance, property, identity, media, social, security, energy, insurance, health, etc.

## Definition

There are a series of criteria that must be met in order for an application to be considered a DApp. Traditional definitions of a decentralised application require a DApp to be open-source. That is, the application operates autonomously without a centralised entity in control of the majority of the application's associated tokens. DApps also have a public, decentralised blockchain that is used by the application to keep a cryptographic record of data, including historical transactions.

Although traditional DApps are typically open-source, DApps that are fully closed-source and partially closed-source have emerged as the cryptocurrency industry evolves. As of 2019, only 15.7% of DApps are fully open-source while 25% of DApps are closed source. In other words, the proportion of DApps with publicly available code is less than the proportion of Dapps without publicly available code. DApps that are open-source generally have higher transaction volumes than closed-source DApps. Bitcoin, the first cryptocurrency, is an example of a DApp.

## Usage

DApps can be classified based on whether they operate on their own block chain, or whether they operate on the block chain of another DApp.

### Smart Contracts

Smart contracts are used by developers to maintain data on the block chain and to execute operations. Multiple smart contracts can be developed for a single DApp to handle more complex operations. Over 75% of DApps are supported by a single smart contract, with the remainder using multiple smart contracts. DApps incur gas, that is fees paid to the validators of the block chain, due to the cost of deploying and executing the DApp's smart contracts. The amount of gas required of a DApp's functions is dependent on the complexity of its smart contracts. A complex smart contract of a DApp that operates on the Ethereum blockchain may fail to be deployed if it costs too much gas, leading to lower throughput and longer wait times for execution.

### Operation

Consensus mechanisms are used by DApps to establish consensus on the network. The two most common mechanisms to establish consensus are proof-of-work (POW) and proof-of-stake (POS). Proof-of-work utilises computational power to establish consensus through the process of mining. Bitcoin uses the proof-of-work mechanism. Proof-of-stake is a consensus mechanism that supports DApps through validators that secure the network by having a stake and percent ownership over the application.

DApps distribute their tokens through three main mechanisms: mining, fund-raising and development. In mining, tokens are distributed as per a predetermined algorithm as rewards to miners that secure the network through transaction verification. Tokens can also be distributed through fundraising, whereby tokens are distributed in exchange for funding in the initial development phase of the DApp, as in an initial coin offering. Lastly, the development mechanism distributes tokens that are set aside for the purpose of developing the DApp through a pre-determined schedule.

There are three main steps that always occur in the formation and development of any DApp: the publishing of the DApp's whitepaper, the distribution of initial tokens, and the distribution of ownership. Firstly, the whitepaper is published, describing the DApp's protocols, features and implementation. Then, required software and scripts are made available to the miners and stakeholders that support the validation and fundraising of the network. In exchange, they are rewarded with the initial tokens distributed by the system. Lastly, as greater numbers of participants join the network, either through utilisation of the DApp or through contributions to the DApp's development, token ownership dilutes, and the system becomes less centralised.

### Characteristics

DApps have their backend code running on a decentralized peer-to-peer network, as opposed to typical applications where the backend code is running on centralized servers. A DApp can have frontend code and user interfaces written in any language that can make calls to its backend.

DApps have been utilized in decentralized finance (DeFi), in which dapps perform financial functions on blockchains. Decentralized finance protocols validating peer-to-peer transactions, such as Aave Protocol, are expected to disrupt centralized finance and lower costs.

The performance of a DApp is tied to its latency, throughput, and sequential performance. Bitcoin's system for transaction validation is designed so that the average time for a Bitcoin to be mined is 10 minutes. Ethereum offers a reduced latency of one transaction every 15 seconds. For comparison, Visa handles approximately 10,000 transactions per second. More recent DApp projects, such as Solana, have attempted to exceed that rate.

Internet connectivity is a core dependency of blockchain systems, which includes DApps. High monetary costs also act as a barrier. Transactions of small monetary values can comprises a large proportion of the transferred amount. Greater demand for the service also leads to increased fees due to increased network traffic. This is an issue for Ethereum, which is attributed to increased network traffic caused by DApps built on the Ethereum blockchain, such as those used by Non-fungible tokens (NFTs). Transaction fees are affected by the complexity of a DApp's smart contracts, and by the particular blockchain.

## Trends

Ethereum is the distributed ledger technology (DLT) that has the largest DApp market. The first DApp on the Ethereum blockchain was published on April 22, 2016. From May 2017, the number of DApps being developed have grown at a higher rate. After February 2018, DApps have been published every day. Less than one fifth of DApps capture almost all the DApp users on the Ethereum blockchain. About 5% of DApps capture 80% of Ethereum transactions. 80% of DApps on Ethereum are used by less than 1000 users. On Ethereum, DApps that are exchanges capture 61.5% of transaction volume, finance DApps capture 25.6%, gambling DApps capture 5%, high-risk DApps capture 4.1%, and games capture 2.5%.

DApps have not achieved wide adoption. Potential users may not have the skill or knowledge to be able to effectively analyse the differences between DApps and traditional applications, and also may not value those differences. This skill and information can be difficult to access for mainstream users. Additionally, the user experience for DApps is often poor, as they are often developed to prioritize functionality, maintenance and stability.

Many DApps struggle to attract users, particularly in their founding stages, and even those that attract widespread initial popularity struggle to retain it. A notable example was the DApp *CryptoKitties*, which heavily slowed down the Ethereum network at the height of its popularity. *CryptoKitties* and another similar gaming-based DApp Dice Games have failed to attract similar traction since.

## Examples

- **Augur**—prediction market platform.

- **Cryptokitties**–game built on Ethereum. It slowed Ethereum down due to insufficient transaction processing and exposed the scaling limitations of public blockchains.
- **Stacks project**–a platform for developing decentralized applications.
- **Freelance**–platform on smart contract.
- **Steemit**–blogging and social media.
- **Uniswap**–cryptocurrency exchange.
- **Session**–blockchain-based end-to-end encrypted messenger.

## 3.3 PUBLIC VS. PRIVATE BLOCKCHAINS

### 3.3.1 Public Blockchains

Public blockchains are decentralized networks that allow anyone to participate, validate transactions, and maintain a transparent, immutable ledger of all activities on the network. They are the backbone of many popular cryptocurrencies and have far-reaching implications beyond digital currencies, affecting various industries with their potential to revolutionize how data and value are managed and transferred. Public blockchains represent a transformative technology with the potential to revolutionize various industries by providing decentralized, transparent, and secure systems. While challenges like scalability, energy consumption, and regulatory uncertainty persist, ongoing advancements and innovations are addressing these issues. As public blockchains continue to evolve, their applications will expand, driving further adoption and integration into mainstream society.

#### Key Characteristics of Public Blockchains

- **Decentralization:** Public blockchains operate without a central authority, distributing control across a network of nodes (computers) that validate and record transactions. Each node holds a copy of the entire blockchain, ensuring that no single entity has control over the network.
- **Transparency:** Transactions on a public blockchain are visible to everyone. This transparency fosters trust and accountability, as anyone can verify transactions and view the history of the blockchain.
- **Immutability:** Once data is recorded on a public blockchain, it cannot be altered or deleted. This immutability is achieved through cryptographic hashing and consensus mechanisms that secure the integrity of the blockchain.
- **Open Participation:** Anyone with the requisite hardware and software

can join a public blockchain network. This openness promotes inclusivity and democratizes access to the blockchain's benefits.

- **Consensus Mechanisms:** Public blockchains rely on consensus mechanisms to validate transactions and secure the network. Common mechanisms include Proof of Work (PoW), used by Bitcoin, and Proof of Stake (PoS), used by Ethereum 2.0 and other blockchains.

### Benefits of Public Blockchains

- **Security:** The decentralized nature of public blockchains makes them highly secure against attacks. Compromising a public blockchain requires gaining control of a majority of the network's nodes, which is extremely difficult and resource-intensive.
- **Trustless Transactions:** Public blockchains eliminate the need for intermediaries by enabling trustless transactions. Participants can transact directly with each other, relying on the blockchain's consensus mechanisms and cryptographic security.
- **Transparency and Accountability:** The transparency of public blockchains ensures that all transactions are publicly verifiable. This feature is particularly valuable in industries where accountability and traceability are critical, such as supply chain management and finance.
- **Innovation:** Public blockchains foster innovation by providing a platform for developing decentralized applications (dApps), smart contracts, and other blockchain-based solutions. Ethereum, for example, has become a hub for DeFi (decentralized finance) and NFT (non-fungible token) projects.

### Challenges of Public Blockchains

- **Scalability:** Public blockchains often face scalability issues due to their decentralized nature. High transaction volumes can lead to network congestion, slow transaction times, and increased fees. Efforts to address scalability include layer 2 solutions like the Lightning Network for Bitcoin and sharding for Ethereum.
- **Energy Consumption:** Proof of Work (PoW) consensus mechanisms require significant computational power, leading to high energy consumption. This has raised environmental concerns, prompting some blockchains to explore more energy-efficient alternatives like Proof of Stake (PoS).
- **Regulatory Uncertainty:** The regulatory landscape for public blockchains and cryptocurrencies is still evolving. Regulatory

uncertainty can hinder the adoption and development of blockchain projects, as businesses and developers navigate complex legal frameworks.

- **Privacy Concerns:** While public blockchains offer transparency, this can also be a drawback for users seeking privacy. Transaction details and wallet balances are visible to anyone on the network. Solutions like zk-SNARKs (zero-knowledge succinct non-interactive arguments of knowledge) and privacy-focused blockchains like Monero aim to address these concerns.

## Applications of Public Blockchains

- **Cryptocurrencies:** The most well-known application of public blockchains is digital currencies like Bitcoin and Ethereum. These cryptocurrencies facilitate peer-to-peer transactions, serving as alternatives to traditional fiat currencies.
- **Decentralized Finance (DeFi):** DeFi platforms leverage public blockchains to offer financial services such as lending, borrowing, trading, and yield farming without intermediaries. Examples include Aave, Compound, and Uniswap, which operate on the Ethereum blockchain.
- **Supply Chain Management:** Public blockchains enhance supply chain transparency and traceability. Companies can track products from origin to destination, ensuring authenticity and reducing fraud. IBM's Food Trust blockchain is an example of blockchain technology applied to supply chain management.
- **Smart Contracts:** Smart contracts are self-executing contracts with the terms directly written into code. They run on public blockchains like Ethereum, enabling automated, trustless transactions for various applications, from financial agreements to real estate transactions.
- **Digital Identity:** Public blockchains can provide secure and immutable digital identity solutions. Individuals can control their identity information, reducing the risk of identity theft and streamlining processes that require identity verification.
- **Voting Systems:** Blockchain-based voting systems aim to enhance the security, transparency, and integrity of elections. By recording votes on a public blockchain, the process becomes tamper-proof and verifiable.

## Case Studies

- **Bitcoin:** Bitcoin, the first and most widely known cryptocurrency, operates on a public blockchain using PoW for consensus. Its primary use case is as a decentralized digital currency and store of value, often referred to as "digital gold."

- **Ethereum:** Ethereum extends the functionality of blockchain technology with its support for smart contracts and dApps. It has become the foundation for numerous DeFi projects, NFTs, and other blockchain innovations.
- **Hyperledger Fabric:** While Hyperledger Fabric is often used as a private blockchain, it has elements that can interact with public blockchains. It is designed for enterprise use, offering modular architecture and permissioned access control.

### Future Directions

- **Layer 2 Solutions:** To address scalability issues, layer 2 solutions like the Lightning Network (for Bitcoin) and rollups (for Ethereum) are being developed. These solutions aim to increase transaction throughput and reduce costs by handling transactions off the main blockchain.
- **Interoperability:** Efforts to enhance interoperability between different blockchain networks are underway, enabling seamless communication and transactions across multiple blockchains. Projects like Polkadot and Cosmos are at the forefront of this development.
- **Sustainability:** The shift from PoW to PoS and other energy-efficient consensus mechanisms aims to reduce the environmental impact of public blockchains. Ethereum 2.0, for example, is transitioning to PoS to achieve greater sustainability.

## 3.3.2 Private Blockchains

Private blockchains, also known as permissioned blockchains, are designed to be more controlled and restrictive compared to their public counterparts. Unlike public blockchains, where anyone can participate, validate transactions, and access data, private blockchains restrict access to specific participants.

Private blockchains offer a controlled, secure, and efficient environment for organizations to leverage blockchain technology. With their restricted access, enhanced privacy, and customizable features, private blockchains are well-suited for enterprise applications across various industries. While they present certain challenges, ongoing advancements and innovations are addressing these issues, paving the way for broader adoption. As organizations continue to explore the potential of private blockchains, their impact on business processes, data management, and industry practices is expected to be profound and far-reaching.

## Characteristics of Private Blockchains

- **Restricted Access:** Participation in a private blockchain is controlled by a central authority or a consortium of entities. Only approved participants can join the network, validate transactions, and access data.
- **Permissioned Network:** Private blockchains operate on a permissioned basis, meaning that nodes must have permission to participate in the network. This contrasts with public blockchains, where anyone can join without prior approval.
- **Centralized Governance:** Governance in private blockchains is typically centralized or managed by a group of stakeholders. This centralization allows for more efficient decision-making processes and control over the network.
- **Privacy and Confidentiality:** Private blockchains offer enhanced privacy and confidentiality, as transactions and data are visible only to authorized participants. This makes them suitable for use cases requiring data privacy and protection.
- **Scalability and Efficiency:** Private blockchains can achieve higher scalability and efficiency compared to public blockchains. Since the number of participants is limited and controlled, consensus mechanisms can be optimized for faster transaction processing.

## Advantages of Private Blockchains

- **Enhanced Privacy:** The restricted access and permissioned nature of private blockchains provide enhanced privacy for participants. Sensitive data can be shared among authorized entities without public exposure.
- **Improved Performance:** Private blockchains can handle a higher volume of transactions with lower latency due to their controlled environment. This makes them suitable for enterprise applications that require high performance and reliability.
- **Regulatory Compliance:** Private blockchains can be designed to comply with specific regulatory requirements. Organizations can implement governance frameworks that align with industry standards and legal obligations.
- **Customizable Features:** Private blockchains offer flexibility in terms of customization. Organizations can tailor the blockchain's features, consensus mechanisms, and security protocols to meet their specific needs.

- **Controlled Environment:** The centralized governance model of private blockchains ensures that network rules and protocols are strictly enforced. This control reduces the risk of malicious activities and network disruptions.

### Challenges of Private Blockchains

- **Centralization Concerns:** The centralized nature of private blockchains can lead to concerns about trust and control. Participants must trust the central authority or consortium managing the network.
- **Limited Decentralization:** Private blockchains do not offer the same level of decentralization as public blockchains. This can be seen as a drawback for use cases that require a high degree of trustlessness and transparency.
- **Interoperability Issues:** Interoperability between private and public blockchains, as well as between different private blockchains, can be challenging. Ensuring seamless data and value transfer across networks requires additional effort and standardization.
- **Security Risks:** While private blockchains offer enhanced privacy, they are not immune to security risks. Insider threats and compromised nodes within the network can pose significant risks.
- **Initial Setup and Maintenance:** Setting up and maintaining a private blockchain can be resource-intensive. Organizations need to invest in infrastructure, governance frameworks, and ongoing maintenance.

### Applications of Private Blockchains

- **Supply Chain Management:** Private blockchains are used to enhance transparency and traceability in supply chains. Companies can track the movement of goods, verify authenticity, and ensure compliance with regulations.
- **Financial Services:** Banks and financial institutions use private blockchains to streamline processes, reduce fraud, and improve the efficiency of cross-border transactions and settlements.
- **Healthcare:** Private blockchains enable secure and private sharing of medical records and patient data among authorized healthcare providers. This enhances patient care and data management.
- **Enterprise Resource Planning (ERP):** Organizations integrate private blockchains with ERP systems to improve data integrity, streamline operations, and enhance collaboration among business units.

- **Digital Identity Management:** Private blockchains provide a secure and verifiable platform for managing digital identities. They enable users to control their identity information and share it securely with trusted entities.
- **Governance and Voting:** Private blockchains are used for secure and transparent voting systems within organizations, ensuring that only authorized members can participate in the voting process.

## Case Studies

- **IBM Food Trust:** IBM Food Trust is a blockchain-based solution for enhancing transparency and traceability in the food supply chain. It uses a private blockchain to enable secure sharing of data among food producers, suppliers, and retailers.
- **JPMorgan's Quorum:** Quorum is an enterprise-focused version of Ethereum developed by JPMorgan. It is designed for use in permissioned environments and offers privacy enhancements and efficient consensus mechanisms for financial applications.
- **Hyperledger Fabric:** Hyperledger Fabric is a modular blockchain framework developed by the Linux Foundation. It supports private and permissioned networks, allowing organizations to build customized blockchain solutions for various industries.
- **R3 Corda:** Corda is a blockchain platform designed for business applications, particularly in the financial sector. It enables secure and private transactions between trusted parties on a permissioned network.

## Future Directions

- **Interoperability Enhancements:** Efforts to improve interoperability between private and public blockchains, as well as among different private blockchains, are ongoing. This will facilitate seamless data exchange and collaboration across networks.
- **Integration with IoT:** The integration of private blockchains with Internet of Things (IoT) devices is expected to enhance data security and integrity in IoT ecosystems. This will enable secure and reliable data sharing among connected devices.
- **Advancements in Privacy Technologies:** The development of advanced privacy-preserving technologies, such as zero-knowledge proofs and secure multi-party computation, will enhance the privacy and security of private blockchains.

- **Regulatory Frameworks:** As blockchain technology matures, regulatory frameworks specific to private blockchains will evolve. This will provide clearer guidelines for compliance and foster greater adoption in regulated industries.
- **Industry-Specific Solutions:** The development of industry-specific blockchain solutions tailored to the unique requirements of different sectors will drive the adoption of private blockchains. This will enable more efficient and secure processes across various industries.

## 3.4 PERMISSIONED VS. PERMISSIONLESS SYSTEMS

The distinction between permissioned and permissionless blockchain systems is fundamental to understanding how different blockchain networks operate and the purposes they serve. These two types of systems offer varying degrees of access, security, control, and scalability, catering to different use cases and industry requirements.

The choice between permissioned and permissionless blockchain systems depends on the specific requirements and goals of the application. Permissionless blockchains excel in providing open access, decentralization, and transparency, making them ideal for applications that benefit from these characteristics. On the other hand, permissioned blockchains offer enhanced privacy, regulatory compliance, and scalability, making them suitable for enterprise and industry-specific applications.

As blockchain technology continues to evolve, both permissioned and permissionless systems will play crucial roles in the broader ecosystem. Hybrid solutions that combine elements of both systems are also emerging, aiming to leverage the strengths of each approach. Ultimately, the decision to use a permissioned or permissionless blockchain should be guided by the specific needs of the project, the regulatory environment, and the desired level of decentralization and control.

### 3.4.1 Permissionless Blockchains

#### Characteristics

- **Open Access:** Permissionless blockchains, also known as public blockchains, are open to anyone. Any individual or entity can join the network, validate transactions, and participate in the consensus process without requiring approval from a central authority.
- **Decentralization:** These systems are highly decentralized, with no single entity having control over the network. Decisions are made collectively by the participants through consensus mechanisms.

- **Transparency:** All transactions and data on a permissionless blockchain are publicly accessible. This transparency ensures that the blockchain's history is open for anyone to audit and verify.
- **Immutability:** Once data is added to the blockchain, it cannot be altered or deleted. This immutability is achieved through cryptographic hashing and decentralized consensus.
- **Incentive Mechanisms:** Participants are often incentivized to contribute to the network's security and operation through rewards, such as mining rewards in Proof of Work (PoW) systems or staking rewards in Proof of Stake (PoS) systems.

## Advantages

- **Security:** The decentralized nature of permissionless blockchains makes them highly secure against attacks. Compromising the network would require controlling a significant portion of the nodes, which is economically and technically challenging.
- **Censorship Resistance:** Without a central authority, permissionless blockchains are resistant to censorship. No single entity can alter or suppress transactions.
- **Global Participation:** Anyone with an internet connection can participate in the network, promoting inclusivity and democratization of access to blockchain technology.
- **Trustless Environment:** Participants do not need to trust a central authority or each other, as the blockchain's consensus mechanisms and cryptographic security provide the necessary trust.

## Disadvantages

- **Scalability Issues:** Permissionless blockchains often face scalability challenges. High transaction volumes can lead to network congestion, slow transaction times, and increased fees.
- **Energy Consumption:** Consensus mechanisms like PoW require significant computational power, resulting in high energy consumption and environmental concerns.
- **Regulatory Uncertainty:** The open and anonymous nature of permissionless blockchains can complicate regulatory compliance, leading to legal and regulatory challenges.

### 3.4.2 Permissioned Blockchains

#### Characteristics

- **Restricted Access:** Permissioned blockchains, also known as private or consortium blockchains, restrict access to authorized participants. Only approved entities can join the network, validate transactions, and access data.
- **Centralized Governance:** Governance is often centralized or controlled by a consortium of stakeholders. This allows for efficient decision-making and enforcement of network rules.
- **Privacy and Confidentiality:** Transactions and data on a permissioned blockchain are visible only to authorized participants, ensuring privacy and confidentiality.
- **Customizable Features:** Organizations can customize the blockchain's features, consensus mechanisms, and security protocols to meet their specific needs and regulatory requirements.

#### Advantages

- **Enhanced Privacy:** The restricted access and permissioned nature of these blockchains provide enhanced privacy for participants, making them suitable for use cases requiring data confidentiality.
- **Improved Performance:** Permissioned blockchains can achieve higher transaction throughput and lower latency due to their controlled environment. This makes them ideal for enterprise applications.
- **Regulatory Compliance:** Organizations can design permissioned blockchains to comply with specific regulatory requirements, ensuring adherence to industry standards and legal obligations.
- **Controlled Environment:** Centralized governance ensures that network rules and protocols are strictly enforced, reducing the risk of malicious activities and network disruptions.

#### Disadvantages

- **Centralization Concerns:** The centralized nature of permissioned blockchains can lead to concerns about trust and control, as participants must trust the managing entities.
- **Limited Decentralization:** Permissioned blockchains do not offer the same level of decentralization as permissionless blockchains, which can be a drawback for use cases requiring high degrees of trustlessness and transparency.

- **Interoperability Issues:** Ensuring seamless data and value transfer between different permissioned blockchains, and between permissioned and permissionless blockchains, can be challenging.
- **Security Risks:** While permissioned blockchains offer enhanced privacy, they are not immune to security risks. Insider threats and compromised nodes within the network can pose significant risks.

### 3.4.3 Comparative Analysis

#### Use Cases

- **Permissionless Blockchains:** Ideal for applications that require open access, transparency, and decentralization. Examples include cryptocurrencies like Bitcoin and Ethereum, decentralized finance (DeFi) platforms, and public voting systems.
- **Permissioned Blockchains:** Suitable for enterprise applications that require privacy, regulatory compliance, and controlled participation. Examples include supply chain management, financial services, healthcare data management, and digital identity solutions.

#### Security and Trust

- **Permissionless Blockchains:** Offer high security through decentralization and consensus mechanisms. Trust is established through cryptographic protocols and distributed validation.
- **Permissioned Blockchains:** Rely on the trustworthiness of the central authority or consortium. Security is maintained through controlled access and centralized governance.

#### Scalability and Performance

- **Permissionless Blockchains:** Often face scalability challenges due to their decentralized nature. Efforts to improve scalability include layer 2 solutions and alternative consensus mechanisms.
- **Permissioned Blockchains:** Can achieve higher scalability and performance by optimizing consensus mechanisms and controlling network participation. This makes them suitable for high-throughput applications.

#### Governance and Control

- **Permissionless Blockchains:** Governed collectively by the participants through consensus mechanisms. Changes to the network require broad agreement among participants.

- **Permissioned Blockchains:** Governed by a central authority or consortium, allowing for efficient decision-making and enforcement of network rules. Changes can be implemented more quickly.

# CHAPTER 4
# CRYPTOGRAPHY IN BLOCKCHAIN

## 4.1 CRYPTOGRAPHIC HASH FUNCTIONS

A cryptographic hash function (CHF) is a hash algorithm (a map of an arbitrary binary string to a binary string with a fixed size of n $n$ bits) that has special properties desirable for a cryptographic application:

- the probability of a particular n $n$-bit output result (hash value) for a random input string ("message") is 2 − n (as for any good hash), so the hash value can be used as a representative of the message;
- finding an input string that matches a given hash value (a *pre-image*) is unfeasible, *assuming all input strings are equally likely.* The *resistance* to such search is quantified as security strength, a cryptographic hash with n $n$ bits of hash value is expected to have a *preimage resistance* strength of n 2 bits, unless the space of possible input values is significantly smaller than 2 (a practical example can be found in § Attacks on hashed passwords);
- a *second preimage* resistance strength, with the same expectations, refers to a similar problem of finding a second message that matches the given hash value when one message is already known; and
- finding any pair of different messages that yield the same hash value (a *collision*) is also unfeasible, a cryptographic hash is expected to have a *collision resistance* strength of *n/2* bits (lower due to the birthday paradox).

Cryptographic hash functions have many information-security applications, notably in digital signatures, message authentication codes (MACs), and other forms of authentication. They can also be used as ordinary hash functions, to index data in hash tables, for fingerprinting, to detect duplicate data or uniquely identify files, and as checksums to detect accidental data corruption. Indeed, in information-security contexts, cryptographic hash values are sometimes called *(digital) fingerprints*, *checksums*, or just *hash values*, even though all these terms stand for more general functions with rather different properties and purposes.

Non-cryptographic hash functions are used in hash tables and to detect accidental errors, their construction frequently provides no resistance to a deliberate attack.

For example, a denial-of-service attack on hash tables is possible if the collisions are easy to find, like in the case of linear cyclic redundancy check (CRC) functions.

### 4.1.1 Properties

Most cryptographic hash functions are designed to take a string of any length as input and produce a fixed-length hash value.

A cryptographic hash function must be able to withstand all known types of cryptanalytic attack. In theoretical cryptography, the security level of a cryptographic hash function has been defined using the following properties:

- **Pre-Image Resistance:** Given a hash value $h$, it should be difficult to find any message $m$ such that $h$ = hash($m$). This concept is related to that of a one-way function. Functions that lack this property are vulnerable to preimage attacks.
- **Second Pre-Image Resistance:** Given an input $m_1$, it should be difficult to find a different input $m_2$ such that hash($m_1$) = hash($m_2$). This property is sometimes referred to as *weak collision resistance.* Functions that lack this property are vulnerable to second-preimage attacks.
- **Collision Resistance:** It should be difficult to find two different messages $m_1$ and $m_2$ such that hash($m_1$) = hash($m_2$). Such a pair is called a cryptographic hash collision. This property is sometimes referred to as *strong collision resistance.* It requires a hash value at least twice as long as that required for pre-image resistance; otherwise collisions may be found by a birthday attack.

Collision Resistance implies second pre-image resistance but does not imply pre-image resistance. The weaker assumption is always preferred in theoretical cryptography, but in practice, a hash-function which is only second pre-image resistant is considered insecure and is therefore not recommended for real applications.

Informally, these properties mean that a malicious adversary cannot replace or modify the input data without changing its digest. Thus, if two strings have the same digest, one can be very confident that they are identical. Second pre-image resistance prevents an attacker from crafting a document with the same hash as a document the attacker cannot control. Collision resistance prevents an attacker from creating two distinct documents with the same hash.

In practice, collision resistance is insufficient for many practical uses. In addition to collision resistance, it should be impossible for an adversary to find two messages with substantially similar digests; or to infer any useful information about the data, given only its digest. In particular, a hash function should behave as much as possible like a random function (often called a random oracle in proofs of security) while still being deterministic and efficiently computable. This rules out functions like the SWIFFT function, which can be rigorously proven to be collision-resistant assuming that certain problems on ideal lattices are computationally difficult, but, as a linear function, does not satisfy these additional properties.

Checksum algorithms, such as CRC32 and other cyclic redundancy checks, are designed to meet much weaker requirements and are generally unsuitable as cryptographic hash functions. For example, a CRC was used for message integrity in the WEP encryption standard, but an attack was readily discovered, which exploited the linearity of the checksum.

### Degree of Difficulty

In cryptographic practice, "difficult" generally means "almost certainly beyond the reach of any adversary who must be prevented from breaking the system for as long as the security of the system is deemed important". The meaning of the term is therefore somewhat dependent on the application since the effort that a malicious agent may put into the task is usually proportional to their expected gain. However, since the needed effort usually multiplies with the digest length, even a thousand-fold advantage in processing power can be neutralized by adding a dozen bits to the latter.

For messages selected from a limited set of messages, for example passwords or other short messages, it can be feasible to invert a hash by trying all possible messages in the set. Because cryptographic hash functions are typically designed to be computed quickly, special key derivation functions that require greater computing resources have been developed that make such brute-force attacks more difficult.

In some theoretical analyses "difficult" has a specific mathematical meaning, such as "not solvable in asymptotic polynomial time". Such interpretations of *difficulty* are important in the study of provably secure cryptographic hash functions but do not usually have a strong connection to practical security. For example, an exponential-time algorithm can sometimes still be fast enough to make a feasible attack. Conversely, a polynomial-time algorithm (e.g., one that requires $n$ steps for $n$-digit keys) may be too slow for any practical use.

## 4.1.2 Illustration

An illustration of the potential use of a cryptographic hash is as follows: Alice poses a tough math problem to Bob and claims that she has solved it. Bob would like to try it himself, but would yet like to be sure that Alice is not bluffing. Therefore, Alice writes down her solution, computes its hash, and tells Bob the hash value (whilst keeping the solution secret). Then, when Bob comes up with the solution himself a few days later, Alice can prove that she had the solution earlier by revealing it and having Bob hash it and check that it matches the hash value given to him before. (This is an example of a simple commitment scheme; in actual practice, Alice and Bob will often be computer programs, and the secret would be something less easily spoofed than a claimed puzzle solution.)

### 4.1.3 Applications

#### Verifying the Integrity of Messages and Files

An important application of secure hashes is the verification of message integrity. Comparing message digests (hash digests over the message) calculated before, and after, transmission can determine whether any changes have been made to the message or file. MD5, SHA-1, or SHA-2 hash digests are sometimes published on websites or forums to allow verification of integrity for downloaded files, including files retrieved using file sharing such as mirroring. This practice establishes a chain of trust as long as the hashes are posted on a trusted site - usually the originating site - authenticated by HTTPS. Using a cryptographic hash and a chain of trust detects malicious changes to the file. Non-cryptographic error-detecting codes such as cyclic redundancy checks only prevent against *non-malicious* alterations of the file, since an intentional spoof can readily be crafted to have the colliding code value.

#### Signature Generation and Verification

Almost all digital signature schemes require a cryptographic hash to be calculated over the message. This allows the signature calculation to be performed on the relatively small, statically sized hash digest. The message is considered authentic if the signature verification succeeds given the signature and recalculated hash digest over the message. So the message integrity property of the cryptographic hash is used to create secure and efficient digital signature schemes.

#### Password Verification

Password verification commonly relies on cryptographic hashes. Storing all user passwords as cleartext can result in a massive security breach if the password file is compromised. One way to reduce this danger is to only store the hash digest of each password. To authenticate a user, the password presented by the user is hashed and compared with the stored hash. A password reset method is required when password hashing is performed; original passwords cannot be recalculated from the stored hash value.

However, use of standard cryptographic hash functions, such as the SHA series, is no longer considered safe for password storage. These algorithms are designed to be computed quickly, so if the hashed values are compromised, it is possible to try guessed passwords at high rates. Common graphics processing units can try billions of possible passwords each second. Password hash functions that perform key stretching – such as PBKDF2, scrypt or Argon2 – commonly use repeated invocations of a cryptographic hash to increase the time (and in some cases computer memory) required to perform brute-force attacks on stored password hash digests.

A password hash also requires the use of a large random, non-secret salt value which can be stored with the password hash. The salt is hashed with the password, altering the password hash mapping for each password, thereby making it infeasible for an adversary to store tables of precomputed hash values to which the password hash digest can be compared or to test a large number of purloined hash values in parallel.

### Proof-of-Work

A proof-of-work system (or protocol, or function) is an economic measure to deter denial-of-service attacks and other service abuses such as spam on a network by requiring some work from the service requester, usually meaning processing time by a computer. A key feature of these schemes is their asymmetry: the work must be moderately hard (but feasible) on the requester side but easy to check for the service provider. One popular system – used in Bitcoin mining and Hashcash – uses partial hash inversions to prove that work was done, to unlock a mining reward in Bitcoin, and as a good-will token to send an e-mail in Hashcash. The sender is required to find a message whose hash value begins with a number of zero bits. The average work that the sender needs to perform in order to find a valid message is exponential in the number of zero bits required in the hash value, while the recipient can verify the validity of the message by executing a single hash function. For instance, in Hashcash, a sender is asked to generate a header whose 160-bit SHA-1 hash value has the first 20 bits as zeros. The sender will, on average, have to try 2 times to find a valid header.

### File or Data Identifier

A message digest can also serve as a means of reliably identifying a file; several source code management systems, including Git, Mercurial and Monotone, use the sha1sum of various types of content (file content, directory trees, ancestry information, etc.) to uniquely identify them. Hashes are used to identify files on peer-to-peer filesharing networks. For example, in an ed2k link, an MD4-variant hash is combined with the file size, providing sufficient information for locating file sources, downloading the file, and verifying its contents. Magnet links are another example. Such file hashes are often the top hash of a hash list or a hash tree which allows for additional benefits.

One of the main applications of a hash function is to allow the fast look-up of data in a hash table. Being hash functions of a particular kind, cryptographic hash functions lend themselves well to this application too. However, compared with standard hash functions, cryptographic hash functions tend to be much more expensive computationally. For this reason, they tend to be used in contexts where it is necessary for users to protect themselves against the possibility of forgery (the creation of data with the same digest as the expected data) by potentially malicious participants.

### Content-Addressable Storage

Content-addressable storage (CAS), also referred to as content-addressed storage or fixed-content storage, is a way to store information so it can be retrieved based on its content, not its name or location. It has been used for high-speed storage and retrieval of fixed content, such as documents stored for compliance with government regulations. Content-addressable storage is similar to content-addressable memory.

CAS systems work by passing the content of the file through a cryptographic hash function to generate a unique key, the "content address". The file system's directory stores these addresses and a pointer to the physical storage of the content. Because an attempt to store the same file will generate the same key, CAS systems ensure that the files within them are unique, and because changing the file will result in a new key, CAS systems provide assurance that the file is unchanged.

CAS became a significant market during the 2000s, especially after the introduction of the 2002 Sarbanes–Oxley Act in the United States which required the storage of enormous numbers of documents for long periods and retrieved only rarely. Ever-increasing performance of traditional file systems and new software systems have eroded the value of legacy CAS systems, which have become increasingly rare after roughly 2018. However, the principles of content addressability continue to be of great interest to computer scientists, and form the core of numerous emerging technologies, such as peer-to-peer file sharing, cryptocurrencies, and distributed computing.

## 4.1.4 Hash Functions based on Block Ciphers

There are several methods to use a block cipher to build a cryptographic hash function, specifically a one-way compression function. The methods resemble the block cipher modes of operation usually used for encryption. Many well-known hash functions, including MD4, MD5, SHA-1 and SHA-2, are built from block-cipher-like components designed for the purpose, with feedback to ensure that the resulting function is not invertible. SHA-3 finalists included functions with block-cipher-like components (e.g., Skein, BLAKE) though the function finally selected,

Keccak, was built on a cryptographic sponge instead. A standard block cipher such as AES can be used in place of these custom block ciphers; that might be useful when an embedded system needs to implement both encryption and hashing with minimal code size or hardware area. However, that approach can have costs in efficiency and security. The ciphers in hash functions are built for hashing: they use large keys and blocks, can efficiently change keys every block, and have been designed and vetted for resistance to related-key attacks. General-purpose ciphers tend to have different design goals. In particular, AES has key and block sizes that make it nontrivial to use to generate long hash values; AES encryption becomes less efficient when the key changes each block; and related-key attacks make it potentially less secure for use in a hash function than for encryption.

## 4.1.5 Hash Function Design

### Merkle–Damgård Construction

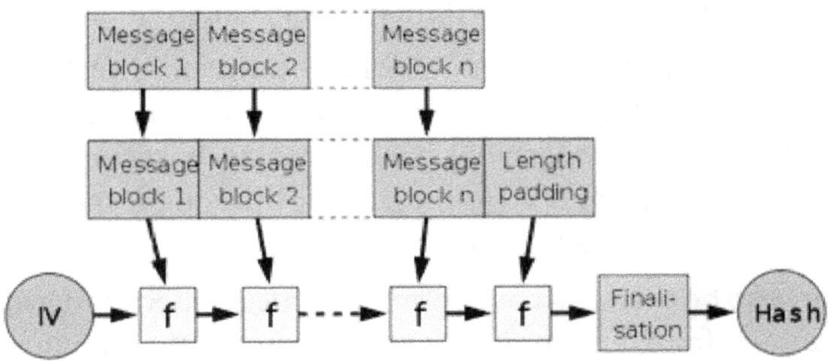


**Fig: The Merkle–Damgård Hash Construction**

A hash function must be able to process an arbitrary-length message into a fixed-length output. This can be achieved by breaking the input up into a series of equally sized blocks, and operating on them in sequence using a one-way compression function. The compression function can either be specially designed for hashing or be built from a block cipher. A hash function built with the Merkle–Damgård construction is as resistant to collisions as is its compression function; any collision for the full hash function can be traced back to a collision in the compression function.

The last block processed should also be unambiguously length padded; this is crucial to the security of this construction. This construction is called the Merkle–Damgård construction. Most common classical hash functions, including SHA-1 and MD5, take this form.

### Wide Pipe versus Narrow Pipe

A straightforward application of the Merkle–Damgård construction, where the size of hash output is equal to the internal state size (between each compression step), results in a narrow-pipe hash design. This design causes many inherent flaws, including length-extension, multicollisions, long message attacks, generate-and-paste attacks, and also cannot be parallelized. As a result, modern hash functions are built on wide-pipe constructions that have a larger internal state size - which range from tweaks of the Merkle–Damgård construction to new constructions such as the sponge construction and HAIFA construction. None of the entrants in the NIST hash function competition use a classical Merkle–Damgård construction. Meanwhile, truncating the output of a longer hash, such as used in SHA-512/256, also defeats many of these attacks.

### 4.1.6 Use in building other cryptographic primitives

Hash functions can be used to build other cryptographic primitives. For these other primitives to be cryptographically secure, care must be taken to build them correctly. Message authentication codes (MACs) (also called keyed hash functions) are often built from hash functions. HMAC is such a MAC.

Just as block ciphers can be used to build hash functions, hash functions can be used to build block ciphers. Luby-Rackoff constructions using hash functions can be provably secure if the underlying hash function is secure. Also, many hash functions (including SHA-1 and SHA-2) are built by using a special-purpose block cipher in a Davies–Meyer or other construction.

That cipher can also be used in a conventional mode of operation, without the same security guarantees; for example, SHACAL, BEAR and LION. Pseudorandom number generators (PRNGs) can be built using hash functions. This is done by combining a (secret) random seed with a counter and hashing it.

Some hash functions, such as Skein, Keccak, and RadioGatún, output an arbitrarily long stream and can be used as a stream cipher, and stream ciphers can also be built from fixed-length digest hash functions. Often this is done by first building a cryptographically secure pseudorandom number generator and then using its stream of random bytes as keystream.

SEAL is a stream cipher that uses SHA-1 to generate internal tables, which are then used in a keystream generator more or less unrelated to the hash algorithm. SEAL is not guaranteed to be as strong (or weak) as SHA-1. Similarly, the key expansion of the HC-128 and HC-256 stream ciphers makes heavy use of the SHA-256 hash function.

### 4.1.7 Concatenation

Concatenating outputs from multiple hash functions provide collision resistance as good as the strongest of the algorithms included in the concatenated result. For example, older versions of Transport Layer Security (TLS) and Secure Sockets

Layer (SSL) used concatenated MD5 and SHA-1 sums. This ensures that a method to find collisions in one of the hash functions does not defeat data protected by both hash functions.

For Merkle–Damgård construction hash functions, the concatenated function is as collision-resistant as its strongest component, but not more collision-resistant. Antoine Joux observed that 2-collisions lead to $n$-collisions: if it is feasible for an attacker to find two messages with the same MD5 hash, then they can find as many additional messages with that same MD5 hash as they desire, with no greater difficulty. Among those $n$ messages with the same MD5 hash, there is likely to be a collision in SHA-1. The additional work needed to find the SHA-1 collision (beyond the exponential birthday search) requires only polynomial time.

### 4.1.8 Cryptographic Hash Algorithms

There are many cryptographic hash algorithms; this section lists a few algorithms that are referenced relatively often. A more extensive list can be found on the page containing a comparison of cryptographic hash functions.

#### MD5

MD5 was designed by Ronald Rivest in 1991 to replace an earlier hash function, MD4, and was specified in 1992 as RFC 1321. Collisions against MD5 can be calculated within seconds which makes the algorithm unsuitable for most use cases where a cryptographic hash is required. MD5 produces a digest of 128 bits (16 bytes).

#### SHA-1

SHA-1 was developed as part of the U.S. Government's Capstone project. The original specification – now commonly called SHA-0 – of the algorithm was published in 1993 under the title Secure Hash Standard, FIPS PUB 180, by U.S. government standards agency NIST (National Institute of Standards and Technology). It was withdrawn by the NSA shortly after publication and was superseded by the revised version, published in 1995 in FIPS PUB 180-1 and commonly designated SHA-1. Collisions against the full SHA-1 algorithm can be produced using the shattered attack and the hash function should be considered broken. SHA-1 produces a hash digest of 160 bits (20 bytes). Documents may refer to SHA-1 as just "SHA", even though this may conflict with the other Secure Hash Algorithms such as SHA-0, SHA-2, and SHA-3.

#### RIPEMD-160

RIPEMD (RACE Integrity Primitives Evaluation Message Digest) is a family of cryptographic hash functions developed in Leuven, Belgium, by Hans Dobbertin, Antoon Bosselaers, and Bart Preneel at the COSIC research group at the Katholieke Universiteit Leuven, and first published in 1996. RIPEMD was based upon the design principles used in MD4 and is similar in performance to the more popular SHA-1. RIPEMD-160 has, however, not been broken. As the name implies, RIPEMD-160 produces a hash digest of 160 bits (20 bytes).

### Whirlpool

Whirlpool is a cryptographic hash function designed by Vincent Rijmen and Paulo S. L. M. Barreto, who first described it in 2000. Whirlpool is based on a substantially modified version of the Advanced Encryption Standard (AES). Whirlpool produces a hash digest of 512 bits (64 bytes).

### SHA-2

SHA-2 (Secure Hash Algorithm 2) is a set of cryptographic hash functions designed by the United States National Security Agency (NSA), first published in 2001. They are built using the Merkle–Damgård structure, from a one-way compression function itself built using the Davies–Meyer structure from a (classified) specialized block cipher.

SHA-2 basically consists of two hash algorithms: SHA-256 and SHA-512. SHA-224 is a variant of SHA-256 with different starting values and truncated output. SHA-384 and the lesser-known SHA-512/224 and SHA-512/256 are all variants of SHA-512. SHA-512 is more secure than SHA-256 and is commonly faster than SHA-256 on 64-bit machines such as AMD64. The output size in bits is given by the extension to the "SHA" name, so SHA-224 has an output size of 224 bits (28 bytes); SHA-256, 32 bytes; SHA-384, 48 bytes; and SHA-512, 64 bytes.

### SHA-3

SHA-3 (Secure Hash Algorithm 3) was released by NIST on August 5, 2015. SHA-3 is a subset of the broader cryptographic primitive family Keccak. The Keccak algorithm is the work of Guido Bertoni, Joan Daemen, Michael Peeters, and Gilles Van Assche. Keccak is based on a sponge construction which can also be used to build other cryptographic primitives such as a stream cipher. SHA-3 provides the same output sizes as SHA-2: 224, 256, 384, and 512 bits. Configurable output sizes can also be obtained using the SHAKE-128 and SHAKE-256 functions. Here the -128 and -256 extensions to the name imply the security strength of the function rather than the output size in bits.

### BLAKE2

BLAKE2, an improved version of BLAKE, was announced on December 21, 2012. It was created by Jean-Philippe Aumasson, Samuel Neves, Zooko Wilcox-O'Hearn, and Christian Winnerlein with the goal of replacing the widely used but broken MD5 and SHA-1 algorithms. When run on 64-bit x64 and ARM architectures, BLAKE2b is faster than SHA-3, SHA-2, SHA-1, and MD5. Although BLAKE and BLAKE2 have not been standardized as SHA-3 has, BLAKE2 has been used in many protocols including the Argon2 password hash, for the high efficiency that it offers on modern CPUs. As BLAKE was a candidate for SHA-3, BLAKE and BLAKE2 both offer the same output sizes as SHA-3 – including a configurable output size.

### BLAKE3

BLAKE3, an improved version of BLAKE2, was announced on January 9, 2020. It was created by Jack O'Connor, Jean-Philippe Aumasson, Samuel Neves, and Zooko Wilcox-O'Hearn. BLAKE3 is a single algorithm, in contrast to BLAKE and BLAKE2, which are algorithm families with multiple variants.

The BLAKE3 compression function is closely based on that of BLAKE2s, with the biggest difference being that the number of rounds is reduced from 10 to 7. Internally, BLAKE3 is a Merkle tree, and it supports higher degrees of parallelism than BLAKE2.

## 4.1.9 Attacks on Cryptographic Hash Algorithms

Even if a hash function has never been broken, a successful attack against a weakened variant may undermine the experts' confidence. For instance, in August 2004 collisions were found in several then-popular hash functions, including MD5. These weaknesses called into question the security of stronger algorithms derived from the weak hash functions – in particular, SHA-1 (a strengthened version of SHA-0), RIPEMD-128, and RIPEMD-160 (both strengthened versions of RIPEMD).

On August 12, 2004, Joux, Carribault, Lemuel, and Jalby announced a collision for the full SHA-0 algorithm. Joux et al. accomplished this using a generalization of the Chabaud and Joux attack. They found that the collision had complexity 2 and took about 80,000 CPU hours on a supercomputer with 256 Itanium 2 processors – equivalent to 13 days of full-time use of the supercomputer.

In February 2005, an attack on SHA-1 was reported that would find collision in about 2 hashing operations, rather than the 2 expected for a 160-bit hash function. In August 2005, another attack on SHA-1 was reported that would find collisions in 2 operations. Other theoretical weaknesses of SHA-1 have been known: and in February 2017 Google announced a collision in SHA-1. Security researchers recommend that new applications can avoid these problems by using later members of the SHA family, such as SHA-2, or using techniques such as randomized hashing that do not require collision resistance.

A successful, practical attack broke MD5 used within certificates for Transport Layer Security in 2008. Many cryptographic hashes are based on the Merkle–Damgård construction. All cryptographic hashes that directly use the full output of a Merkle–Damgård construction are vulnerable to length extension attacks. This makes the MD5, SHA-1, RIPEMD-160, Whirlpool, and the SHA-256 / SHA-512 hash algorithms all vulnerable to this specific attack. SHA-3, BLAKE2, BLAKE3, and the truncated SHA-2 variants are not vulnerable to this type of attack.

### 4.1.10 Attacks on Hashed Passwords

Rather than store plain user passwords, controlled access system frequently store the hash of each user's password in a file or database. When someone requests access, the password they submit is hashed and compared with the stored value. If the database is stolen (an all too frequent occurrence), the thief will only have the hash values, not the passwords.

Passwords may still be retrieved by an attacker from the hashes, because most people choose passwords in predictable ways. Lists of common passwords are widely circulated and many passwords are short enough that even all possible combinations may be tested if calculation of the hash does not take too much time.

The use of cryptographic salt prevents some attacks, such as building files of precomputing hash values, e.g., rainbow tables. But searches on the order of 100 billion tests per second are possible with high-end graphics processors, making direct attacks possible even with salt. The United States National Institute of Standards and Technology recommends storing passwords using special hashes called key derivation functions (KDFs) that have been created to slow brute force searches. Slow hashes include pbkdf2, bcrypt, scrypt, argon2, Balloon and some recent modes of Unix crypt. For KDFs that perform multiple hashes to slow execution, NIST recommends an iteration count of 10,000 or more.

## 4.2 PUBLIC KEY CRYPTOGRAPHY

Public-key cryptography, or asymmetric cryptography, is the field of cryptographic systems that use pairs of related keys. Each key pair consists of a public key and a corresponding private key. Key pairs are generated with cryptographic algorithms based on mathematical problems termed one-way functions. Security of public-key cryptography depends on keeping the private key secret; the public key can be openly distributed without compromising security.

In a public-key encryption system, anyone with a public key can encrypt a message, yielding a ciphertext, but only those who know the corresponding private key can decrypt the ciphertext to obtain the original message.

For example, a journalist can publish the public key of an encryption key pair on a web site so that sources can send secret messages to the news organization in ciphertext. Only the journalist who knows the corresponding private key can decrypt the ciphertexts to obtain the sources' messages—an eavesdropper reading email on its way to the journalist cannot decrypt the ciphertexts.

In a digital signature system, a sender can use a private key together with a message to create a signature. Anyone with the corresponding public key can verify whether the signature matches the message, but a forger who does not know the private key cannot find any message/signature pair that will pass verification with the public key.

For example, a software publisher can create a signature key pair and include the public key in software installed on computers. Later, the publisher can distribute an update to the software signed using the private key, and any computer receiving an update can confirm it is genuine by verifying the signature using the public key. As long as the software publisher keeps the private key secret, even if a forger can distribute malicious updates to computers, they cannot convince the computers that any malicious updates are genuine.

Public key algorithms are fundamental security primitives in modern cryptosystems, including applications and protocols that offer assurance of the confidentiality, authenticity and non-repudiability of electronic communications and data storage. They underpin numerous Internet standards, such as Transport Layer Security (TLS), SSH, S/MIME and PGP. Some public key algorithms provide key distribution and secrecy (e.g., Diffie–Hellman key exchange), some provide digital signatures (e.g., Digital Signature Algorithm), and some provide both (e.g., RSA). Compared to symmetric encryption, asymmetric encryption is rather slower than good symmetric encryption, too slow for many purposes. Today's cryptosystems (such as TLS, Secure Shell) use both symmetric encryption and asymmetric encryption, often by using asymmetric encryption to securely exchange a secret key, which is then used for symmetric encryption.

### 4.2.1 Description

Before the mid-1970s, all cipher systems used symmetric key algorithms, in which the same cryptographic key is used with the underlying algorithm by both the sender and the recipient, who must both keep it secret. Of necessity, the key in every such system had to be exchanged between the communicating parties in some secure way prior to any use of the system – for instance, via a secure channel. This requirement is never trivial and very rapidly becomes unmanageable as the number of participants increases, or when secure channels are not available, or when, (as is sensible cryptographic practice), keys are frequently changed. In particular, if messages are meant to be secure from other users, a separate key is required for each possible pair of users.

By contrast, in a public key system, the public keys can be disseminated widely and openly, and only the corresponding private keys need be kept secret by its owner.

Two of the best-known uses of public key cryptography are:

- Public key encryption, in which a message is encrypted with the intended recipient's public key. For properly chosen and used algorithms, messages cannot in practice be decrypted by anyone who does not possess the matching private key, who is thus presumed to be the owner of that key and so the person associated with the public key. This can be used to ensure confidentiality of a message.
- Digital signatures, in which a message is signed with the sender's private key and can be verified by anyone who has access to the sender's public key. This verification proves that the sender had access to the private key, and therefore is very likely to be the person associated with the public key. It also proves that the signature was prepared for that exact message, since a signature that passes verification with the public key on one message will not pass verification with the public key on other messages.

One important issue is confidence/proof that a particular public key is authentic, i.e., that it is correct and belongs to the person or entity claimed, and has not been tampered with or replaced by some (perhaps malicious) third party. There are several possible approaches, including:

A public key infrastructure (PKI), in which one or more third parties - known as certificate authorities - certify ownership of key pairs. TLS relies upon this. This implies that the PKI system (software, hardware, and management) is trust-able by all involved.

A "web of trust" decentralizes authentication by using individual endorsements of links between a user and the public key belonging to that user. PGP uses this approach, in addition to lookup in the domain name system (DNS). The DKIM system for digitally signing emails also uses this approach.

### 4.2.2 Applications

The most obvious application of a public key encryption system is for encrypting communication to provide confidentiality – a message that a sender encrypts using the recipient's public key, which can be decrypted only by the recipient's paired private key.

Another application in public key cryptography is the digital signature. Digital signature schemes can be used for sender authentication. Non-repudiation systems use digital signatures to ensure that one party cannot successfully dispute its authorship of a document or communication.

Further applications built on this foundation include: digital cash, password-authenticated key agreement, time-stamping services and non-repudiation protocols.

### 4.2.3 Hybrid Cryptosystems

Because asymmetric key algorithms are nearly always much more computationally intensive than symmetric ones, it is common to use a public/private *asymmetric* key-exchange algorithm to encrypt and exchange a *symmetric key*, which is then used by symmetric-key cryptography to transmit data using the now-shared *symmetric key* for a symmetric key encryption algorithm. PGP, SSH, and the SSL/TLS family of schemes use this procedure; they are thus called *hybrid cryptosystems*. The initial *asymmetric* cryptography-based key exchange to share a server-generated *symmetric* key from the server to client has the advantage of not requiring that a symmetric key be pre-shared manually, such as on printed paper or discs transported by a courier, while providing the higher data throughput of symmetric key cryptography over asymmetric key cryptography for the remainder of the shared connection.

### 4.2.4 History

During the early history of cryptography, two parties would rely upon a key that they would exchange by means of a secure, but non-cryptographic, method such as a face-to-face meeting, or a trusted courier. This key, which both parties must then keep absolutely secret, could then be used to exchange encrypted messages. A number of significant practical difficulties arise with this approach to distributing keys.

#### Anticipation

In his 1874 book *The Principles of Science*, William Stanley Jevons wrote:

- Can the reader say what two numbers multiplied together will produce the number 8616460799? I think it unlikely that anyone but myself will ever know.

Here he described the relationship of one-way functions to cryptography, and went on to discuss specifically the factorization problem used to create a trapdoor function. In July 1996, mathematician Solomon W. Golomb said: "Jevons anticipated a key feature of the RSA Algorithm for public key cryptography, although he certainly did not invent the concept of public key cryptography."

#### Classified Discovery

In 1970, James H. Ellis, a British cryptographer at the UK Government Communications Headquarters (GCHQ), conceived of the possibility of "non-secret encryption", (now called public key cryptography), but could see no way to implement it.

In 1973, his colleague Clifford Cocks implemented what has become known as the RSA encryption algorithm, giving a practical method of "non-secret encryption", and in 1974 another GCHQ mathematician and cryptographer, Malcolm J. Williamson, developed what is now known as Diffie–Hellman key exchange. The scheme was also passed to the US's National Security Agency. Both organisations had a military focus and only limited computing power was available in any case; the potential of public key cryptography remained unrealised by either organization:

- I judged it most important for military use ... if you can share your key rapidly and electronically, you have a major advantage over your opponent. Only at the end of the evolution from Berners-Lee designing an open internet architecture for CERN, its adaptation and adoption for the Arpanet ... did public key cryptography realise its full potential. —Ralph Benjamin

These discoveries were not publicly acknowledged for 27 years, until the research was declassified by the British government in 1997.

## Public Discovery

In 1976, an asymmetric key cryptosystem was published by Whitfield Diffie and Martin Hellman who, influenced by Ralph Merkle's work on public key distribution, disclosed a method of public key agreement.

This method of key exchange, which uses exponentiation in a finite field, came to be known as Diffie–Hellman key exchange. This was the first published practical method for establishing a shared secret-key over an authenticated (but not confidential) communications channel without using a prior shared secret. Merkle's "public key-agreement technique" became known as Merkle's Puzzles, and was invented in 1974 and only published in 1978. This makes asymmetric encryption a rather new field in cryptography although cryptography itself dates back more than 2,000 years.

In 1977, a generalization of Cocks's scheme was independently invented by Ron Rivest, Adi Shamir and Leonard Adleman, all then at MIT. The latter authors published their work in 1978 in Martin Gardner's Scientific American column, and the algorithm came to be known as RSA, from their initials. RSA uses exponentiation modulo a product of two very large primes, to encrypt and decrypt, performing both public key encryption and public key digital signatures.

Its security is connected to the extreme difficulty of factoring large integers, a problem for which there is no known efficient general technique. A description of the algorithm was published in the Mathematical Games column in the August 1977 issue of Scientific American.

Since the 1970s, a large number and variety of encryption, digital signature, key agreement, and other techniques have been developed, including the Rabin cryptosystem, ElGamal encryption, DSA and ECC.

### 4.2.5 Weaknesses

As with all security-related systems, there are various potential weaknesses in public-key cryptography. Aside from poor choice of an asymmetric key algorithm (there are few that are widely regarded as satisfactory) or too short a key length, the chief security risk is that the private key of a pair becomes known. All security of messages, authentication, etc., will then be lost. Additionally, with the advent of quantum computing, many asymmetric key algorithms are considered vulnerable to attacks, and new quantum-resistant schemes are being developed to overcome the problem.

#### Algorithms

All public key schemes are in theory susceptible to a "brute-force key search attack". However, such an attack is impractical if the amount of computation needed to succeed – termed the "work factor" by Claude Shannon – is out of reach of all potential attackers. In many cases, the work factor can be increased by simply choosing a longer key.

But other algorithms may inherently have much lower work factors, making resistance to a brute-force attack (e.g., from longer keys) irrelevant. Some special and specific algorithms have been developed to aid in attacking some public key encryption algorithms; both RSA and ElGamal encryption have known attacks that are much faster than the brute-force approach. None of these are sufficiently improved to be actually practical, however.

Major weaknesses have been found for several formerly promising asymmetric key algorithms. The "knapsack packing" algorithm was found to be insecure after the development of a new attack. As with all cryptographic functions, public-key implementations may be vulnerable to side-channel attacks that exploit information leakage to simplify the search for a secret key. These are often independent of the algorithm being used. Research is underway to both discover, and to protect against, new attacks.

#### Alteration of Public Keys

Another potential security vulnerability in using asymmetric keys is the possibility of a "man-in-the-middle" attack, in which the communication of public keys is intercepted by a third party (the "man in the middle") and then modified to provide different public keys instead. Encrypted messages and responses must, in all instances, be intercepted, decrypted, and re-encrypted by the attacker using the correct public keys for the different communication segments so as to avoid suspicion.

A communication is said to be insecure where data is transmitted in a manner that allows for interception (also called "sniffing"). These terms refer to reading the sender's private data in its entirety. A communication is particularly unsafe when interceptions can not be prevented or monitored by the sender.

A man-in-the-middle attack can be difficult to implement due to the complexities of modern security protocols. However, the task becomes simpler when a sender is using insecure media such as public networks, the Internet, or wireless communication. In these cases an attacker can compromise the communications infrastructure rather than the data itself. A hypothetical malicious staff member at an Internet Service Provider (ISP) might find a man-in-the-middle attack relatively straightforward. Capturing the public key would only require searching for the key as it gets sent through the ISP's communications hardware; in properly implemented asymmetric key schemes, this is not a significant risk.

In some advanced man-in-the-middle attacks, one side of the communication will see the original data while the other will receive a malicious variant. Asymmetric man-in-the-middle attacks can prevent users from realizing their connection is compromised. This remains so even when one user's data is known to be compromised because the data appears fine to the other user. This can lead to confusing disagreements between users such as "it must be on your end!" when neither user is at fault. Hence, man-in-the-middle attacks are only fully preventable when the communications infrastructure is physically controlled by one or both parties; such as via a wired route inside the sender's own building. In summation, public keys are easier to alter when the communications hardware used by a sender is controlled by an attacker.

## Public Key Infrastructure

One approach to prevent such attacks involves the use of a public key infrastructure (PKI); a set of roles, policies, and procedures needed to create, manage, distribute, use, store and revoke digital certificates and manage public-key encryption. However, this has potential weaknesses.

For example, the certificate authority issuing the certificate must be trusted by all participating parties to have properly checked the identity of the key-holder, to have ensured the correctness of the public key when it issues a certificate, to be secure from computer piracy, and to have made arrangements with all participants to check all their certificates before protected communications can begin. Web browsers, for instance, are supplied with a long list of "self-signed identity certificates" from PKI providers – these are used to check the *bona fides* of the certificate authority and then, in a second step, the certificates of potential communicators. An attacker who could subvert one of those certificate authorities into issuing a certificate for a bogus public key could then mount a "man-in-the-middle" attack as easily as if the certificate scheme were not used at all. An attacker who penetrates an authority's servers and obtains its store of certificates and keys (public and private) would be able to spoof, masquerade, decrypt, and forge transactions without limit, assuming that they were able to place themselves in the communication stream.

Despite its theoretical and potential problems, Public key infrastructure is widely used. Examples include TLS and its predecessor SSL, which are commonly used to provide security for web browser transactions (for example, most websites utilize TLS for HTTPS).

Aside from the resistance to attack of a particular key pair, the security of the certification hierarchy must be considered when deploying public key systems. Some certificate authority – usually a purpose-built program running on a server computer – vouches for the identities assigned to specific private keys by producing a digital certificate. Public key digital certificates are typically valid for several years at a time, so the associated private keys must be held securely over that time. When a private key used for certificate creation higher in the PKI server hierarchy is compromised, or accidentally disclosed, then a "man-in-the-middle attack" is possible, making any subordinate certificate wholly insecure.

### Unencrypted metadata

Most of the available public-key encryption software does not conceal metadata in the message header, which might include the identities of the sender and recipient, the sending date, subject field, and the software they use etc. Rather, only the body of the message is concealed and can only be decrypted with the private key of the intended recipient. This means that a third party could construct quite a detailed model of participants in a communication network, along with the subjects being discussed, even if the message body itself is hidden.

However, there has been a recent demonstration of messaging with encrypted headers, which obscures the identities of the sender and recipient, and significantly reduces the available metadata to a third party. The concept is based around an open repository containing separately encrypted metadata blocks and encrypted messages. Only the intended recipient is able to decrypt the metadata block, and having done so they can identify and download their messages and decrypt them. Such a messaging system is at present in an experimental phase and not yet deployed. Scaling this method would reveal to the third party only the inbox server being used by the recipient and the timestamp of sending and receiving. The server could be shared by thousands of users, making social network modelling much more challenging.

## 4.2.6 Examples

Examples of well-regarded asymmetric key techniques for varied purposes include:

- Diffie–Hellman key exchange protocol
- DSS (Digital Signature Standard), which incorporates the Digital Signature Algorithm
- ElGamal
- Elliptic-curve cryptography
  - Elliptic Curve Digital Signature Algorithm (ECDSA)
  - Elliptic-curve Diffie–Hellman (ECDH)
  - Ed25519 and Ed448 (EdDSA)
  - X25519 and X448 (ECDH/EdDH)
- Various password-authenticated key agreement techniques
- Paillier cryptosystem
- RSA encryption algorithm (PKCS#1)
- Cramer–Shoup cryptosystem
- YAK authenticated key agreement protocol

Examples of asymmetric key algorithms not yet widely adopted include:

- NTRUEncrypt cryptosystem
- Kyber
- McEliece cryptosystem

Examples of notable – yet insecure – asymmetric key algorithms include:

- Merkle–Hellman knapsack cryptosystem

Examples of protocols using asymmetric key algorithms include:

- S/MIME
- GPG, an implementation of OpenPGP, and an Internet Standard
- EMV, EMV Certificate Authority
- IPsec
- PGP
- ZRTP, a secure VoIP protocol
- Transport Layer Security standardized by IETF and its predecessor Secure Socket Layer
- SILC
- SSH
- Bitcoin
- Off-the-Record Messaging

## 4.3 DIGITAL SIGNATURES AND SECURE TRANSACTIONS

### 4.3.1 Digital Signatures

A digital signature is a mathematical scheme for verifying the authenticity of digital messages or documents. A valid digital signature on a message gives a recipient confidence that the message came from a sender known to the recipient.

Digital signatures are a standard element of most cryptographic protocol suites, and are commonly used for software distribution, financial transactions, contract management software, and in other cases where it is important to detect forgery or tampering.

Digital signatures are often used to implement electronic signatures, which include any electronic data that carries the intent of a signature, but not all electronic signatures use digital signatures. Electronic signatures have legal significance in some countries, including Brazil, Canada, South Africa, the United States, Algeria, Turkey, India, Indonesia, Mexico, Saudi Arabia, Uruguay, Switzerland, Chile and the countries of the European Union.

Digital signatures employ asymmetric cryptography. In many instances, they provide a layer of validation and security to messages sent through a non-secure channel: Properly implemented, a digital signature gives the receiver reason to believe the message was sent by the claimed sender. Digital signatures are equivalent to traditional handwritten signatures in many respects, but properly implemented digital signatures are more difficult to forge than the handwritten type.

Digital signature schemes, in the sense used here, are cryptographically based, and must be implemented properly to be effective. They can also provide non-repudiation, meaning that the signer cannot successfully claim they did not sign a message, while also claiming their private key remains secret. Further, some non-repudiation schemes offer a timestamp for the digital signature, so that even if the private key is exposed, the signature is valid. Digitally signed messages may be anything representable as a bitstring: examples include electronic mail, contracts, or a message sent via some other cryptographic protocol.

#### Definition

A digital signature scheme typically consists of three algorithms:

- A *key generation* algorithm that selects a *private key* uniformly at random from a set of possible private keys. The algorithm outputs the private key and a corresponding *public key*.
- A *signing* algorithm that, given a message and a private key, produces a signature.

- A *signature verifying* algorithm that, given the message, public key and signature, either accepts or rejects the message's claim to authenticity.

Two main properties are required:

- First, the authenticity of a signature generated from a fixed message and fixed private key can be verified by using the corresponding public key.
- Secondly, it should be computationally infeasible to generate a valid signature for a party without knowing that party's private key. A digital signature is an authentication mechanism that enables the creator of the message to attach a code that acts as a signature. The Digital Signature Algorithm (DSA), developed by the National Institute of Standards and Technology, is one of many examples of a signing algorithm.

In the following discussion, 1 refers to a unary number. Formally, a digital signature scheme is a triple of probabilistic polynomial time algorithms, $(G, S, V)$, satisfying:

- $G$ (key-generator) generates a public key ($pk$), and a corresponding private key ($sk$), on input 1, where $n$ is the security parameter.
- $S$ (signing) returns a tag, $t$, on the inputs: the private key ($sk$), and a string ($x$).
- $V$ (verifying) outputs *accepted* or *rejected* on the inputs: the public key ($pk$), a string ($x$), and a tag ($t$).

For correctness, $S$ and $V$ must satisfy

- $\Pr[\ (pk, sk) \leftarrow G(1),\ V(\ pk, x, S(sk, x)\ ) = accepted\ ] = 1.$

A digital signature scheme is secure if for every non-uniform probabilistic polynomial time adversary, $A$

- $\Pr[\ (pk, sk) \leftarrow G(1), (x, t) \leftarrow A(pk, 1), x \notin Q, V(pk, x, t) = accepted] < \text{negl}(n),$

where $A$ denotes that $A$ has access to the oracle, $S(sk, \cdot\ )$, $Q$ denotes the set of the queries on $S$ made by $A$, which knows the public key, $pk$, and the security parameter, $n$, and $x \notin Q$ denotes that the adversary may not directly query the string, $x$, on $S$.

## History

In 1976, Whitfield Diffie and Martin Hellman first described the notion of a digital signature scheme, although they only conjectured that such schemes existed based on functions that are trapdoor one-way permutations.

Soon afterwards, Ronald Rivest, Adi Shamir, and Len Adleman invented the RSA algorithm, which could be used to produce primitive digital signatures (although only as a proof-of-concept – "plain" RSA signatures are not secure). The first widely marketed software package to offer digital signature was Lotus Notes 1.0, released in 1989, which used the RSA algorithm. Other digital signature schemes were soon developed after RSA, the earliest being Lamport signatures, Merkle signatures (also known as “Merkle trees” or simply “Hash trees”), and Rabin signatures.

In 1988, Shafi Goldwasser, Silvio Micali, and Ronald Rivest became the first to rigorously define the security requirements of digital signature schemes. They described a hierarchy of attack models for signature schemes, and also presented the GMR signature scheme, the first that could be proved to prevent even an existential forgery against a chosen message attack, which is the currently accepted security definition for signature schemes. The first such scheme which is not built on trapdoor functions but rather on a family of function with a much weaker required property of one-way permutation was presented by Moni Naor and Moti Yung.

## Method

One digital signature scheme (of many) is based on RSA. To create signature keys, generate an RSA key pair containing a modulus, $N$, that is the product of two random secret distinct large primes, along with integers, $e$ and $d$, such that $e\,d \equiv 1 \pmod{\varphi(N)}$, where $\varphi$ is Euler’s totient function. The signer’s public key consists of $N$ and $e$, and the signer’s secret key contains $d$.

Used directly, this type of signature scheme is vulnerable to key-only existential forgery attack. To create a forgery, the attacker picks a random signature $\sigma$ and uses the verification procedure to determine the message, $m$, corresponding to that signature. In practice, however, this type of signature is not used directly, but rather, the message to be signed is first hashed to produce a short digest, that is then padded to larger width comparable to $N$, then signed with the reverse trapdoor function. This forgery attack, then, only produces the padded hash function output that corresponds to $\sigma$, but not a message that leads to that value, which does not lead to an attack. In the random oracle model, hash-then-sign (an idealized version of that practice where hash and padding combined have close to $N$ possible outputs), this form of signature is existentially unforgeable, even against a chosen-plaintext attack.

There are several reasons to sign such a hash (or message digest) instead of the whole document.

- **For Efficiency:** The signature will be much shorter and thus save time since hashing is generally much faster than signing in practice.
- **For Compatibility:** Messages are typically bit strings, but some signature schemes operate on other domains (such as, in the case of RSA, numbers modulo a composite number $N$). A hash function can be used to convert an arbitrary input into the proper format.

- **For Integrity:** Without the hash function, the text "to be signed" may have to be split (separated) in blocks small enough for the signature scheme to act on them directly. However, the receiver of the signed blocks is not able to recognize if all the blocks are present and in the appropriate order.

## Applications

As organizations move away from paper documents with ink signatures or authenticity stamps, digital signatures can provide added assurances of the evidence to provenance, identity, and status of an electronic document as well as acknowledging informed consent and approval by a signatory. The United States Government Printing Office (GPO) publishes electronic versions of the budget, public and private laws, and congressional bills with digital signatures. Universities including Penn State, University of Chicago, and Stanford are publishing electronic student transcripts with digital signatures. Below are some common reasons for applying a digital signature to communications:

### Authentication

A message may have letterhead or a handwritten signature identifying its sender, but letterheads and handwritten signatures can be copied and pasted onto forged messages. Even legitimate messages may be modified in transit.

If a bank's central office receives a letter claiming to be from a branch office with instructions to change the balance of an account, the central bankers need to be sure, before acting on the instructions, that they were actually sent by a branch banker, and not forged—whether a forger fabricated the whole letter, or just modified an existing letter in transit by adding some digits.

With a digital signature scheme, the central office can arrange beforehand to have a public key on file whose private key is known only to the branch office. The branch office can later sign a message and the central office can use the public key to verify the signed message was not a forgery before acting on it. A forger who *doesn't* know the sender's private key can't sign a different message, or even change a single digit in an existing message without making the recipient's signature verification fail.

Encryption can hide the content of the message from an eavesdropper, but encryption on its own may not let recipient verify the message's authenticity, or even detect selective modifications like changing a digit—if the bank's offices simply encrypted the messages they exchange, they could still be vulnerable to forgery.

In other applications, such as software updates, the messages are not secret—when a software author publishes a patch for all existing installations of the software to apply, the patch itself is not secret, but computers running the software must verify the authenticity of the patch before applying it, lest they become victims to malware.

**Limitations:**

- **Replays:** A digital signature scheme on its own does not prevent a valid signed message from being recorded and then maliciously reused in a replay attack. For example, the branch office may legitimately request that bank transfer be issued once in a signed message. If the bank doesn't use a system of transaction ids in their messages to detect which transfers have already happened, someone could illegitimately reuse the same signed message many times to drain an account.
- **Uniqueness and Malleability of Signatures:** A signature itself cannot be used to uniquely identify the message it signs—in some signature schemes, every message has a large number of possible valid signatures from the same signer, and it may be easy, even without knowledge of the private key, to transform one valid signature into another. If signatures are misused as transaction ids in an attempt by a bank-like system such as a Bitcoin exchange to detect replays, this can be exploited to replay transactions.
- **Authenticating a Public Key:** Prior knowledge of a *public key* can be used to verify authenticity of a *signed message*, but not the other way around—prior knowledge of a *signed message* cannot be used to verify authenticity of a *public key*. In some signature schemes, given a signed message, it is easy to construct a public key under which the signed message will pass verification, even without knowledge of the private key that was used to make the signed message in the first place.

## Non-Repudiation

Non-repudiation, or more specifically non-repudiation of origin, is an important aspect of digital signatures. By this property, an entity that has signed some information cannot at a later time deny having signed it. Similarly, access to the public key only does not enable a fraudulent party to fake a valid signature.

Note that these authentication, non-repudiation etc. properties rely on the secret key *not having been revoked* prior to its usage. Public revocation of a key-pair is a required ability, else leaked secret keys would continue to implicate the claimed owner of the key-pair. Checking revocation status requires an "online" check; e.g., checking a certificate revocation list or via the Online Certificate Status Protocol. Very roughly this is analogous to a vendor who receives credit-cards first checking online with the credit-card issuer to find if a given card has been reported lost or stolen. Of course, with stolen key pairs, the theft is often discovered only after the secret key's use, e.g., to sign a bogus certificate for espionage purpose.

### Notions of Security

In their foundational paper, Goldwasser, Micali, and Rivest lay out a hierarchy of attack models against digital signatures:

- In a *key-only* attack, the attacker is only given the public verification key.
- In a *known message* attack, the attacker is given valid signatures for a variety of messages known by the attacker but not chosen by the attacker.
- In an *adaptive chosen message* attack, the attacker first learns signatures on arbitrary messages of the attacker's choice.

They also describe a hierarchy of attack results:

- A *total break* results in the recovery of the signing key.
- A universal forgery attack results in the ability to forge signatures for any message.
- A selective forgery attack results in a signature on a message of the adversary's choice.
- An existential forgery merely results in some valid message/signature pair not already known to the adversary.

The strongest notion of security, therefore, is security against existential forgery under an adaptive chosen message attack.

### Additional Security Precautions

#### Putting the Private Key on a Smart Card

All public key / private key cryptosystems depend entirely on keeping the private key secret. A private key can be stored on a user's computer, and protected by a local password, but this has two disadvantages:

- the user can only sign documents on that particular computer
- the security of the private key depends entirely on the security of the computer

A more secure alternative is to store the private key on a smart card. Many smart cards are designed to be tamper-resistant (although some designs have been broken, notably by Ross Anderson and his students). In a typical digital signature implementation, the hash calculated from the document is sent to the smart card, whose CPU signs the hash using the stored private key of the user, and then returns the signed hash. Typically, a user must activate their smart card by entering a personal identification number or PIN code (thus providing two-factor authentication). It can be arranged that the private key never leaves the smart card, although this is not always implemented. If the smart card is stolen, the thief will still need the PIN code to generate a digital signature. This reduces the security of the scheme to that of the PIN system, although it still requires an attacker to possess the card. A mitigating factor is that private keys, if generated and stored on smart cards, are usually regarded as difficult to copy, and are assumed to exist in exactly one copy. Thus, the loss of the smart card may be detected by the owner and the corresponding certificate can be immediately revoked. Private keys that are protected by software only may be easier to copy, and such compromises are far more difficult to detect.

### Using Smart Card Readers with a Separate Keyboard

Entering a PIN code to activate the smart card commonly requires a numeric keypad. Some card readers have their own numeric keypad. This is safer than using a card reader integrated into a PC, and then entering the PIN using that computer's keyboard. Readers with a numeric keypad are meant to circumvent the eavesdropping threat where the computer might be running a keystroke logger, potentially compromising the PIN code. Specialized card readers are also less vulnerable to tampering with their software or hardware and are often EAL3 certified.

### Other Smart Card Designs

Smart card design is an active field, and there are smart card schemes which are intended to avoid these particular problems, despite having few security proofs so far.

### Using Digital Signatures Only with Trusted Applications

One of the main differences between a digital signature and a written signature is that the user does not "see" what they sign. The user application presents a hash code to be signed by the digital signing algorithm using the private key. An attacker who gains control of the user's PC can possibly replace the user application with a foreign substitute, in effect replacing the user's own communications with those of the attacker.

This could allow a malicious application to trick a user into signing any document by displaying the user's original on-screen, but presenting the attacker's own documents to the signing application.

To protect against this scenario, an authentication system can be set up between the user's application (word processor, email client, etc.) and the signing application.

The general idea is to provide some means for both the user application and signing application to verify each other's integrity. For example, the signing application may require all requests to come from digitally signed binaries.

### Using a Network Attached Hardware Security Module

One of the main differences between a cloud based digital signature service and a locally provided one is risk. Many risk averse companies, including governments, financial and medical institutions, and payment processors require more secure standards, like FIPS 140-2 level 3 and FIPS 201 certification, to ensure the signature is validated and secure.

### WYSIWYS

Technically speaking, a digital signature applies to a string of bits, whereas humans and applications "believe" that they sign the semantic interpretation of those bits. In order to be semantically interpreted, the bit string must be transformed into a form that is meaningful for humans and applications, and this is done through a combination of hardware and software based processes on a computer system. The problem is that the semantic interpretation of bits can change as a function of the processes used to transform the bits into semantic content. It is relatively easy to change the interpretation of a digital document by implementing changes on the computer system where the document is being processed. From a semantic perspective this creates uncertainty about what exactly has been signed. WYSIWYS (What You See Is What You Sign) means that the semantic interpretation of a signed message cannot be changed. In particular this also means that a message cannot contain hidden information that the signer is unaware of, and that can be revealed after the signature has been applied. WYSIWYS is a requirement for the validity of digital signatures, but this requirement is difficult to guarantee because of the increasing complexity of modern computer systems. The term WYSIWYS was coined by Peter Landrock and Torben Pedersen to describe some of the principles in delivering secure and legally binding digital signatures for Pan-European projects.

### Digital Signatures versus Ink on Paper Signatures

An ink signature could be replicated from one document to another by copying the image manually or digitally, but to have credible signature copies that can resist some scrutiny is a significant manual or technical skill, and to produce ink signature copies that resist professional scrutiny is very difficult.

Digital signatures cryptographically bind an electronic identity to an electronic document and the digital signature cannot be copied to another document. Paper contracts sometimes have the ink signature block on the last page, and the previous pages may be replaced after a signature is applied. Digital signatures can be applied to an entire document, such that the digital signature on the last page will indicate tampering if any data on any of the pages have been altered, but this can also be achieved by signing with ink and numbering all pages of the contract.

## Some Digital Signature Algorithms

- RSA
- DSA
- ECDSA
- EdDSA
- RSA with SHA
- ECDSA with SHA
- ElGamal signature scheme as the predecessor to DSA, and variants Schnorr signature and Pointcheval–Stern signature algorithm
- Rabin signature algorithm
- Pairing-based schemes such as BLS
- NTRUSign is an example of a digital signature scheme based on hard lattice problems
- Undeniable signatures
- Aggregate signatureru—a signature scheme that supports aggregation: Given n signatures on n messages from n users, it is possible to aggregate all these signatures into a single signature whose size is constant in the number of users. This single signature will convince the verifier that the n users did indeed sign the n original messages. A scheme by Mihir Bellare and Gregory Neven may be used with Bitcoin.
- Signatures with efficient protocols—are signature schemes that facilitate efficient cryptographic protocols such as zero-knowledge proofs or secure computation.

## The Current State of Use—Legal and Practical

Most digital signature schemes share the following goals regardless of cryptographic theory or legal provision:

- **Quality Algorithms:** Some public-key algorithms are known to be insecure, as practical attacks against them have been discovered.
- **Quality Implementations:** An implementation of a good algorithm (or protocol) with mistake(s) will not work.
- Users (and their Software) must carry out the signature protocol properly.

- **The Private Key Must Remain Private:** If the private key becomes known to any other party, that party can produce *perfect* digital signatures of anything.
- **The Public Key Owner Must be Verifiable:** A public key associated with Bob actually came from Bob. This is commonly done using a public key infrastructure (PKI) and the public key↔user association is attested by the operator of the PKI (called a certificate authority). For 'open' PKIs in which anyone can request such an attestation (universally embodied in a cryptographically protected public key certificate), the possibility of mistaken attestation is non-trivial. Commercial PKI operators have suffered several publicly known problems. Such mistakes could lead to falsely signed, and thus wrongly attributed, documents. 'Closed' PKI systems are more expensive, but less easily subverted in this way.

Only if all of these conditions are met will a digital signature actually be any evidence of who sent the message, and therefore of their assent to its contents. Legal enactment cannot change this reality of the existing engineering possibilities, though some such have not reflected this actuality.

Legislatures, being importuned by businesses expecting to profit from operating a PKI, or by the technological avant-garde advocating new solutions to old problems, have enacted statutes and/or regulations in many jurisdictions authorizing, endorsing, encouraging, or permitting digital signatures and providing for (or limiting) their legal effect. The first appears to have been in Utah in the United States, followed closely by the states Massachusetts and California. Other countries have also passed statutes or issued regulations in this area as well and the UN has had an active model law project for some time. These enactments (or proposed enactments) vary from place to place, have typically embodied expectations at variance (optimistically or pessimistically) with the state of the underlying cryptographic engineering, and have had the net effect of confusing potential users and specifiers, nearly all of whom are not cryptographically knowledgeable.

Adoption of technical standards for digital signatures have lagged behind much of the legislation, delaying a more or less unified engineering position on interoperability, algorithm choice, key lengths, and so on what the engineering is attempting to provide.

## Industry Standards

Some industries have established common interoperability standards for the use of digital signatures between members of the industry and with regulators. These include the Automotive Network Exchange for the automobile industry and the SAFE-BioPharma Association for the healthcare industry.

### Using Separate Key Pairs for Signing and Encryption

In several countries, a digital signature has a status somewhat like that of a traditional pen and paper signature, as in the 1999 EU digital signature directive and 2014 EU follow-on legislation. Generally, these provisions mean that anything digitally signed legally binds the signer of the document to the terms therein. For that reason, it is often thought best to use separate key pairs for encrypting and signing. Using the encryption key pair, a person can engage in an encrypted conversation (e.g., regarding a real estate transaction), but the encryption does not legally sign every message he or she sends. Only when both parties come to an agreement do they sign a contract with their signing keys, and only then are they legally bound by the terms of a specific document. After signing, the document can be sent over the encrypted link. If a signing key is lost or compromised, it can be revoked to mitigate any future transactions. If an encryption key is lost, a backup or key escrow should be utilized to continue viewing encrypted content. Signing keys should never be backed up or escrowed unless the backup destination is securely encrypted.

## 4.3.2 Secure Transactions

A secured transaction is a loan or a credit transaction in which the lender acquires a security interest in collateral owned by the borrower and is entitled to foreclose on or repossess the collateral in the event of the borrower's default.

The terms of the relationship are governed by a contract, or security agreement. In the United States, secured transactions in personal property (that is, anything other than real property) are governed by Article 9 of the Uniform Commercial Code (U.C.C.).

### Security Interest Protection in Bankruptcy Proceedings

One of the main benefits of becoming a secured creditor through a secured transaction is protection during a bankruptcy proceeding. In the event of a bankruptcy proceeding, a secured creditor needs to file a proof of claim describing the debt and the remaining balance owed.

In the United States the Bankruptcy Code §506(b) entitles a secured creditor with a court approved claim to accrue post-filing interest, attorney's fees, and costs on its claim when three conditions are met:

- The attorney fees and costs are "reasonable";
- payment of the attorneys fees and costs by borrower (or debtor) must be provided in the lien or by statute which the claim arose; and
- interest, attorneys fees, and costs can be accrued to the extent that the value of the collateral exceeds the amount secured by it.

Claims can be undersecured, where the value of the collateral is worth less than the amount due for the lien. Such as someone uses their car valued at $30,000, while the lien is for $40,000, meaning $10,000 of the debt is unsecured. Claims also can be oversecured, where the value of the collateral is worth more than the amount due for the lien. Example, someone uses their boat valued at $50,000 for a lien valued at $45,000, making $5,000 oversecured.

One feature that applies in bankruptcy proceedings that impacts creditors is the automatic stay. If the security interest is not adequately protected, a secured creditor may ask the court to lift the automatic stay. In the United States an automatic stay must be lifted by the courts if:

- there is no equity in the collateral that might be realized for unsecured creditors, and
- the collateral is not necessary for an effective reorganization.

### How to Become a Secured Creditor

A security interest can be created by contracts, liens created by statutes, and liens created by judicial acts. UCC §9-203(b) requires three things to create a security interest in the United States:

- possession of the collateral or an authenticated security agreement with a description of the collateral,
- value of the collateral, and
- the borrower (debtor) must have rights in the collateral.

### Types of Collateral

A secured transaction includes several forms of collateral. The definition of collateral in the U.C.C. is:

the property subject to a security interest or agricultural lien. The term includes:

- proceeds to which a security interest attaches;
- accounts, chattel paper, payment intangibles, and promissory notes that have been sold; and
- goods that are the subject of a consignment.—*§ 9-102. (12) Definitions and Index of Definitions. Collateral, U.C.C. Text § 9-102*

This definition includes things such as home loans, car loans, inventory loans, farm crop loans, and many more. Depending on the type of collateral special rules may apply to the secured transaction. Article 9 of the U.C.C. defines many types of collateral, which are not always the same as the common meaning. An example of this would be the definition of "farm products", which includes not only the eggs a chicken lays, but the chicken too. In the United States, when a U.C.C. collateral term is used in the security agreement, usually the courts will apply the Article 9 term meaning rather than the common one.

Various types of property can serve as collateral for a security interest, such as a when a person takes a mortgage out to purchase a house the house becomes collateral. Another example of collateral for a security interest would be the car if someone takes out a car lien to help cover the costs.

The law treats differently those creditors who are secured (i.e., have an authenticated, perfected security interest) from those creditors who are unsecured. An unsecured creditor is simply a person who is owed money and has not received payment according to the terms of the agreed upon transaction. Upon default of a debtor who has multiple creditors, the distinction between being a secured creditor and an unsecured creditor is legally significant. The secured creditor will generally always have priority to getting his money before the unsecured creditors do. In other words, the unsecured creditor is at the back of the line of priority – his only remedy is to obtain a judgment from the court for the amount of the defaulted loan.

The following example is given:

- A debtor borrows $10,000 from a car dealership to purchase an automobile, using the automobile itself as collateral for the loan (in other words the dealership retains a right to repossess the automobile in the event the debtor defaults on the loan). The dealership makes this loan using an authenticated security agreement – a signed agreement giving the dealership the secured right to repossess the car in the event of default of the debtor. The debtor also has two unsecured creditors who have made loans of $1000 each to the debtor. Neither of these creditors has a security agreement – their only method of recovering their money in the event that the debtor defaults on the loan is through the judicial system, whereas the secured creditor can simply repossess the car at his option (This is called self-help repossession and is completely legal provided the secured creditor does not breach the peace in doing so). The debtor is in debt $10K to the secured creditor and $2000 to the unsecured creditors. Assume the debtor defaults and his only asset is the automobile. The dealership can repossess the auto and sell it to satisfy its debt. Two things can happen here: 1) The dealership sells the collateral (car) for more than the amount of the debt (let's say $15K). In this case, the debtor would receive the excess $5K (surplus) which he would use to satisfy the debts of his unsecured creditors (and then would have $3K left over). 2) The dealership repossess the car and sells it for less than the amount of the debt, let's say $9K (more likely scenario). In this case, the secured creditor dealership keeps the $9K, and the remaining $1K (deficiency) that the dealership is owed becomes unsecured – it is on the same level of priority as the other two unsecured loans. Those three unsecured claims of $1K each will be paid off equally. Thus, if the debtor has $1500 to satisfy its debts – each unsecured creditor would get $500 (1/3 of amount each). The remaining debt will probably never be repaid because, in cases such as these with the debtor having multiple loans on default, the debtor has most likely filed for Ch. 7 Bankruptcy.

It is crucial, if you are a lender, to have a security agreement in collateral that you are confident is worth at least as much as the amount of the loan you made to the debtor. If not, your deficiency in that amount is unsecured. In the previous example – the dealership loaned $10K on a car that had a fair market value of only $9K. Thus, they were deficient $1K which becomes unsecured. To perfect a security agreement, the filing of a public notice is usually required.

## 4.4 PRIVACY AND ANONYMITY IN CRYPTOCURRENCIES

Privacy and anonymity in cryptocurrencies are critical topics that have garnered significant attention as digital currencies gain popularity. Cryptocurrencies, such as Bitcoin and Ethereum, offer a decentralized means of transferring value without the need for intermediaries like banks. While these currencies provide various benefits, including faster transactions and reduced fees, they also raise important questions about privacy and anonymity.

Privacy and anonymity are fundamental aspects of the cryptocurrency landscape, offering significant benefits for users while also presenting challenges for regulators. By understanding and addressing these challenges, the cryptocurrency community can work towards a future where privacy and security coexist with regulatory compliance and financial integrity. As technology advances and regulatory approaches evolve, the interplay between privacy, anonymity, and oversight will shape the future of digital finance.

### 4.4.1 Understanding Privacy and Anonymity

Privacy and anonymity, while related, are distinct concepts. Privacy in the context of cryptocurrencies refers to the ability to keep one's financial activities concealed from public view and unauthorized access. Anonymity, on the other hand, involves the ability to conduct transactions without revealing one's identity.

#### Privacy

Privacy focuses on protecting the details of transactions and the identities of the parties involved. This can be achieved through various cryptographic techniques that obscure transaction data, making it difficult for external observers to track the flow of funds or associate transactions with specific individuals.

### Anonymity

Anonymity ensures that even if transaction data is accessible, it cannot be easily linked to the identities of the users involved. This is often achieved through the use of pseudonyms or temporary addresses that change with each transaction, making it challenging to build a comprehensive profile of a user's activity.

## 4.4.2 Privacy Mechanisms in Cryptocurrencies

Several cryptocurrencies have implemented mechanisms to enhance privacy. These mechanisms range from basic obfuscation techniques to advanced cryptographic protocols.

### Bitcoin

Bitcoin, the first and most widely known cryptocurrency, does not offer true privacy or anonymity. All transactions are recorded on a public ledger, known as the blockchain, which allows anyone to view the transaction history. However, Bitcoin transactions are pseudonymous. Users are identified by their public keys (addresses) rather than personal information. Despite this, sophisticated analysis techniques can sometimes link these addresses to real-world identities.

### Privacy Coins

Privacy coins are cryptocurrencies specifically designed to enhance privacy and anonymity. Examples include Monero, Zcash, and Dash.

- **Monero (XMR):** Monero employs several techniques to enhance privacy. These include Ring Signatures, which mix a user's transaction with others, making it difficult to trace, and Confidential Transactions, which obscure the transaction amount. Monero also uses Stealth Addresses, which generate one-time addresses for each transaction, further protecting user privacy.
- **Zcash (ZEC):** Zcash offers users the choice between transparent and shielded transactions. Shielded transactions use a cryptographic method called zk-SNARKs (zero-knowledge succinct non-interactive arguments of knowledge) to hide the sender, receiver, and transaction amount.
- **Dash (DASH):** Dash provides an optional privacy feature called PrivateSend, which mixes multiple transactions together to obscure the origin and destination of funds. This is similar to CoinJoin, a method used by some Bitcoin mixers.

### 4.4.3 Implications for Users

#### Benefits

- **Financial Privacy:** Enhanced privacy protects users from unwanted scrutiny and potential exploitation of their financial data. This is particularly important in regions with oppressive regimes or high levels of financial surveillance.
- **Security:** By keeping transaction details private, users reduce the risk of becoming targets for crime, such as hacking or physical attacks aimed at coercing individuals into transferring funds.
- **Freedom:** Privacy and anonymity provide users with the freedom to transact without censorship or interference from third parties, promoting financial independence and autonomy.

#### Drawbacks

- **Illicit Activities:** The same features that protect legitimate users' privacy can also facilitate illegal activities, such as money laundering, drug trafficking, and financing terrorism. This has led to increased scrutiny from regulators and law enforcement agencies.
- **Regulatory Challenges:** Privacy coins pose significant challenges for regulatory compliance, particularly with anti-money laundering (AML) and know-your-customer (KYC) regulations. This has resulted in some exchanges delisting privacy-focused cryptocurrencies.

### 4.4.4 Implications for Regulators

Regulators face a complex challenge in balancing the benefits of financial privacy with the need to prevent illicit activities. Several approaches have been proposed to address these challenges:

- **Enhanced Monitoring:** Governments and financial institutions are developing advanced analytical tools to trace cryptocurrency transactions and identify patterns indicative of illegal activities.
- **Regulatory Frameworks:** Regulatory frameworks are evolving to address the unique challenges posed by cryptocurrencies. This includes the implementation of stricter KYC and AML requirements for exchanges and other cryptocurrency service providers.
- **Banning or Restricting Privacy Coins:** Some jurisdictions have considered or implemented bans or restrictions on privacy-focused cryptocurrencies. However, this approach can drive users to unregulated markets or alternative privacy-enhancing technologies.

### 4.4.5 The Future of Privacy and Anonymity in Cryptocurrencies

The future of privacy and anonymity in cryptocurrencies will likely involve a balancing act between technological innovation and regulatory compliance. As the cryptocurrency ecosystem evolves, new privacy-enhancing technologies will emerge, potentially offering even greater levels of anonymity and security.

Simultaneously, regulatory frameworks will need to adapt to these innovations to ensure that they can effectively mitigate the risks associated with illicit activities without stifling the legitimate use of cryptocurrencies. Collaborative efforts between industry stakeholders, regulators, and privacy advocates will be essential in achieving this balance.

# CHAPTER 5

# MINING AND CONSENSUS ALGORITHMS

## 5.1 MINING PROCESSES AND MINERS

Cryptocurrency mining is a fundamental process that underpins decentralized digital currencies, such as Bitcoin, Ethereum, and many others. Mining not only secures the blockchain but also ensures the integrity and stability of the cryptocurrency network.

Cryptocurrency mining is a complex and multifaceted process that is integral to the functioning of decentralized digital currencies. Miners perform essential tasks, including transaction verification, network security, and maintaining decentralization. The mining process relies on specialized hardware and significant computational power, raising concerns about energy consumption and environmental impact. As the cryptocurrency ecosystem evolves, there is a growing emphasis on developing more sustainable and energy-efficient mining practices. By understanding the technical, economic, and environmental aspects of mining, we can appreciate the challenges and opportunities facing this dynamic industry.

### 5.1.1 Understanding Cryptocurrency Mining

Cryptocurrency mining is the process by which new digital coins are created and transactions are verified and added to the blockchain. This process relies on complex cryptographic algorithms and requires significant computational power.

#### The Blockchain

A blockchain is a distributed ledger that records all transactions made with a specific cryptocurrency. Each block contains a list of transactions, a timestamp, and a reference to the previous block, forming a chain. The blockchain is maintained by a network of nodes, which are computers running the cryptocurrency software.

#### Proof of Work (PoW)

The most common consensus mechanism for securing and validating transactions in cryptocurrencies is Proof of Work (PoW). Miners compete to solve complex mathematical problems, and the first to solve the problem gets to add a new block to the blockchain and receive a reward in the form of newly created cryptocurrency and transaction fees.

### 5.1.2 The Mining Process

The mining process involves several steps, each requiring specialized hardware and software.

- **Step 1:** Transaction Verification: Miners collect pending transactions from a pool known as the memory pool (mempool). These transactions are checked for validity, ensuring that the sender has sufficient funds and that the transactions follow the network's rules.
- **Step 2:** Block Creation: Once a set of transactions is verified, miners group them into a candidate block. This block includes a reference to the previous block, a timestamp, and a nonce (a random number used in the PoW algorithm).
- **Step 3:** Solving the PoW Algorithm: Miners must find a nonce that, when combined with the block's data and passed through a cryptographic hash function (such as SHA-256 for Bitcoin), produces a hash value that meets the network's difficulty target. This target is adjusted periodically to ensure that blocks are added at a consistent rate, typically every 10 minutes for Bitcoin.
- **Step 4:** Broadcasting the Block: The first miner to find a valid hash broadcasts the new block to the network. Other nodes verify the block and the solution to the PoW problem. Once verified, the block is added to the blockchain, and the miner receives the block reward and transaction fees.

### 5.1.3 Mining Hardware

Cryptocurrency mining requires specialized hardware capable of performing the necessary calculations at high speed.

- **Central Processing Units (CPUs):** Initially, cryptocurrency mining could be performed using standard CPUs found in personal computers. However, as the difficulty of mining increased, CPUs became less efficient.
- **Graphics Processing Units (GPUs):** GPUs, which are more efficient at handling parallel processing tasks, became the preferred choice for mining cryptocurrencies like Ethereum. GPUs offer a significant increase in hashing power compared to CPUs.
- **Application-Specific Integrated Circuits (ASICs):** For cryptocurrencies like Bitcoin, ASICs have become the dominant mining hardware. ASICs

are custom-built chips designed specifically for mining a particular algorithm, offering unparalleled performance and energy efficiency.

### 5.1.4 The Role of Miners

Miners play a crucial role in maintaining the integrity and security of cryptocurrency networks. Their responsibilities include:

- **Transaction Validation:** Miners ensure that all transactions are legitimate, preventing double-spending and fraud.
- **Network Security:** By solving complex cryptographic problems, miners make it extremely difficult for any single entity to control the blockchain or alter transaction history.
- **Decentralization:** Mining distributes the control of the network across a wide range of participants, reducing the risk of centralization and enhancing the resilience of the cryptocurrency.

### 5.1.5 Economic Aspects of Mining

Cryptocurrency mining is not only a technical process but also an economic one. The profitability of mining depends on several factors:

- **Block Rewards and Transaction Fees:** Miners earn rewards in the form of new cryptocurrency and transaction fees. For example, Bitcoin miners currently receive 6.25 BTC per block (as of the last halving in 2020) plus any transaction fees included in the block.
- **Mining Difficulty:** As more miners join the network, the difficulty of the PoW algorithm increases, making it harder to find a valid hash. This helps maintain a steady rate of block creation but can reduce individual miner profitability.
- **Energy Costs:** Mining is an energy-intensive process, and electricity costs can significantly impact profitability. Miners often seek locations with low energy costs to maximize their earnings.
- **Hardware Costs:** The initial investment in mining hardware can be substantial, particularly for ASICs. Additionally, hardware must be regularly updated to remain competitive as mining difficulty increases.

### 5.1.6 Environmental Impact of Mining

Cryptocurrency mining has raised concerns about its environmental impact due to the significant energy consumption required.

- **Energy Consumption:** Mining operations consume vast amounts of electricity, leading to concerns about their carbon footprint. For example, the Bitcoin network's energy consumption has been compared to that of entire countries.

- **Renewable Energy:** To mitigate environmental impacts, some mining operations are turning to renewable energy sources, such as hydropower, solar, and wind. These efforts aim to reduce the carbon footprint of mining and promote sustainable practices.
- **Energy-Efficient Technologies:** The development of more energy-efficient mining technologies, such as next-generation ASICs and improvements in PoW algorithms, can help reduce the environmental impact of mining.

### 5.1.7 Alternatives to Proof of Work

Given the environmental concerns associated with PoW, alternative consensus mechanisms have been developed:

- **Proof of Stake (PoS):** In PoS systems, validators (rather than miners) are chosen to create new blocks and validate transactions based on the number of coins they hold and are willing to "stake" as collateral. PoS is considered more energy-efficient than PoW since it does not require extensive computational power.
- **Delegated Proof of Stake (DPoS):** DPoS is a variation of PoS where stakeholders elect a small number of delegates to validate transactions and create new blocks. This method aims to improve efficiency and scalability while maintaining decentralization.

## 5.2 BLOCK REWARDS AND HALVING EVENTS

### 5.2.1 Block Rewards

Block rewards are a fundamental component of cryptocurrency ecosystems, serving as the primary incentive mechanism for miners who maintain and secure blockchain networks.

Block rewards are a foundational element of cryptocurrency ecosystems, providing critical incentives for miners to secure and maintain blockchain networks. They play a significant role in the economic and technical dynamics of cryptocurrencies, influencing monetary supply, market behavior, and network security. As the cryptocurrency landscape evolves, addressing the challenges associated with block rewards, such as sustainability and centralization, will be crucial for the continued growth and stability of digital currencies. Future innovations in consensus mechanisms and mining technologies will shape the next generation of cryptocurrencies, striving to balance efficiency, security, and decentralization.

## Understanding Block Rewards

Block rewards are the incentives given to miners for successfully adding a new block to the blockchain. These rewards consist of newly minted cryptocurrency and transaction fees collected from the transactions included in the block. Block rewards play a crucial role in ensuring the continued operation and security of decentralized networks by motivating miners to participate in the mining process.

## How Block Rewards Work

### Mining and Proof of Work (PoW)

In Proof of Work (PoW) systems, such as Bitcoin, miners compete to solve complex cryptographic puzzles. The first miner to solve the puzzle gets to add the new block to the blockchain and receives the block reward. This reward serves as compensation for the computational resources expended during the mining process.

- **Block Creation:** When a miner successfully solves the cryptographic puzzle, a new block is created and added to the blockchain.
- **Reward Distribution:** The miner who solved the puzzle receives the block reward, which includes newly created cryptocurrency and transaction fees from the transactions in the block.

### Proof of Stake (PoS) and Other Consensus Mechanisms

In Proof of Stake (PoS) systems, block creators (validators) are chosen based on the number of coins they hold and are willing to "stake" as collateral. Block rewards in PoS systems often consist solely of transaction fees, as the creation of new coins is typically less frequent compared to PoW systems. Other consensus mechanisms, such as Delegated Proof of Stake (DPoS) and Proof of Authority (PoA), have their own reward structures but generally follow a similar principle of incentivizing network participation.

## Importance of Block Rewards

Block rewards are vital for several reasons:

- **Network Security:** Block rewards incentivize miners to secure the network by investing in computational resources. This makes it difficult for malicious actors to gain control of the blockchain.
- **Decentralization:** Rewards encourage widespread participation in the mining process, promoting decentralization and reducing the risk of centralization.
- **Monetary Supply:** Block rewards play a key role in the issuance of new cryptocurrency units, influencing the overall monetary supply and inflation rate of the cryptocurrency.

## Block Rewards in Different Cryptocurrencies

- **Bitcoin (BTC):** Bitcoin, the first and most well-known cryptocurrency, uses a PoW consensus mechanism. The initial block reward was 50 BTC per block, but this reward halves approximately every four years in an event known as the "halving." The most recent halving occurred in May 2020, reducing the reward to 6.25 BTC per block. Halvings will continue until the total supply of 21 million BTC is reached, projected around 2140.
- **Ethereum (ETH):** Ethereum initially used a PoW mechanism with a block reward of 5 ETH, which has been reduced over time through various network upgrades. Ethereum is transitioning to a PoS system (Ethereum 2.0), where block rewards will consist primarily of transaction fees and staking rewards, with new issuance rates set to be significantly lower than the current PoW system.
- **Litecoin (LTC):** Litecoin, often referred to as the silver to Bitcoin's gold, also uses a PoW mechanism with a block reward structure similar to Bitcoin. The current block reward for Litecoin is 12.5 LTC per block, which halves approximately every four years. The next halving is expected in August 2023.
- **Zcash (ZEC):** Zcash, a privacy-focused cryptocurrency, uses a PoW mechanism with a current block reward of 3.125 ZEC per block, which halves every four years. Zcash also includes a "Founders' Reward" where a portion of the block reward is allocated to the Zcash development team and other stakeholders to fund ongoing development and operations.

## Economic and Technical Impacts of Block Rewards

**Economic Impacts:**

- **Incentive Structure:** Block rewards create an incentive structure that encourages miners to invest in hardware and energy to secure the network, driving technological advancements in mining equipment.
- **Monetary Policy:** The issuance of new cryptocurrency through block rewards affects the overall monetary supply and inflation rate. Halvings in PoW systems reduce the rate of new issuance, potentially increasing scarcity and value over time.
- **Market Dynamics:** Changes in block rewards can impact the supply-demand dynamics of a cryptocurrency. For example, Bitcoin halvings are often followed by increased market interest and price appreciation.

**Technical Impacts:**

- **Security and Stability:** Consistent block rewards contribute to network security and stability by ensuring that miners remain incentivized to participate and secure the blockchain.

- **Network Upgrades:** Adjustments to block rewards and consensus mechanisms often accompany network upgrades and hard forks, requiring coordination and technical expertise from the community.
- **Energy Consumption:** In PoW systems, the pursuit of block rewards drives significant energy consumption. This has led to increased scrutiny and the exploration of more energy-efficient consensus mechanisms like PoS.

### Challenges and Future Directions

- **Sustainability Concerns:** The high energy consumption associated with PoW mining has raised sustainability concerns. Cryptocurrencies are exploring alternative consensus mechanisms, such as PoS, which require less computational power and energy.
- **Centralization Risks:** As mining becomes more resource-intensive, there is a risk of centralization, where a few large entities control a significant portion of the network's hashing power. This undermines the decentralized nature of cryptocurrencies. Addressing this requires continued innovation in mining hardware and consensus algorithms.
- **Economic Incentives:** As block rewards decrease over time, particularly in Bitcoin, transaction fees are expected to become the primary incentive for miners. This transition poses challenges for maintaining network security and requires careful consideration of fee structures and network usage patterns.

## 5.2.2 Halving Events

Halving events are a significant and anticipated occurrence in the cryptocurrency world, particularly in Proof of Work (PoW) systems like Bitcoin and Litecoin. These events reduce the block reward miners receive for adding a new block to the blockchain by half.

Halving events are a pivotal aspect of the cryptocurrency ecosystem, shaping the supply dynamics, miner incentives, and market behavior. By reducing the rate at which new coins are created, halvings introduce a deflationary element that can drive price appreciation and market speculation. While these events present challenges, such as potential impacts on miner revenue and network security, they are integral to the economic model of many PoW cryptocurrencies. As the industry evolves, addressing the implications of halving events will be crucial for ensuring the long-term viability and stability of cryptocurrency networks.

## Understanding Halving Events

Halving events are programmed reductions in the block reward given to miners. These events are built into the cryptocurrency's protocol to control the supply of new coins and mimic the scarcity of precious metals like gold.

### Mechanics of Halving

- **Block Reward Reduction:** At each halving event, the reward for mining a new block is reduced by 50%. For example, if the reward was 12.5 coins per block before the halving, it would drop to 6.25 coins afterward.
- **Scheduled Intervals:** Halvings occur at predetermined intervals based on the number of blocks mined. For Bitcoin, a halving occurs approximately every 210,000 blocks, which translates to roughly every four years.
- **Finite Supply:** Halving events continue until the maximum supply of the cryptocurrency is reached. For Bitcoin, this is 21 million coins. As the block reward decreases over time, the rate of new coin issuance slows down, ultimately ceasing when the total supply is mined.

## Historical Halving Events

### Bitcoin Halvings

Bitcoin has experienced three halving events to date:

- **First Halving (2012):** The first halving occurred on November 28, 2012, reducing the block reward from 50 BTC to 25 BTC. This event was notable for increasing public awareness of Bitcoin and contributing to its subsequent price increase.
- **Second Halving (2016):** On July 9, 2016, the second halving reduced the block reward from 25 BTC to 12.5 BTC. This halving was followed by a significant bull market, culminating in Bitcoin reaching nearly $20,000 in December 2017.
- **Third Halving (2020):** The third halving took place on May 11, 2020, further reducing the block reward to 6.25 BTC. This event occurred amid growing institutional interest in Bitcoin and a significant price rally, with Bitcoin surpassing $60,000 in 2021.

### Litecoin Halvings

Litecoin, a prominent altcoin, also undergoes halving events:

- **First Halving (2015):** Litecoin's first halving occurred on August 25, 2015, reducing the block reward from 50 LTC to 25 LTC.

- **Second Halving (2019):** The second halving took place on August 5, 2019, cutting the block reward to 12.5 LTC. Similar to Bitcoin, Litecoin halvings have historically been followed by increased market interest and price appreciation.

## Impact of Halving Events

Halving events have several significant impacts on the cryptocurrency ecosystem, influencing miner behavior, market dynamics, and long-term supply.

### Economic Impact

- **Supply and Demand:** By reducing the rate at which new coins are created, halvings effectively limit the supply. Given constant or increasing demand, this scarcity can lead to price increases.
- **Miner Incentives:** Lower block rewards mean miners receive fewer coins for their efforts, potentially affecting their profitability. Miners with higher operational costs may be forced to shut down, leading to a temporary decrease in the network's hash rate.
- **Market Speculation:** Halving events often generate considerable market speculation and media attention, contributing to increased trading volumes and volatility. Historical data shows that halvings are frequently followed by significant price rallies.

### Technical Impact

- **Hash Rate and Security:** A reduction in block rewards can lead to a decline in the network's hash rate if miners exit the market. However, as inefficient miners leave, the difficulty adjustment mechanism recalibrates, maintaining network security and block times.
- **Transaction Fees:** As block rewards decrease, transaction fees become a more critical component of miner revenue. This shift underscores the importance of a healthy fee market to sustain network security in the long term.

## Challenges and Considerations

While halving events contribute to the deflationary nature of cryptocurrencies, they also present several challenges:

- **Miner Revenue:** Sustained reductions in block rewards necessitate that miners rely more heavily on transaction fees. In periods of low transaction volume, this can pose financial challenges for miners.
- **Network Security:** A significant drop in the number of active miners could lead to decreased hash rates and potential security vulnerabilities, making the network more susceptible to attacks.

- **Market Volatility:** The anticipation and aftermath of halving events can lead to increased market volatility, impacting investor sentiment and market stability.

### Future Implications

As cryptocurrencies continue to evolve, the role and impact of halving events will remain a focal point for the community, developers, and investors.

- **Sustainability of Mining:** The long-term sustainability of PoW mining, especially in the face of diminishing block rewards, will likely drive innovation in mining technologies and energy efficiency.
- **Transition to Alternative Consensus Mechanisms:** Some cryptocurrencies are exploring alternatives to PoW, such as Proof of Stake (PoS), which may alter or eliminate the need for traditional halving events. Ethereum's transition to Ethereum 2.0 and its PoS mechanism is a prominent example.
- **Economic Models:** The economic models underpinning cryptocurrencies may evolve to ensure that miner incentives remain aligned with network security and stability. This could include changes to transaction fee structures or the introduction of new incentive mechanisms.

## 5.3 FORKS IN BLOCKCHAIN: HARD FORKS VS. SOFT FORKS

In blockchain, a fork is defined variously as:

- "What happens when a blockchain diverges into two potential paths forward",
- "A change in protocol", or
- A situation that "occurs when two or more blocks have the same block height".

Forks are related to the fact that different parties need to use common rules to maintain the history of the blockchain. When parties are not in agreement, alternative chains may emerge. While most forks are short-lived some are permanent.

Short-lived forks are due to the difficulty of reaching fast consensus in a distributed system. Whereas permanent forks (in the sense of protocol changes) have been used to add new features to a blockchain, they can also be used to reverse the effects of hacking such as the case with Ethereum and Ethereum Classic, or avert catastrophic bugs on a blockchain as was the case with the bitcoin fork on 6 August 2010. The concept of blockchain technology was first introduced in 2008 by an unknown person or group of people using the pseudonym "Satoshi Nakamoto" in a white paper describing the design of a decentralized digital currency called Bitcoin. Blockchain forks have been widely discussed in the context of the bitcoin scalability problem.

### 5.3.1 Types of Forks

Forks can be classified as *accidental* or *intentional*. *Accidental fork* happens when two or more miners find a block at nearly the same time. The fork is resolved when subsequent block(s) are added and one of the chains becomes longer than the alternative(s).

The network abandons the blocks that are not in the longest chain (they are called *orphaned* blocks). Intentional forks that modify the rules of a blockchain can be classified as follows:

#### Hard Fork

A *hard fork* is a change to the blockchain protocol that is not backward compatible and requires all users to upgrade their software in order to continue participating in the network. In a hard fork, the network splits into two separate versions: one that follows the new rules and one that follows the old rules.

For example, Ethereum was hard forked in 2016 to "make whole" the investors in The DAO, which had been hacked by exploiting a vulnerability in its code. In this case, the fork resulted in a split creating Ethereum and Ethereum Classic chains. In 2014 the Nxt community was asked to consider a hard fork that would have led to a rollback of the blockchain records to mitigate the effects of a theft of 50 million NXT from a major cryptocurrency exchange.

The hard fork proposal was rejected, and some of the funds were recovered after negotiations and ransom payment. Alternatively, to prevent a permanent split, a majority of nodes using the new software may return to the old rules, as was the case of bitcoin split on 12 March 2013.

A more recent hard-fork example is of Bitcoin in 2017, which resulted in a split creating Bitcoin Cash. The network split was mainly due to a disagreement in how to increase the transactions per second to accommodate for demand.

#### Soft Fork

A *soft fork* is a backward-compatible change to the blockchain protocol that allows new rules to be introduced without requiring all users to upgrade their software. In a soft fork, a majority of the network's miners implement the new rules and begin following the updated version of the blockchain.

The rest of the network can continue to follow the blockchain, but they will be unable to validate that new blocks follow the updated rules. Because a soft fork is backward-compatible, it does not result in the creation of a new blockchain or the splitting of the network. Instead, it allows the network to gradually transition to the new rules while still maintaining compatibility with the old rules.

### 5.3.2 Cryptocurrency Splits

A *permanent chain split* is described as a case when there are two or more permanent versions of a blockchain sharing the same history up to a certain time, after which the histories start to differ. Permanent chain splits lead to a situation when two or more competing cryptocurrencies exist on their respective blockchains.

#### Taxation

The taxation of cryptocurrency splits varies substantially from state to state. A few examples include:

##### Australian Taxation Office (ATO)

The ATO does not classify cryptocurrency splits as taxation events. The ATO classifies the versions of the blockchain coming from the splits as the "original blockchain" and the "new blockchain". In relation to the cost base, the cryptocurrency on the original blockchain should be assigned all the original cost base, while the cryptocurrency on the new blockchain should be assigned cost base zero.

##### HM Revenue & Customs (HMRC)

The UK HMRC does not classify cryptocurrency splits as taxation events. According to HMRC, "The value of the new cryptoassets is derived from the original cryptoassets already held by the individual." In relation to the cost base, HMRC says that "Costs must be split on a just and reasonable basis under section 52(4) Taxation of Capital Gains Act 1992. HMRC does not prescribe any particular apportionment method. HMRC has the power to enquire into an apportionment method that it believes is not just and reasonable."

As of September 2021, it is believed that more than 2.3 million people in the UK own a cryptoasset. As these assets don't physically exist, HMRC has been forced to issue guidance stating that cryptoassets will follow the residence of the beneficial owner. So, if you live in the UK and trade cryptoassets, no matter where these assets are "held", you will be liable to UK taxes. However, there is a growing belief that this guidance may well be challenged in the courts. This could impact future HMRC tax income from those not domiciled in the UK for tax purposes. "

##### Internal Revenue Service (IRS)

The US Internal Revenue Service (IRS) classifies cryptocurrency splits as "airdrops" and as taxable events. According to the guidance published by IRS, provided the taxpayer is in possession of the keys, they are obliged to pay tax for the new cryptocurrency using the fair market value of the cryptocurrency as their income.

## 5.4 OTHER CONSENSUS ALGORITHMS: PRACTICAL BYZANTINE FAULT TOLERANCE (PBFT), DELEGATED PROOF OF STAKE (DPOS), ETC

### 5.4.1 Other Consensus Algorithms

Consensus algorithms are the backbone of distributed systems and blockchain networks, ensuring that all participating nodes agree on the state of the system despite potential failures or malicious behavior. These algorithms are essential for maintaining the integrity, security, and functionality of decentralized networks.

Consensus algorithms are critical for the operation and security of blockchain networks and distributed systems.

Each algorithm has its strengths and weaknesses, making it suitable for different applications and network requirements. PoW offers robust security but at the cost of high energy consumption, while PoS and DPoS provide energy-efficient alternatives with varying degrees of decentralization and scalability. PBFT, PoA, Raft, and Tendermint offer specialized solutions for fault tolerance, efficiency, and specific use cases.

As the blockchain ecosystem continues to evolve, ongoing research and development aim to address the limitations of existing consensus algorithms and introduce innovative approaches to achieve secure, scalable, and decentralized consensus. Understanding the trade-offs and principles of each algorithm is essential for designing effective and resilient distributed systems.

### The Need for Consensus Algorithms

In a decentralized network, multiple nodes operate independently and need to agree on the same data or transactions to maintain consistency and avoid conflicts. Without a central authority to enforce this agreement, consensus algorithms play a crucial role in ensuring that all nodes reach a common decision.

### Proof of Work (PoW)

**Principles and Mechanics:**

- **Mechanism:** Nodes (miners) compete to solve complex mathematical puzzles. The first one to solve the puzzle gets to add the next block to the blockchain and is rewarded with cryptocurrency.
- **Difficulty Adjustment:** The difficulty of the puzzles adjusts periodically to maintain a consistent block creation time.

**Advantages:**

- **Security:** High computational requirements make it difficult for attackers to take control of the network.

- **Decentralization:** PoW encourages decentralization by allowing anyone with computational resources to participate.

**Challenges:**

- **Energy Consumption:** PoW is highly energy-intensive, leading to environmental concerns.
- **Scalability:** The need for extensive computations limits transaction throughput.

## Proof of Stake (PoS)

**Principles and Mechanics:**

- **Mechanism:** Validators are chosen to create new blocks based on the number of coins they hold and are willing to "stake" as collateral.
- **Selection:** The probability of being chosen to validate a block is proportional to the amount of cryptocurrency staked.

**Advantages:**

- **Energy Efficiency:** PoS consumes significantly less energy than PoW.
- **Security:** Large stakeholders have a vested interest in maintaining network integrity.

**Challenges:**

- **Centralization Risk:** Wealthier participants can have disproportionate influence over the network.
- **Initial Distribution:** Fair initial distribution of coins is crucial to prevent early centralization.

## Proof of Authority (PoA)

**Principles and Mechanics:**

- **Mechanism:** A limited number of pre-approved nodes (authorities) validate transactions and produce blocks.
- **Authority:** Validators are typically known and trusted entities.

**Advantages:**

- **Efficiency:** High transaction throughput and low latency.
- **Simplicity:** Straightforward implementation and operation.

**Challenges:**

- **Centralization:** Centralized nature reduces decentralization benefits.
- **Trust:** Requires trust in a limited number of validators.

### Raft

**Principles and Mechanics:**

- **Mechanism:** Designed for distributed systems, Raft divides consensus into leader election, log replication, and safety.
- **Leader Election:** One node is elected as the leader to manage log replication.

**Advantages:**

- **Simplicity:** Easy to understand and implement compared to other consensus algorithms.
- **Fault Tolerance:** Can tolerate node failures and maintain consensus.

**Challenges:**

- **Scalability:** Primarily designed for smaller distributed systems, not large blockchain networks.
- **Centralization:** Leader-based approach can lead to temporary centralization.

### Tendermint

**Principles and Mechanics:**

- **Mechanism:** Combines PBFT with a PoS-like system where validators are selected based on their stake.
- **Finality:** Provides instant finality through multiple voting rounds.

**Advantages:**

- **Scalability:** High transaction throughput and fast finality.
- **Security:** Byzantine fault tolerance enhances security.

**Challenges:**

- **Complexity:** Implementation can be more complex than simpler consensus mechanisms.
- **Centralization Risk:** Similar to PoS, larger stakeholders can have more influence.

## 5.4.2 Practical Byzantine Fault Tolerance (PBFT)

Practical Byzantine Fault Tolerance (PBFT) is an algorithm designed to solve the Byzantine Generals Problem in distributed systems, ensuring that a network of nodes can reach consensus even if some of the nodes behave maliciously or arbitrarily.

Developed by Miguel Castro and Barbara Liskov in the late 1990s, PBFT has become a foundational component of several distributed ledger technologies and blockchain systems.

Practical Byzantine Fault Tolerance (PBFT) is a robust and efficient consensus algorithm that addresses the challenges of achieving consensus in distributed systems with Byzantine faults. By providing fault tolerance, low latency, and deterministic finality, PBFT has become a cornerstone of various blockchain and distributed ledger technologies. Despite its challenges, ongoing research and development continue to enhance its scalability and efficiency, ensuring its relevance and applicability in the evolving landscape of decentralized systems.

## Understanding Byzantine Fault Tolerance

- **The Byzantine Generals Problem:** The Byzantine Generals Problem is a classic problem in distributed computing and cryptography, illustrating the challenges of achieving consensus in the presence of faulty or malicious nodes. Named after an allegory where generals of the Byzantine army must agree on a coordinated attack plan despite some traitorous generals, the problem highlights the difficulty of ensuring all non-faulty nodes (or generals) reach the same decision.
- **Byzantine Fault Tolerance (BFT):** BFT refers to the ability of a distributed system to continue functioning correctly even if some of its components fail or act maliciously. A system is considered Byzantine fault-tolerant if it can reach consensus despite the presence of Byzantine faults.

## Principles of Practical Byzantine Fault Tolerance

PBFT is a specific implementation of Byzantine fault-tolerant consensus designed to be practical for real-world systems. It operates efficiently in asynchronous environments, where there is no assumption about the timing of messages between nodes.

**Core Principles:**

- **Fault Tolerance:** PBFT can tolerate up to ff Byzantine faults in a system with 3f+13f+1 total nodes. This means that it can handle a fraction of nodes behaving arbitrarily, including malicious behavior.
- **Asynchronous Operation:** PBFT does not rely on synchronized clocks or timing assumptions, making it robust in varied network conditions.
- **Consensus Through Replication:** PBFT uses a replicated state machine approach, where multiple nodes (replicas) maintain copies of the state and execute operations in a coordinated manner.

### The PBFT Protocol

The PBFT protocol operates through a series of phases to ensure consensus:

- **Request Phase—Client Request:** A client sends a request to the primary (leader) node to perform a specific operation.
- **Pre-Prepare Phase—Primary Broadcast:** The primary node assigns a sequence number to the request and broadcasts a pre-prepare message to all other nodes (replicas).
- **Prepare Phase—Replica Verification:** Each replica verifies the pre-prepare message and broadcasts a prepare message to all other replicas, indicating it has received the request and agrees with the proposed sequence number.
- **Commit Phase:**
  - **Consensus Building:** Once a replica receives 2f prepare messages from different replicas (including itself), it broadcasts a commit message.
  - **Commit Confirmation:** When a replica receives 2f+1 commit messages (including its own), it considers the request committed and executes the operation.
- **Reply Phase—Client Response:** After executing the request, the replica sends a reply to the client. The client considers the operation successful once it receives f+1 matching replies.

### Advantages of PBFT

PBFT offers several advantages that make it suitable for various applications:

- **Fault Tolerance:** PBFT can handle up to f Byzantine faults, ensuring robustness and reliability even in the presence of malicious nodes.
- **Efficiency:** Unlike earlier BFT algorithms, PBFT is optimized for practical use, providing low latency and high throughput in real-world systems.
- **No Proof of Work:** PBFT does not rely on computationally intensive proof-of-work (PoW) mechanisms, making it more energy-efficient compared to PoW-based consensus algorithms like Bitcoin's.
- **Deterministic Finality:** PBFT provides deterministic finality, meaning that once consensus is reached, the decision is final and cannot be reversed.

### Applications of PBFT

PBFT has been implemented in various blockchain and distributed ledger technologies due to its practical benefits:

- **Hyperledger Fabric:** Hyperledger Fabric, a popular enterprise blockchain platform, uses a variant of PBFT for its consensus mechanism. Fabric's PBFT implementation ensures transaction finality and fault tolerance in permissioned blockchain networks, where participants are known and trusted to some extent.
- **Zilliqa:** Zilliqa, a high-throughput public blockchain platform, employs a modified version of PBFT combined with sharding. This hybrid approach allows Zilliqa to achieve high transaction processing speeds while maintaining security and fault tolerance.
- **Tendermint:** Tendermint, a consensus engine used by the Cosmos network, implements a version of PBFT. Tendermint's consensus algorithm ensures fast finality and high fault tolerance, making it suitable for various decentralized applications.

## Challenges and Limitations

While PBFT offers significant advantages, it also faces certain challenges and limitations:

- **Scalability:** PBFT's communication complexity grows quadratically with the number of nodes (O(n), making it less efficient for large-scale networks.
- **Leader Election:** The protocol relies on a primary (leader) node, and the system's performance can be affected if the primary behaves maliciously or fails. Leader election protocols are necessary to handle primary failures.
- **Trust Assumptions:** PBFT assumes that nodes can be somewhat trusted (i.e., there are fewer than f Byzantine nodes). In fully open and permissionless environments, ensuring these trust assumptions can be challenging.

## Future Directions and Improvements

Research and development efforts continue to address the challenges and limitations of PBFT, focusing on scalability, security, and efficiency improvements:

- **Sharding:** Implementing sharding techniques can help scale PBFT by dividing the network into smaller, manageable subsets (shards) that run the PBFT protocol independently.
- **Optimized Communication:** Reducing communication overhead through optimized message-passing protocols and techniques can enhance PBFT's scalability.

- **Hybrid Consensus:** Combining PBFT with other consensus mechanisms, such as Proof of Stake (PoS) or asynchronous Byzantine fault-tolerant (ABFT) protocols, can provide a balanced approach to consensus.

### 5.4.3 Delegated Proof of Stake (DPoS)

Delegated Proof of Stake (DPoS) is a consensus mechanism developed to enhance the efficiency and scalability of blockchain networks. Proposed by Daniel Larimer in 2014, DPoS addresses some of the limitations of traditional Proof of Work (PoW) and Proof of Stake (PoS) systems by introducing a more democratic and performance-oriented approach to achieving consensus.

Delegated Proof of Stake (DPoS) is a powerful and innovative consensus mechanism that addresses many of the limitations of traditional PoW and PoS systems. By introducing a democratic and performance-oriented approach to achieving consensus, DPoS enhances scalability, energy efficiency, and decentralized governance. Despite facing challenges such as centralization risks and voter apathy, DPoS has proven to be a valuable consensus mechanism for several blockchain platforms, enabling fast and efficient transaction processing. As research and development continue, DPoS is likely to evolve further, incorporating new innovations to address its challenges and expand its applications in the blockchain ecosystem.

#### Understanding Consensus Mechanisms

Before diving into DPoS, it is important to understand the context of consensus mechanisms in blockchain technology:

- **Proof of Work (PoW):** PoW requires miners to solve complex cryptographic puzzles to validate transactions and add new blocks to the blockchain. It is energy-intensive and can be slow, with a tendency towards centralization due to mining pool dominance.
- **Proof of Stake (PoS):** PoS selects validators based on the number of coins they hold and are willing to "stake" as collateral. While more energy-efficient than PoW, PoS can still face issues with centralization and scalability.

#### Principles of Delegated Proof of Stake (DPoS)

DPoS builds on the PoS concept but adds a layer of democratic governance and delegation to improve performance and decentralization.

##### Core Principles

- **Delegation:** Token holders in a DPoS system vote for a small number of delegates or witnesses who are responsible for validating transactions and producing blocks. This delegation of responsibilities helps streamline the consensus process.

- **Voting Power:** Voting power is proportional to the number of tokens held by each participant. Larger stakeholders have a greater influence on the selection of delegates.
- **Incentives:** Delegates are rewarded for their efforts in maintaining the network. These rewards often come from transaction fees and newly minted tokens.
- **Accountability:** Delegates can be voted out and replaced if they fail to perform their duties effectively, ensuring accountability and responsiveness to the community.

## The DPoS Process

The DPoS process involves several key steps to achieve consensus.

**Voting:**

- **Token Holders Vote:** Token holders cast votes to elect a fixed number of delegates (e.g., 21 in EOS, 100 in Lisk). The voting process can be continuous, allowing for real-time adjustments in delegate selection based on performance and community trust.

**Block Production:**

- **Delegate Rotation:** Elected delegates take turns producing blocks in a round-robin fashion. This rotation ensures that all elected delegates have the opportunity to participate in the consensus process.
- **Block Time:** Block times in DPoS systems are typically shorter than in PoW and PoS systems, leading to faster transaction confirmations. For example, EOS has a block time of 0.5 seconds.

**Consensus and Finality:**

- **Block Validation:** Delegates validate transactions and produce blocks. The network achieves consensus as long as a majority of delegates (typically two-thirds) agree on the validity of the transactions.
- **Finality:** Once a block is confirmed by the required number of delegates, it is considered final and irreversible.

## Advantages of DPoS

DPoS offers several significant advantages over traditional consensus mechanisms:

- **Scalability:** By limiting the number of nodes participating in the consensus process, DPoS can achieve higher transaction throughput and faster block times, making it more suitable for large-scale applications.

- **Energy Efficiency:** Unlike PoW, DPoS does not require intensive computational work, making it more energy-efficient and environmentally friendly.
- **Decentralized Governance:** The voting mechanism allows for democratic participation, with stakeholders having a direct say in the selection of delegates. This can enhance the decentralization and resilience of the network.
- **Flexibility:** The ability to vote out underperforming or malicious delegates ensures that the network remains adaptable and responsive to the needs of its users.

## Applications of DPoS

DPoS has been implemented in various blockchain platforms, each leveraging its unique features to enhance performance and governance:

- **EOS:** EOS is one of the most well-known implementations of DPoS. It aims to provide a decentralized operating system that supports industrial-scale decentralized applications (dApps). With a block time of 0.5 seconds and support for thousands of transactions per second, EOS showcases the scalability potential of DPoS.
- **BitShares:** BitShares, created by Daniel Larimer, was one of the first blockchain platforms to implement DPoS. It serves as a decentralized exchange and financial platform, leveraging DPoS to achieve fast and efficient transaction processing.
- **Steem:** Steem, another project by Daniel Larimer, uses DPoS to power a social media platform where users are rewarded for creating and curating content. The DPoS consensus mechanism ensures that the platform can handle high transaction volumes associated with social media interactions.
- **Lisk:** Lisk uses a modified version of DPoS to enable developers to build blockchain applications using JavaScript. The platform focuses on accessibility and ease of use, leveraging DPoS to provide a scalable and user-friendly environment for application development.

## Challenges and Considerations

Despite its advantages, DPoS also faces several challenges and considerations:

- **Centralization Risks:** While DPoS aims to enhance decentralization, there is a risk that large stakeholders can dominate the voting process, leading to centralization of power among a few influential delegates.

- **Security Concerns:** The smaller number of validators in DPoS systems can potentially make the network more vulnerable to coordinated attacks if a significant portion of delegates collude or are compromised.
- **Voter Apathy:** In practice, many token holders may not actively participate in the voting process, leading to a concentration of voting power among a few active participants and potentially reducing the overall representativeness of the governance process.

### Future Directions and Improvements

Ongoing research and development efforts are focused on addressing the challenges of DPoS and further enhancing its capabilities:

- **Incentive Structures:** Improving incentive mechanisms to encourage wider voter participation and prevent centralization of voting power.
- **Hybrid Models:** Combining DPoS with other consensus mechanisms to balance scalability, security, and decentralization. For example, integrating DPoS with PoS or Proof of Authority (PoA) models.
- **Advanced Governance Models:** Developing more sophisticated governance frameworks that enhance transparency, accountability, and community involvement.

# CHAPTER 6
# POPULAR CRYPTOCURRENCIES

## 6.1 BITCOIN (BTC)

Bitcoin is the first decentralized cryptocurrency. Nodes in the peer-to-peer bitcoin network verify transactions through cryptography and record them in a public distributed ledger, called a blockchain, without central oversight. Consensus between nodes is achieved using a computationally intensive process based on proof of work, called mining, that guarantees the security of the bitcoin blockchain. Mining consumes increasing quantities of electricity and has been criticized for its environmental effects.

Based on a free market ideology, bitcoin was invented in 2008 by Satoshi Nakamoto, an unknown person. Use of bitcoin as a currency began in 2009, with the release of its open-source implementation. In 2021, El Salvador adopted it as legal tender. Bitcoin is currently used more as a store of value and less as a medium of exchange or unit of account.

It is mostly seen as an investment and has been described by many scholars as an economic bubble. As bitcoin is pseudonymous, its use by criminals has attracted the attention of regulators, leading to its ban by several countries as of 2021.

### 6.1.1 History

#### Background

Before bitcoin, several digital cash technologies were released, starting with David Chaum's ecash in the 1980s. The idea that solutions to computational puzzles could have some value was first proposed by cryptographers Cynthia Dwork and Moni Naor in 1992.

The concept was independently rediscovered by Adam Back who developed Hashcash, a proof-of-work scheme for spam control in 1997. The first proposals for distributed digital scarcity-based cryptocurrencies came from cypherpunks Wei Dai (b-money) and Nick Szabo (bit gold) in 1998. In 2004, Hal Finney developed the first currency based on reusable proof of work. These various attempts were not successful: Chaum's concept required centralized control and no banks wanted to sign on, Hashcash had no protection against double-spending, while b-money and bit gold were not resistant to Sybil attacks.

## 2008–2009: Creation

The domain name *bitcoin.org* was registered on 18 August 2008. On 31 October 2008, a link to a white paper authored by Satoshi Nakamoto titled *Bitcoin: A Peer-to-Peer Electronic Cash System* was posted to a cryptography mailing list. Nakamoto implemented the bitcoin software as open-source code and released it in January 2009. Nakamoto's identity remains unknown. All individual components of bitcoin originated in earlier academic literature. Nakamoto's innovation was their complex interplay resulting in the first decentralized, Sybil resistant, Byzantine fault tolerant digital cash system, that would eventually be referred to as the first blockchain. Nakamoto's paper was not peer reviewed and was initially ignored by academics, who argued that it could not work.

On 3 January 2009, the bitcoin network was created when Nakamoto mined the starting block of the chain, known as the *genesis block*. Embedded in this block was the text "The Times 03/Jan/2009 Chancellor on brink of second bailout for banks", which is the date and headline of an issue of *The Times* newspaper. Nine days later, Hal Finney received the first bitcoin transaction: ten bitcoins from Nakamoto. Wei Dai and Nick Szabo were also early supporters. On May 22, 2010, the first known commercial transaction using bitcoin occurred when programmer Laszlo Hanyecz bought two Papa John's pizzas for 10,000, in what would later be celebrated as "Bitcoin Pizza Day".

## 2010–2012: Early Growth

Blockchain analysts estimate that Nakamoto had mined about one million bitcoins before disappearing in 2010 when he handed the network alert key and control of the code repository over to Gavin Andresen. Andresen later became lead developer at the Bitcoin Foundation, an organization founded in September 2012 to promote bitcoin.

After early "proof-of-concept" transactions, the first major users of bitcoin were black markets, such as the dark web Silk Road. During its 30 months of existence, beginning in February 2011, Silk Road exclusively accepted bitcoins as payment, transacting 9.9 million, worth about $214 million.

## 2013–2014: First Regulatory Actions

In March 2013, the US Financial Crimes Enforcement Network (FinCEN) established regulatory guidelines for "decentralized virtual currencies" such as bitcoin, classifying American bitcoin miners who sell their generated bitcoins as money services businesses, subject to registration and other legal obligations. In May 2013, US authorities seized the unregistered exchange Mt. Gox. In June 2013, the US Drug Enforcement Administration seized 11.02 from a man attempting to use them to buy illegal substances. This marked the first time a government agency had seized bitcoins. The FBI seized about 30,000 in October 2013 from Silk Road, following the arrest of its founder Ross Ulbricht.

In December 2013, the People's Bank of China prohibited Chinese financial institutions from using bitcoin. After the announcement, the value of bitcoin dropped, and Baidu no longer accepted bitcoins for certain services. Buying real-world goods with any virtual currency had been illegal in China since at least 2009.

## 2015–2019

Research produced by the University of Cambridge estimated that in 2017, there were 2.9 to 5.8 million unique users using a cryptocurrency wallet, most of them using bitcoin. In August 2017, the SegWit software upgrade was activated. Segwit was intended to support the Lightning Network as well as improve scalability. SegWit opponents, who supported larger blocks as a scalability solution, forked to create Bitcoin Cash, one of many forks of bitcoin.

In December 2017, the first futures on bitcoin was introduced by the Chicago Mercantile Exchange (CME). In February 2018, the price crashed after China imposed a complete ban on Bitcoin trading. The percentage of bitcoin trading in the Chinese renminbi fell from over 90% in September 2017 to less than 1% in June 2018. During the same year, Bitcoin prices were negatively affected by several hacks or thefts from cryptocurrency exchanges.

## 2020–Present

In 2020, some major companies and institutions started to acquire bitcoin: MicroStrategy invested $250 million in bitcoin as a treasury reserve asset, Square, Inc., $50 million, and MassMutual, $100 million. In November 2020, PayPal added support for bitcoin in the US.

In February 2021, Bitcoin's market capitalization reached $1 trillion for the first time. In November 2021, the Taproot soft-fork upgrade was activated, adding support for Schnorr signatures, improved functionality of smart contracts and Lightning Network. Before, Bitcoin only used a custom elliptic curve with the ECDSA algorithm to produce signatures. In September 2021, Bitcoin became legal tender in El Salvador, alongside the US dollar. In October 2021, the first bitcoin futures Exchange-traded fund (ETF), called BITO, from ProShares was approved by the SEC and listed on the CME.

In May and June 2022, the bitcoin price fell following the collapses of TerraUSD, a stablecoin, and the Celsius Network, a cryptocurrency loan company. In 2023, ordinals—non-fungible tokens (NFTs)—on Bitcoin, went live. In January 2024, the first 11 US spot bitcoin ETFs began trading, offering direct exposure to bitcoin for the first time on American stock exchanges.

### 6.1.2 Design

#### Units and Divisibility

The unit of account of the bitcoin system is the *bitcoin*. However, the BTC code does not conform to ISO 4217 as BT is the country code of Bhutan, and ISO 4217 requires the first letter used in global commodities to be 'X'. XBT, a code that conforms to ISO 4217 though not officially part of it, is used by Bloomberg L.P.

No uniform capitalization convention exists; some sources use *Bitcoin*, capitalized, to refer to the technology and network, and *bitcoin*, lowercase, for the unit of account. The *Cambridge Advanced Learner's Dictionary* and the *Oxford Advanced Learner's Dictionary* use the capitalized and lowercase variants without distinction.

One bitcoin is divisible to eight decimal places. Units for smaller amounts of bitcoin are the millibitcoin (mBTC), equal to 1/1000 bitcoin, and the satoshi (sat), representing 1/100000000 (one hundred millionth) bitcoin, the smallest amount possible. 100,000 satoshis are one mBTC.

#### Blockchain

As a decentralized system, bitcoin operates without a central authority or single administrator, so that anyone can create a new bitcoin address and transact without needing any approval. This is accomplished through a specialized distributed ledger called a *blockchain* that records bitcoin transactions.

The blockchain is implemented as an ordered list of *blocks*. Each block contains a SHA-256 hash of the previous block, chaining them in chronological order. The blockchain is maintained by a peer-to-peer network. Individual blocks, public addresses, and transactions within blocks are public information, and can be examined using a blockchain explorer.

Nodes validate and broadcast transactions, each maintaining a copy of the blockchain for ownership verification. A new block is created every 10 minutes on average, updating the blockchain across all nodes without central oversight. This process tracks bitcoin spending, ensuring each bitcoin is spent only once. Unlike a traditional ledger that tracks physical currency, bitcoins exist digitally as unspent outputs of transactions.

#### Addresses and Transactions

In the blockchain, bitcoins are linked to specific addresses that are hashes of a public key. Creating an address involves generating a random private key and then computing the corresponding address. This process is almost instant, but the reverse (finding the private key for a given address) is nearly impossible. Publishing a bitcoin address does not risk its private key, and it is extremely unlikely to accidentally generate a used key with funds. To use bitcoins, owners need their private key to digitally sign transactions, which are verified by the network using the public key, keeping the private key secret.

Bitcoin transactions use a Forth-like scripting language, involving one or more inputs and outputs. When sending bitcoins, a user specifies the recipients' addresses and the amount for each output. This allows sending bitcoins to several recipients in a single transaction.

To prevent double-spending, each input must refer to a previous unspent output in the blockchain. Using multiple inputs is similar to using multiple coins in a cash transaction. As in a cash transaction, the sum of inputs can exceed the intended sum of payments. In such a case, an additional output can return the change back to the payer. Unallocated input satoshis in the transaction become the transaction fee.

Losing a private key means losing access to the bitcoins, with no other proof of ownership accepted by the protocol. For instance, in 2013, a user lost 7,500, valued at US$7.5 million, by accidentally discarding a hard drive with the private key. It is estimated that around 20% of all bitcoins are lost. The private key must also be kept secret as its exposure, such as through a data breach, can lead to theft of the associated bitcoins. As of December 2017, approximately 980,000 had been stolen from cryptocurrency exchanges.

## Mining

The mining process in Bitcoin involves maintaining the blockchain through computer processing power. Miners group and broadcast new transactions into blocks, which are then verified by the network. Each block must contain a proof of work (PoW) to be accepted, involving finding a nonce number that, combined with the block content, produces a hash numerically smaller than the network's *difficulty target*. This PoW is simple to verify but hard to generate, requiring many attempts. PoW forms the basis of Bitcoin's consensus mechanism.

The difficulty of generating a block is deterministically adjusted based on the mining power on the network by changing the difficulty target, which is recalibrated every 2,016 blocks (approximately two weeks) to maintain an average time of ten minutes between new blocks. The process requires significant computational power and specialized hardware.

Miners who successfully find a new block can collect transaction fees from the included transactions and a set reward in bitcoins. To claim this reward, a special transaction called a *coinbase* is included in the block, with the miner as the payee. All bitcoins in existence have been created through this type of transaction. This reward is halved every 210,000 blocks until 21 million, with new bitcoin issuance slated to end around 2140. Afterward, miners will only earn from transaction fees.

These fees are determined by the transaction's size and the amount of data stored, measured in satoshis per byte.

The proof of work system and the chaining of blocks make blockchain modifications very difficult, as altering one block requires changing all subsequent blocks. As more blocks are added, modifying older blocks becomes increasingly challenging. In case of disagreement, nodes trust the longest chain, which required the greatest amount of effort to produce. To tamper or censor the ledger, one needs to control the majority of the global hashrate. The high cost required to reach this level of computational power guarantees the security of the bitcoin blockchain.

Bitcoin mining's environmental impact is controversial and has attracted the attention of regulators, leading to restrictions or incentives in various jurisdictions. As of 2022, a non-peer-reviewed study by the Cambridge Centre for Alternative Finance (CCAF) estimated that bitcoin mining represented 0.4% of global electricity consumption. Another 2022 non-peer-reviewed commentary published in *Joule* estimated that bitcoin mining was responsible for 0.2% of world greenhouse gas emissions. About half of the electricity used is generated through fossil fuels. Moreover, mining hardware's short lifespan results in electronic waste. The amount of electrical energy consumed, and the e-waste generated, is comparable to that of Greece and the Netherlands, respectively.

### Privacy and Fungibility

Bitcoin is pseudonymous, with funds linked to addresses, not real-world identities. While the owners of these addresses are not directly identified, all transactions are public on the blockchain. Patterns of use, like spending coins from multiple inputs, can hint at a common owner. Public data can sometimes be matched with known address owners. Bitcoin exchanges might also need to collect personal data as per legal requirements. For enhanced privacy, users can generate a new address for each transaction.

In the Bitcoin network, each bitcoin is treated equally, ensuring basic fungibility. However, users and applications can choose to differentiate between bitcoins. While wallets and software treat all bitcoins the same, each bitcoin's transaction history is recorded on the blockchain. This public record allows for chain analysis, where users can identify and potentially reject bitcoins from controversial sources. For example, in 2012, Mt. Gox froze accounts containing bitcoins identified as stolen.

### Wallets

Bitcoin wallets were the first cryptocurrency wallets, enabling users to store the information necessary to transact bitcoins. The first wallet program, simply named *Bitcoin*, and sometimes referred to as the *Satoshi client*, was released in 2009 by Nakamoto as open-source software. Bitcoin Core is among the best known clients. Forks of Bitcoin Core exist such as Bitcoin Unlimited. Wallets can be full clients, with a full copy of the blockchain to check the validity of mined blocks, or lightweight clients, just to send and receive transactions without a local copy of the entire blockchain. Third-party internet services called online wallets store users' credentials on their servers, making them susceptible of hacks. Cold storage protects bitcoins from such hacks by keeping private keys offline, either through specialized hardware wallets or paper printouts.

### Scalability and Decentralization Challenges

Nakamoto limited the block size to one megabyte. The limited block size and frequency can lead to delayed processing of transactions, increased fees and a Bitcoin scalability problem. The Lightning Network, second-layer routing network, is a potential scaling solution.

Research shows a trend towards centralization in bitcoin as miners join pools for stable income. If a single miner or pool controls more than 50% of the hashing power, it would allow them to censor transactions and double-spend coins. In 2014, mining pool Ghash.io reached 51% mining power, causing safety concerns, but later voluntarily capped its power at 39.99% for the benefit of the whole network. A few entities also dominate other parts of the ecosystem such as the client software, online wallets, and simplified payment verification (SPV) clients.

## 6.1.3 Economics and Usage

### Bitcoin's Theoretical Roots and Ideology

According to the European Central Bank, the decentralization of money offered by bitcoin has its theoretical roots in the Austrian school of economics, especially with Friedrich von Hayek's book *The Denationalization of Money*, in which he advocates a complete free market in the production, distribution and management of money to end the monopoly of central banks. Sociologist Nigel Dodd, citing the crypto-anarchist *Declaration of Bitcoin's Independence*, argues that the essence of the bitcoin ideology is to remove money from social, as well as governmental, control. *The Economist* describes bitcoin as "a techno-anarchist project to create an online version of cash, a way for people to transact without the possibility of interference from malicious governments or banks". These philosophical ideas initially attracted libertarians and anarchists. Economist Paul Krugman argues that cryptocurrencies like bitcoin are only used by bank skeptics and criminals.

### Recognition as a Currency and Legal Status

Money serves three purposes: a store of value, a medium of exchange, and a unit of account. According to *The Economist* in 2014, bitcoin functions best as a medium of exchange. In 2015, *The Economist* noted that bitcoins had three qualities useful in a currency: they are "hard to earn, limited in supply and easy to verify". However, a 2018 assessment by *The Economist* stated that cryptocurrencies met none of these three criteria. Per some researchers, as of 2015, bitcoin functions more as a payment system than as a currency. In 2014, economist Robert J. Shiller wrote that bitcoin has potential as a unit of account for measuring the relative value of goods, as with Chile's Unidad de Fomento, but that "Bitcoin in its present form ... doesn't really solve any sensible economic problem".

François R. Velde, Senior Economist at the Chicago Fed, described bitcoin as "an elegant solution to the problem of creating a digital currency". David Andolfatto, Vice President at the Federal Reserve Bank of St. Louis, stated that bitcoin is a threat to the establishment, which he argues is a good thing for the Federal Reserve System and other central banks, because it prompts these institutions to operate sound policies.

The legal status of bitcoin varies substantially from one jurisdiction to another. Because of its decentralized nature and its global presence, regulating bitcoin is difficult. However, the use of bitcoin can be criminalized, and shutting down exchanges and the peer-to-peer economy in a given country would constitute a de facto ban.

The use of bitcoin by criminals has attracted the attention of financial regulators, legislative bodies, and law enforcement. Nobel-prize winning economist Joseph Stiglitz says that bitcoin's anonymity encourages money laundering and other crimes. This is the main justification behind bitcoin bans. As of November 2021, nine countries applied an absolute ban (Algeria, Bangladesh, China, Egypt, Iraq, Morocco, Nepal, Qatar, and Tunisia) while another 42 countries had an implicit ban. Bitcoin is only legal tender in El Salvador.

## Use for Payments

As of 2018, Bitcoin is rarely used in transactions with merchants, but it is popular to purchase illegal goods online. Prices are not usually quoted in bitcoin and trades involve conversions into fiat currencies. Commonly cited reasons for not using Bitcoin include high costs, the inability to process chargebacks, high price volatility, long transaction times, and transaction fees (especially for small purchases). *Bloomberg* reported that bitcoin was being used for large-item purchases on the site Overstock.com and for cross-border payments to freelancers. As of 2015, there was little sign of bitcoin use in international remittances despite high fees charged by banks and Western Union who compete in this market.

In September 2021, the Bitcoin Law made bitcoin legal tender in El Salvador, alongside the US dollar. The adoption has been criticized both internationally and within El Salvador. In particular, in 2022, the International Monetary Fund (IMF) urged El Salvador to reverse its decision. As of 2022, the use of Bitcoin in El Salvador remains low: 80% of businesses refused to accept it despite being legally required to. In April 2022, the Central African Republic (CAR) adopted Bitcoin as legal tender alongside the CFA franc, but repealed the reform one year later.

Bitcoin is also used by some governments. For instance, the Iranian government initially opposed cryptocurrencies, but later saw them as an opportunity to circumvent sanctions. Since 2020, Iran has required local bitcoin miners to sell bitcoin to the Central Bank of Iran, allowing the central bank to use it for imports. Some constituent states also accept tax payments in bitcoin, including Colorado (US) and Zug (Switzerland). As of 2023, the US government owned more than $5 billion worth of seized bitcoin.

## Use for Investment and Status as an Economic Bubble

As of 2018, the overwhelming majority of bitcoin transactions took place on cryptocurrency exchanges. Since 2014, regulated bitcoin funds also allow exposure to the asset or to futures as an investment. Individuals and companies such as the Winklevoss twins and Elon Musk's companies SpaceX and Tesla have massively invested in Bitcoin. Bitcoin wealth is highly concentrated, with 0.01% holding 27% of in-circulation currency, as of 2021. As of September 2023, El Salvador had $76.5 million worth of bitcoin in its international reserves.

In 2018, research published in the *Journal of Monetary Economics* concluded that price manipulation occurred during the Mt. Gox bitcoin theft and that the market remained vulnerable to manipulation. Research published in *The Journal of Finance* also suggested that trading associated with increases in the amount of the Tether cryptocurrency and associated trading at the Bitfinex exchange accounted for about half of the price increase in bitcoin in late 2017.

Bitcoin, along with other cryptocurrencies, has been described as an economic bubble by several economists, including Nobel Prize in Economics laureates, such as Joseph Stiglitz, James Heckman, and Paul Krugman.

Another recipient of the prize, Robert Shiller, argues that bitcoin is rather a fad that may become an asset class. He describes its price growth as an "epidemic", driven by contagious narratives.

According to research published in the *International Review of Financial Analysis* in 2018, Bitcoin as an asset is highly volatile and does not behave like any other conventional asset.

According to one 2022 analysis published in *The Journal of Alternative Investments*, bitcoin was less volatile than oil, silver, US Treasuries, and 190 stocks in the S&P 500 during and after the 2020 stock market crash. The term *hodl* was created in December 2013 for holding Bitcoin rather than selling it during periods of volatility.

Economists, investors, and the central bank of Estonia have described bitcoin as a potential Ponzi scheme. Legal scholar Eric Posner disagrees, however, as "a real Ponzi scheme takes fraud; bitcoin, by contrast, seems more like a collective delusion". A 2014 World Bank report also concluded that bitcoin was not a deliberate Ponzi scheme.

## 6.2 ETHEREUM (ETH)

Ethereum is a decentralized blockchain with smart contract functionality. Ether is the native cryptocurrency of the platform. Among cryptocurrencies, ether is second only to bitcoin in market capitalization. It is open-source software. Ethereum was conceived in 2013 by programmer Vitalik Buterin. Ethereum has several founders notably Gavin Wood, Charles Hoskinson, Anthony Di Iorio, and Joseph Lubin. In 2014, development work began and was crowdfunded, and the network went live on 30 July 2015. Ethereum allows anyone to deploy permanent and immutable decentralized applications onto it, with which users can interact. Decentralized finance (DeFi) applications provide financial instruments that do not directly rely on financial intermediaries like brokerages, exchanges, or banks. This facilitates borrowing against cryptocurrency holdings or lending them out for interest. Ethereum also allows users to create and exchange non-fungible tokens (NFTs), which are tokens that can be tied to unique digital assets, such as images. Additionally, many other cryptocurrencies utilize the ERC-20 token standard on top of the Ethereum blockchain and have utilized the platform for initial coin offerings. On 15 September 2022, Ethereum transitioned its consensus mechanism from proof-of-work (PoW) to proof-of-stake (PoS) in an upgrade process known as "the Merge". This has cut Ethereum's energy usage by 99%.

### 6.2.1 History

#### Founding (2013–2014)

Ethereum was initially described in late 2013 in a white paper by Vitalik Buterin, a programmer and co-founder of *Bitcoin Magazine*, that described a way to build decentralized applications. Buterin argued to the Bitcoin Core developers that blockchain technology could benefit from other applications besides money and that it needed a more robust language for application development that could lead to attaching real-world assets, such as stocks and property, to the blockchain. In 2013, Buterin briefly worked with eToro CEO Yoni Assia on the Colored Coins project and drafted its white paper outlining additional use cases for blockchain technology. However, after failing to gain agreement on how the project should proceed, he proposed the development of a new platform with a more robust scripting language—a Turing-complete programming language—that would eventually become Ethereum.

Ethereum was announced at the North American Bitcoin Conference in Miami, in January 2014. During the conference, Gavin Wood, Charles Hoskinson, and Anthony Di Iorio (who financed the project) rented a house in Miami with Buterin at which they could develop a fuller sense of what Ethereum might become. Di Iorio invited friend Joseph Lubin, who invited reporter Morgen Peck, to bear witness. Peck subsequently wrote about the experience in *Wired*. Six months later the founders met again in Zug, Switzerland, where Buterin told the founders that the project would proceed as a non-profit. Hoskinson left the project at that time and soon after founded IOHK, a blockchain company responsible for Cardano.

Ethereum has an unusually long list of founders. Anthony Di Iorio wrote: "Ethereum was founded by Vitalik Buterin, Myself, Charles Hoskinson, Mihai Alisie & Amir Chetrit (the initial 5) in December 2013. Joseph Lubin, Gavin Wood, & Jeffrey Wilcke were added in early 2014 as founders." Buterin chose the name Ethereum after browsing a list of elements from science fiction on Wikipedia. He stated, "I immediately realized that I liked it better than all of the other alternatives that I had seen; I suppose it was that [it] sounded nice and it had the word 'ether', referring to the hypothetical invisible medium that permeates the universe and allows light to travel." Buterin wanted his platform to be the underlying and imperceptible medium for the applications running on top of it.

## Development (2014)

Formal development of the software underlying Ethereum began in early 2014 through a Swiss company, Ethereum Switzerland GmbH (*EthSuisse*). The idea of putting executable smart contracts in the blockchain needed to be specified before it could be implemented in software. This work was done by Gavin Wood, then the chief technology officer, in the Ethereum Yellow Paper that specified the Ethereum Virtual Machine. Subsequently, a Swiss non-profit foundation, the Ethereum Foundation (*Stiftung Ethereum*), was founded. Development was funded by an online public crowd sale from July to August 2014, in which participants bought the Ethereum value token (ether) with another digital currency, bitcoin. While there was early praise for the technical innovations of Ethereum, questions were also raised about its security and scalability.

## Launch and the DAO Event (2014–2016)

Several codenamed prototypes of Ethereum were developed over 18 months in 2014 and 2015 by the Ethereum Foundation as part of their proof-of-concept series. "Olympic" was the last prototype and public beta pre-release. The Olympic network gave users a bug bounty of 25,000 ether for stress-testing the Ethereum blockchain. On 30 July 2015, "Frontier" marked the official launch of the Ethereum platform, and Ethereum created its "genesis block". The genesis block contained

8,893 transactions allocating various amounts of ether to different addresses, and a block reward of 5 ETH.

Since the initial launch, Ethereum has undergone a number of planned protocol upgrades, which are important changes affecting the underlying functionality and/or incentive structures of the platform. Protocol upgrades are accomplished by means of a hard fork.

In 2016, a decentralized autonomous organization called The DAO—a set of smart contracts developed on the platform—raised a record US$150 million in a crowd sale to fund the project. The DAO was exploited in June 2016 when US$50 million of DAO tokens were stolen by an unknown hacker.

The event sparked a debate in the crypto-community about whether Ethereum should perform a contentious "hard fork" to reappropriate the affected funds. The fork resulted in the network splitting into two blockchains: Ethereum with the theft reversed, and Ethereum Classic which continued on the original chain.

## Continued Development and Milestones (2017–Present)

In March 2017, various blockchain startups, research groups, and *Fortune* 500 companies announced the creation of the Enterprise Ethereum Alliance (EEA) with 30 founding members.

By May 2017, the nonprofit organization had 116 enterprise members, including ConsenSys, CME Group, Cornell University's research group, Toyota Research Institute, Samsung SDS, Microsoft, Intel, J. P. Morgan, Cooley LLP, Merck KGaA, DTCC, Deloitte, Accenture, Banco Santander, BNY Mellon, ING, and National Bank of Canada. By July 2017, there were over 150 members in the alliance, including MasterCard, Cisco Systems, Sberbank, and Scotiabank.

### CryptoKitties and the ERC-721 NFT Standard

In 2017, *CryptoKitties*, the blockchain game and decentralized application (dApp) featuring digital cat artwork as NFTs, was launched on the Ethereum network. In cultivating popularity with users and collectors, it gained notable mainstream media attention providing significant exposure to Ethereum in the process. It was considered the most popular smart contract in use on the network but it also highlighted concerns over Ethereum's scalability due to the game's substantial consumption of network capacity at the time.

In January 2018, a community-driven paper (an EIP, "Ethereum Improvement Proposal") under the leadership of civic hacker and lead author William Entriken was published, called *ERC-721: Non-Fungible Token Standard.* It introduced ERC-721, the first official NFT standard on Ethereum. This standardization allowed Ethereum to become central to a multi-billion dollar digital collectibles market.

### Continued Developments

By January 2018, ether was the second-largest cryptocurrency in terms of market capitalization, behind bitcoin. As of 2021, it maintained that relative position. In 2019, Ethereum Foundation employee Virgil Griffith was arrested by the US government for presenting at a blockchain conference in North Korea. He would later plead guilty to one count of conspiring to violate the International Emergency Economic Powers Act in 2021.

In March 2021, Visa Inc. announced that it began settling stablecoin transactions using Ethereum. In April 2021, JP Morgan Chase, UBS, and MasterCard announced that they were investing US$65 million into ConsenSys, a software development firm that builds Ethereum-related infrastructure.

There were two network upgrades in 2021. The first was "Berlin", implemented on 14 April 2021. The second was "London", which took effect on 5 August. The London upgrade included Ethereum Improvement Proposal ("EIP") 1559, a mechanism for reducing transaction fee volatility. The mechanism causes a portion of the ether paid in transaction fees for each block to be destroyed rather than given to the block proposer, reducing the inflation rate of ether and potentially resulting in periods of deflation. On 27 August 2021, the blockchain experienced a brief fork that was the result of clients running different incompatible software versions.

### Ethereum 2.0

Ethereum 2.0 (Eth2) was a set of three or more upgrades, also known as "phases", meant to transition the network's consensus mechanism to proof-of-stake, and to scale the network's transaction throughput with execution sharding and an improved EVM architecture.

The switch from proof-of-work to proof-of-stake on 15 September 2022 has cut Ethereum's energy usage by 99%. This upgrade, known as "The Merge", was the first phase in the series of upgrades.

However, the impact this has on global energy consumption and climate change may be limited since the computers previously used for mining ether may be used to mine other cryptocurrencies that are energy-intensive. On March 13, 2024 the second phase known as "Dencun" or also "Deneb-Cancun" upgrade went live. This upgrade lowered the transaction fees on the many Layer 2 networks built on top of the base Ethereum blockchain.

## 6.2.2 Design

Ethereum is a peer-to-peer network that maintains a database containing the storage values of all Ethereum accounts and processes state-altering transactions. Approximately every 12 seconds, a batch of new transactions, known as a "block", is processed by the network. Each block contains a cryptographic hash identifying the series of blocks that must precede it if the block is to be considered valid. This series of blocks is known as the blockchain.

Each "node" (network participant) connects with a relatively small subset of the network to offer blocks and unvalidated transactions (i.e., transactions not yet in the blockchain) to its peers for download, and it downloads any of these from its peers that it doesn't already have. Each node usually has a unique set of peers, so that offering an item to its peers results in the propagation of that item throughout the entire network within seconds. A node's collection of unvalidated transactions is known as its "mempool".

A node may choose to create a copy of the state for itself. It does this by starting with the genesis state and executing every transaction in the blockchain, in the proper order of blocks and in the order they are listed within each block.

Any Ethereum account may "stake" (deposit) 32 ETH to become a validator. At the end of each "epoch" (32 block slots, each slot lasting 12 seconds), each validator is pseudorandomly assigned to one of the slots of the epoch after the next, either as the block proposer or as an attester. During a slot, the block proposer uses their mempool to create a block that is intended to become the new "head" (latest block) of the blockchain, and the attesters attest to which block is at the head of the chain. If a validator makes self-contradicting proposals or attestations, or if it is inactive, it loses a portion of its stake. It may add to its stake at any time. A validator's attestation is given a weight equal to its stake or 32, whichever is less. According to the Ethereum protocol, the blockchain with the highest accumulated weight of attestations at any given time is to be regarded as the canonical chain. Validators are rewarded for making valid proposals and attestations. A validator's rewards are paid via transactions within the same chain that contains their proposal or attestation, and therefore would have little or no market value unless that chain becomes the canonical chain. This incentivizes validators to support the chain that they think other validators view as the canonical chain, which results in a high degree of consensus.

## Ether

Ether (ETH) is the cryptocurrency generated in accordance with the Ethereum protocol as a reward to validators in a proof-of-stake system for adding blocks to the blockchain. Ether is represented in the state as an unsigned integer associated with each account, this being the account's ETH balance denominated in wei (10 wei = 1 ether). At the end of each epoch, new ETH is generated by the addition of protocol-specified amounts to the balances of all validators for that epoch, with the block proposers receiving the largest portion. Additionally, ether is the only currency accepted by the protocol as payment for the transaction fee. The transaction fee is composed of two parts: the base fee and the tip. The base fee is "burned" (deleted from existence) and the tip goes to the block proposer. The validator reward together with the tips provide the incentive to validators to keep the blockchain growing (i.e., to keep processing new transactions). Therefore, ETH is fundamental to the operation of the network. Ether may be "sent" from one account to another via a transaction, the execution of which simply entails subtracting the *amount to be sent* from the sender's balance and adding the same amount to the recipient's balance. Ether is often erroneously referred to as "Ethereum". The uppercase Greek letter Xi, Ξ, is sometimes used as a currency symbol for ether.

### Accounts

There are two types of accounts on Ethereum: user accounts and contract accounts. Both types have an ETH balance, may transfer ETH to any account, may execute the code of another contract, or create a new contract, and are identified on the blockchain and in the state by an account address.

Contracts are the only type of account that has associated bytecode and storage (to store contract specific state). The code of a contract is evaluated when a transaction is sent to it. The code of the contract may read user specified data from the transaction, and may have a return value. In addition to control flow statements, the bytecode may include instructions to send ETH, read from and write to the contract's storage, create temporary storage (memory) that vanishes at the end of code evaluation, perform arithmetic and hashing operations, send transactions to other contracts (thus executing their code), create new contracts, and query information about the current transaction or the blockchain.

### Addresses

Ethereum addresses are composed of the prefix "`0x`" (a common identifier for hexadecimal) concatenated with the rightmost 20 bytes of the Keccak-256 hash of the ECDSA public key (the curve used is the so-called *secp256k1*). In hexadecimal, two digits represent a byte, and so addresses contain 40 hexadecimal digits after the

**"`0x`", e.g.,** `0xb794f5ea0ba39494ce839613fffba74279579268.`

Contract addresses are in the same format, however, they are determined by sender and creation transaction nonce.

### Virtual Machine

The Ethereum Virtual Machine (EVM) is the runtime environment for transaction execution in Ethereum. The EVM is a stack based virtual machine with an instruction set specifically designed for Ethereum. The instruction set includes, among other things, stack operations, memory operations, and operations to inspect the current execution context, such as remaining gas, information about the current block, and the current transaction. The EVM is designed to be deterministic on a wide variety of hardware and operating systems, so that given a pre-transaction state and a transaction, each node produces the same post-transaction state, thereby enabling network consensus. The formal definition of the EVM is specified in the Ethereum Yellow Paper. EVMs have been implemented in C++, C#, Go, Haskell, Java, JavaScript, Python, Ruby, Rust, Elixir, Erlang, and soon WebAssembly.

### Gas

Gas is a unit of account within the EVM used in the calculation of the transaction fee, which is the amount of ETH a transaction's sender must pay to the network to have the transaction included in the blockchain. Each type of operation which may be performed by the EVM is hardcoded with a certain gas cost, which is intended to be roughly proportional to the monetary value of the resources (e.g., computation and storage) a node must expend or dedicate to perform that operation.

When a sender is creating a transaction, the sender must specify a *gas limit* and *gas price*. The *gas limit* is the maximum amount of gas the sender is willing to use in the transaction, and the *gas price* is the amount of ETH the sender wishes to pay to the network per unit of gas used. A transaction may only be included in the blockchain at a block slot that has a *base gas price* less than or equal to the transaction's *gas price*. The portion of the *gas price* that is in excess of the *base gas price* is known as the tip and goes to the block proposer; the higher the tip, the more incentive a block proposer has to include the transaction in their block, and thus the quicker the transaction will be included in the blockchain. The sender buys the full amount of gas (i.e., their ETH balance is debited the amount: *gas limit* × *gas price*) up-front, at the start of the execution of the transaction, and is refunded at the end for any unused gas. If at any point the transaction does not have enough gas to perform the next operation, the transaction is reverted but the sender is still only refunded for the unused gas. In user interfaces, gas prices are typically denominated in gigawei (Gwei), a subunit of ETH equal to 10 ETH.

## 6.2.3 Applications

The EVM's instruction set is Turing-complete. Popular uses of Ethereum have included the creation of fungible (ERC-20) and non-fungible (ERC-721) tokens with a variety of properties, crowdfunding (e.g., initial coin offerings), decentralized finance, decentralized exchanges, decentralized autonomous organizations (DAOs), games, prediction markets, and gambling.

### Contract Source Code

Ethereum's smart contracts are written in high-level programming languages and then compiled down to EVM bytecode and deployed to the Ethereum blockchain.

They can be written in Solidity (a language library with similarities to C and JavaScript), Serpent (similar to Python, but deprecated), Yul (an intermediate language that can compile to various different backends—EVM 1.0, EVM 1.5, and eWASM are planned), LLL (a low-level Lisp-like language), and Mutan (Go-based, but deprecated). Source code and compiler information are usually published along with the launch of the contract so that users can see the code and verify that it compiles to the bytecode that is on-chain. One issue related to using smart contracts on a public blockchain is that bugs, including security holes, are visible to all but cannot be fixed quickly. One example of this is the 2016 attack on The DAO, which could not be quickly stopped or reversed.

### ERC-20 Tokens

The ERC-20 (Ethereum Request-for-Comments #20) Token Standard allows for fungible tokens on the Ethereum blockchain. The standard, proposed by Fabian Vogelsteller in November 2015, implements an API for tokens within smart contracts. The standard provides functions that include the transfer of tokens from one account to another, getting the current token balance of an account, and getting the total supply of the token available on the network. Smart contracts that correctly implement ERC-20 processes are called ERC-20 Token Contracts, and they keep track of created tokens on Ethereum. Numerous cryptocurrencies have launched as ERC-20 tokens and have been distributed through initial coin offerings.

### Non-Fungible Tokens (NFTs)

Ethereum also allows for the creation of unique and indivisible tokens, called non-fungible tokens (NFTs). Since tokens of this type are unique, they have been used to represent such things as collectibles, digital art, sports memorabilia, virtual real estate, and items within games. ERC-721 is the first official NFT standard for Ethereum and was followed up by ERC-1155 which introduced semi-fungibility, both are widely used, though some fully fungible tokens using ERC-20 have been used for NFTs such as *CryptoPunks*.

The first NFT project, Etheria, a 3D map of tradable and customizable hexagonal tiles, was deployed to the network in October 2015 and demonstrated live at DEVCON1 in November of that year. In 2021, Christie's sold a digital image with an NFT by Beeple for US$69.3 million, making him the third-most-valuable living artist in terms of auction prices at the time, although observers have noted that both the buyer and seller had a vested interest in driving demand for the artist's work.

### Decentralized Finance

Decentralized finance (DeFi) offers financial instruments in a decentralized architecture, outside of companies' and governments' control, such as money market funds which let users earn interest. DeFi applications are typically accessed through a Web3-enabled browser extension or application, such as MetaMask, which allows users to directly interact with the Ethereum blockchain through a website. Many of these DApps can connect and work together to create complex financial services.

Examples of DeFi platforms include MakerDAO. Uniswap, a decentralized exchange for tokens on Ethereum grew from US$20 million in liquidity to US$2.9 billion in 2020. As of October 2020, over US$11 billion was invested in various DeFi protocols. Additionally, through a process called "wrapping", certain DeFi protocols allow synthetic versions of various assets (such as bitcoin, gold, and oil) to be tradeable on Ethereum and also compatible with all of Ethereum's major wallets and applications.

## Enterprise Software

Ethereum-based software and networks, independent from the public Ethereum chain, have been tested by enterprise software companies. Interested parties have included Microsoft, IBM, JPMorgan Chase, Deloitte, R3, and Innovate UK (cross-border payments prototype). Barclays, UBS, Credit Suisse, Amazon, Visa, and other companies have also experimented with Ethereum.

## Permissioned Ledgers

Ethereum-based permissioned blockchain variants are used and being investigated for various projects:

- In 2017, JPMorgan Chase proposed developing JPM Coin on a permissioned-variant of Ethereum blockchain dubbed "Quorum". It is "designed to toe the line between private and public in the realm of shuffling derivatives and payments. The idea is to satisfy regulators who need seamless access to financial goings-on while protecting the privacy of parties that don't wish to reveal their identities nor the details of their transactions to the general public."

## Performance

As of January 2016, the Ethereum protocol could process about 25 transactions per second; this did not change after the move to proof-of-stake. In comparison, the Visa payment platform processes 45,000 payments per second. This has led some to question the scalability of Ethereum.

A proposal to partition global state and computation into shard chains was presented at Ethereum's Devcon 3 in November 2017. If implemented, each node in the network would only have to store and validate a subset of the network. Ethereum's blockchain uses a Merkle-Patricia Tree to store account state in each block. The trie allows for storage savings, set membership proofs (called "Merkle proofs"), and light client synchronization. The network has faced congestion problems, such as in 2017 in relation to *CryptoKitties*.

### 6.2.4 Regulation

In the United States, the proposed Digital Commodities Consumer Protection Act would treat Ethereum and other cryptocurrencies as commodities, which could then be regulated by the Commodity Futures Trading Commission (CFTC).

## 6.3 RIPPLE (XRP)

Ripple is a real-time gross settlement system, currency exchange and remittance network that is open to financial institutions worldwide and was created by Ripple Labs Inc., a US-based technology company. Released in 2012, Ripple is built upon a distributed open source protocol, and supports tokens representing fiat currency, cryptocurrency, commodities, or other units of value such as frequent flier miles or mobile minutes. Ripple purports to enable "secure, instantly and nearly free global financial transactions of any size with no chargebacks". The ledger employs the native cryptocurrency known as XRP.

In December 2020, Ripple Labs and two of its executives were sued by the U.S. Securities and Exchange Commission (SEC) for selling XRP tokens, which the SEC classified as unregistered securities. In July 2023, the court ruled that "XRP, as a digital token, is not in and of itself a 'contract, transaction, or scheme' that embodies the Howey requirements of an investment contract."

### 6.3.1 History

Ripple was conceived by Jed McCaleb and built by Arthur Britto and David Schwartz who then approached Ryan Fugger who had debuted in 2005 as a financial service to provide secure payment options to members of an online community via a global network. Fugger had developed a system called OpenCoin which would transform into Ripple. The company also created its own form of digital currency referred to as XRP to allow financial institutions to transfer money with negligible fees and wait-time. In 2013, the company reported interest from banks for using its payment system.

By 2018, over 100 banks had signed up, but most of them were only using Ripple's XCurrent messaging technology, while avoiding the XRP cryptocurrency due to its volatility problems. Representatives of the Society for Worldwide Interbank Financial Telecommunication (SWIFT), whose market dominance is being challenged by Ripple, have argued that the scalability issues of Ripple and other blockchain solutions remain unsolved, confining them to bilateral and intra-bank applications. A Ripple executive acknowledged in 2018 that "We started out with your classic blockchain, which we love. But the feedback from the banks is you can't put the whole world on a blockchain."

Ripple relies on a common shared ledger, which is a distributed database storing information about all Ripple accounts. Chris Larsen told the Stanford Graduate School of Business that the network was managed by a network of independent servers which compare their transaction records, and that servers could in theory belong to anyone, including banks or market makers. Ripple validates accounts and balances instantly for payment transmission and delivers payment notification within a few seconds. Payments are irreversible, and there are no chargebacks.

Ripple Labs continued as the primary contributor of code to the consensus verification system behind Ripple. In 2014, the protocol gained access to the US banking system amid concerns over security and a lack of regulation.

### 6.3.2 Litigation

A class action was filed against Ripple in May 2018 "alleging that it led a scheme to raise hundreds of millions of dollars through unregistered sales of its XRP tokens". According to the complaint, "the company created billions of coins 'out of thin air' and then profited by selling them to the public in 'what is essentially a never-ending initial coin offering'".

The U.S. Securities and Exchange Commission (SEC) initiated legal proceedings against Ripple Labs, CEO Brad Garlinghouse, and co-founder Chris Larsen on December 21, 2020, for allegedly selling unregistered securities. In the lawsuit, the SEC claimed that XRP was a security instead of a commodity, because it was generated and distributed by Ripple Labs in a centralized fashion and was not being adopted by financial institutions for its advertised use cases. The SEC stated that Ripple executives sold 14.6 billion units of XRP for more than $1.38 billion to fund the company's operations and enrich themselves.

In response, Garlinghouse criticized the SEC and indicated that Ripple Labs would defend itself in court. Coinbase delisted XRP on December 28; an investor filed a class action on December 30 alleging that Coinbase sold XRP tokens with the understanding that they were unregistered securities. On April 13, 2021, SEC Commissioner Hester M. Peirce published the Token Safe Harbor Proposal 2.0, which is "intended to provide Initial Development Teams with a three-year time period within which they can facilitate participation in, and the continued development of, a functional or decentralized network, exempt from the registration provisions of the federal securities laws so long as certain conditions are met."

Judge Analisa Torres issued a decision on motions for summary judgement on 13 July 2023, and stated the XRP token itself is not a security, although the manner in which it is sold could constitute the sale of a security. "XRP, as a digital token, is not in and of itself a 'contract, transaction, or scheme' that embodies the Howey requirements of an investment contract." The ruling further found that the institutional sales of XRP tokens constituted the unregistered offer and sale of investment contracts.

However programmatic sales and other XRP token sales by Ripple Labs did not constitute the offer and sale of investment contracts, she ruled. The case could subsequently go to a full trial, or be appealed.

### 6.3.3 Reception

For its creation and development of the Ripple protocol (RTXP) and the Ripple payment/exchange network Ripple Labs was named as one of 2014's 50 Smartest Companies in the February 2014 edition of *MIT Technology Review.*

A scientific study made by two researchers from Stanford and Stockholm universities that studied the money production from an energy consumption point of view and a macroeconomic level stated that running a server on Ripple was comparable to the energy needs of running an email server.

## 6.4 LITECOIN (LTC)

Litecoin is a decentralized peer-to-peer cryptocurrency and open-source software project released under the MIT/X11 license. Inspired by Bitcoin, Litecoin was among the earliest altcoins, starting in October 2011. In technical details, the Litecoin main chain shares a slightly modified Bitcoin codebase. The practical effects of those codebase differences are lower transaction fees, faster transaction confirmations, and faster mining difficulty retargeting. Due to its underlying similarities to Bitcoin, Litecoin has historically been referred to as the "silver to Bitcoin's gold." In 2022, Litecoin added optional privacy features via soft fork through the MWEB (MimbleWimble extension block) upgrade.

### 6.4.1 Design

#### Units and Divisibility

Currency codes for representing litecoin is LTC. Its Unicode character is Ł. One litecoin is divisible to eight decimal places. Units for smaller amounts of litecoin are:

- lites, or millilitecoin (mŁ), equal to 1/1000 litecoin,
- photons, or microlitecoin (μŁ), equal to 1/1000000, and
- the litoshi, which is the smallest possible division, and named in homage to bitcoin's smallest denomination the satoshi, representing 1/100000000 (one hundred millionth) litecoin.

### 6.4.2 History

#### Pre-Litecoin

By 2011, Bitcoin mining was largely performed by GPUs. This raised concern in some users that mining now had a high barrier to entry, and that CPU resources were becoming obsolete and worthless for mining. Using code from Bitcoin, a new alternative currency was created called *Tenebrix* (TBX). Tenebrix replaced the SHA-256 rounds in Bitcoin's mining algorithm with the *scrypt* function, which had been specifically designed in 2009 to be expensive to accelerate with FPGA or ASIC chips. This would allow Tenebrix to have been "GPU-resistant", and utilize the available CPU resources from bitcoin miners. Tenebrix itself was a successor project to an earlier cryptocurrency which replaced Bitcoin's issuance schedule with a constant block reward (thus creating an unlimited money supply). However, the developers included a clause in the code that would allow them to claim 7.7 million TBX for themselves at no cost, which was criticized by users.

To address this, Charlie Lee, a Google employee who would later become engineering director at Coinbase, created an alternative version of Tenebrix called *Fairbrix* (FBX). Litecoin inherits the scrypt mining algorithm from Fairbrix, but returns to the limited money supply of Bitcoin, with other changes.

#### Creation and Launch

Lee released Litecoin via an open-source client on GitHub on October 7, 2011. The Litecoin network went live on October 13, 2011. Litecoin was a source code fork of the Bitcoin Core client, originally differing by having a decreased block generation time (2.5 minutes), increased maximum number of coins, different hashing algorithm (scrypt, instead of SHA-256), faster difficulty retarget, and a slightly modified GUI.

#### 2011–2016

After launch, the early growth of Litecoin was aided by its increasing exchange availability and liquidity on early exchanges such as BTC-e. During the month of November 2013, the aggregate value of Litecoin experienced massive growth which included a 100% leap within 24 hours. In early 2014, Lee suggested merge mining (auxPOW) Dogecoin with Litecoin to the Dogecoin community at large. In September 2014, Dogecoin began merge-mining with Litecoin.

#### 2017–2021

In 2020, PayPal added the ability for users to purchase a derivative of Litecoin along with Bitcoin, Ethereum and Bitcoin Cash which could not be withdrawn or spent as part of its Crypto feature. In September 2021, a fake press release was published on GlobeNewswire announcing a partnership between Litecoin and Walmart. This caused the price of Litecoin to increase by around 30%, before the press release was revealed as a hoax.

### 2022–Present

In May 2022, MWEB (Mimblewimble Extension Blocks) upgrade was activated on the Litecoin network as a soft fork. This upgrade provides users with the option of sending confidential Litecoin transactions, in which the amount being sent is only known between the sender and receiver.

In June 2022, PayPal added the ability for users to transfer Litecoin along with Bitcoin, Ethereum and Bitcoin Cash between PayPal to other wallets and exchanges.

### 6.4.3 Differences from Bitcoin

Litecoin is different in some ways from Bitcoin:

- The targeted block time is every 2.5 minutes for Litecoin, as opposed to Bitcoin's 10 minutes. This allows Litecoin to confirm transactions four times faster than Bitcoin.
- Scrypt, an alternative proof-of-work algorithm, is used for Litecoin. According to *Motherboard*, "Scrypt was chosen because it theoretically prevents the use of ASICs, those specialized chips that greatly increase mining power and efficiency (though there is debate over the validity of this claim)".
- Litecoin is merge mined with another prominent cryptocurrency, Dogecoin.
- Litecoin has a maximum circulating supply of Ł84,000,000, which is four times larger than Bitcoin's maximum circulating supply of ₿ 21,000,000.
- MWEB optional privacy was added to Litecoin's base layer in May 2022 via soft fork. This allows amounts held within wallets and transaction amounts within MWEB to be private.

Third party vendors providing point of sale infrastructure for Litecoin include BitPay.

## 6.5 EMERGING CRYPTOCURRENCIES AND TRENDS

The cryptocurrency landscape is constantly evolving, with new technologies, projects, and trends emerging regularly. This dynamic environment is driven by innovation in blockchain technology, changing market demands, regulatory developments, and shifts in investor sentiment. The cryptocurrency landscape is characterized by rapid innovation and constant evolution. Emerging cryptocurrencies like Polkadot, Solana, Avalanche, Cardano, and Chainlink are pushing the boundaries of what blockchain technology can achieve. Concurrently, trends such as DeFi, NFTs, interoperability, Layer 2 solutions, regulatory developments, and sustainability are shaping the future of the digital asset ecosystem. As the market continues to grow, these emerging projects and trends will play a crucial role in defining the next phase of the cryptocurrency revolution.

### 6.5.1 Emerging Cryptocurrencies

#### Polkadot (DOT)

Polkadot is a next-generation blockchain protocol designed to enable multiple blockchains to interoperate seamlessly. Developed by Dr. Gavin Wood, one of the co-founders of Ethereum, Polkadot aims to solve the issue of blockchain interoperability by creating a multi-chain framework that allows different blockchains to transfer messages and value in a trust-free fashion.

**Key Features:**

- **Interoperability:** Polkadot enables different blockchains to communicate and share information.
- **Scalability:** It uses a sharded multichain network, allowing for parallel processing of multiple transactions.
- **Governance:** Polkadot has a sophisticated governance model where stakeholders can vote on network upgrades and changes.

#### Solana (SOL)

Solana is a high-performance blockchain designed for scalability and speed. With its unique Proof of History (PoH) consensus mechanism, Solana can process thousands of transactions per second, making it one of the fastest blockchains in the market.

**Key Features:**

- **High Throughput:** Solana can handle over 50,000 transactions per second (TPS).
- **Low Latency:** The network offers sub-second block times.
- **Low Costs:** Solana's efficient design keeps transaction fees minimal.

#### Avalanche (AVAX)

Avalanche is a platform for creating custom blockchain networks and decentralized applications (dApps). It aims to provide a highly scalable and interoperable environment for developers.

**Key Features:**

- **Consensus Protocol:** Avalanche uses a novel consensus protocol that allows for quick and efficient transaction finality.
- **Interoperability:** The platform supports multiple virtual machines, including EVM (Ethereum Virtual Machine), enabling easy integration with Ethereum-based dApps.
- **Subnets:** Developers can create custom blockchains called subnets tailored to specific use cases.

### Cardano (ADA)

Cardano is a blockchain platform developed through a research-driven approach, emphasizing security, scalability, and sustainability. It aims to provide a more balanced and sustainable ecosystem for cryptocurrencies and smart contracts.

**Key Features:**

- **Research-Based Development:** Cardano is built on peer-reviewed academic research.
- **Ouroboros:** Its Proof of Stake (PoS) consensus mechanism is designed for energy efficiency and security.
- **Layered Architecture:** Cardano separates the settlement and computation layers to improve scalability and flexibility.

### Chainlink (LINK)

Chainlink is a decentralized oracle network that enables smart contracts to securely interact with real-world data and external APIs. It bridges the gap between blockchain and off-chain environments, expanding the potential use cases for smart contracts.

**Key Features:**

- **Decentralized Oracles:** Chainlink provides tamper-proof data feeds for smart contracts.
- **Flexibility:** It can connect to any API, enabling a wide range of use cases.
- **Security:** Chainlink's decentralized architecture enhances the reliability and security of data inputs.

## 6.5.2 Trends in the Cryptocurrency Ecosystem

### Decentralized Finance (DeFi)

DeFi refers to a broad category of financial services built on blockchain technology, aiming to recreate traditional financial systems (such as lending, borrowing, and trading) in a decentralized manner.

Key components of the DeFi ecosystem include decentralized exchanges (DEXs), lending platforms, and stablecoins.

- **Growth:** The DeFi sector has seen exponential growth, with the total value locked (TVL) in DeFi protocols reaching billions of dollars.
- **Innovation:** DeFi projects are continually innovating with new financial products, including yield farming, liquidity mining, and synthetic assets.

### Non-Fungible Tokens (NFTs)

NFTs are unique digital assets representing ownership of a specific item or piece of content, stored on the blockchain. They have gained significant attention in the realms of art, gaming, and entertainment.

- **Market Expansion:** The NFT market has expanded rapidly, with high-profile sales and growing interest from artists, musicians, and brands.
- **Use Cases:** Beyond art and collectibles, NFTs are being used for digital identity, gaming, virtual real estate, and more.

### Interoperability Solutions

Interoperability between different blockchain networks is becoming increasingly important as the ecosystem grows.

Projects like Polkadot, Cosmos, and Avalanche focus on enabling seamless interaction between distinct blockchains.

- **Cross-Chain Bridges:** Development of cross-chain bridges to facilitate the transfer of assets and data between different blockchains.
- **Standardization:** Efforts to create standard protocols for interoperability to ensure compatibility and ease of integration.

### Layer 2 Solutions

Layer 2 solutions aim to address the scalability issues of existing blockchain networks by offloading transactions from the main blockchain (Layer 1) to secondary layers. These solutions enhance transaction throughput and reduce costs.

- **Rollups:** Techniques like optimistic rollups and zk-rollups bundle multiple transactions into a single transaction on the main blockchain, improving efficiency.
- **State Channels:** These allow participants to conduct multiple transactions off-chain, with only the final state recorded on the blockchain.

## Regulatory Developments

As the cryptocurrency market matures, regulatory frameworks are evolving to address issues related to security, fraud, and market stability. Governments and regulatory bodies are working to create policies that protect investors while fostering innovation.

- **Compliance:** Increasing emphasis on compliance with anti-money laundering (AML) and know-your-customer (KYC) regulations.
- **Central Bank Digital Currencies (CBDCs):** Exploration and development of CBDCs by various countries, which could coexist with or compete against cryptocurrencies.

## Environmental Concerns and Sustainability

The environmental impact of cryptocurrency mining, especially with energy-intensive PoW systems, has become a significant concern. There is a growing emphasis on developing more sustainable and eco-friendly blockchain technologies.

- **Transition to PoS:** Some networks, like Ethereum, are transitioning from PoW to PoS to reduce their carbon footprint.
- **Green Cryptocurrencies:** Emergence of cryptocurrencies designed with sustainability in mind, utilizing energy-efficient consensus mechanisms.

# CHAPTER 7
# BLOCKCHAIN USE CASES

## 7.1 CRYPTOCURRENCIES AS A MEDIUM OF EXCHANGE

Cryptocurrencies have evolved significantly since the inception of Bitcoin in 2009, and one of their primary intended uses is as a medium of exchange. Cryptocurrencies have the potential to revolutionize the way we conduct transactions by offering a decentralized, efficient, and secure medium of exchange. While there are significant challenges, such as volatility, scalability, regulatory uncertainty, and adoption barriers, the continuous evolution of blockchain technology and increasing integration with traditional financial systems are paving the way for broader acceptance and usage.

Emerging cryptocurrencies like Bitcoin, Litecoin, Dash, and Bitcoin Cash, along with stablecoins, are already demonstrating the viability of digital currencies for everyday transactions. As the ecosystem matures, with advancements in technology, regulatory clarity, and growing adoption, cryptocurrencies could become a mainstream medium of exchange, transforming the global financial landscape.

### 7.1.1 Understanding Cryptocurrencies as a Medium of Exchange

A medium of exchange is an instrument used to facilitate the sale, purchase, or trade of goods and services. For cryptocurrencies to function effectively as a medium of exchange, they must exhibit certain characteristics, such as widespread acceptance, stability in value, divisibility, portability, and security.

### 7.1.2 Advantages of Cryptocurrencies as a Medium of Exchange

- **Decentralization:**
  - *No Central Authority:* Cryptocurrencies operate on decentralized networks, eliminating the need for intermediaries like banks. This reduces transaction fees and processing times.
  - *Global Access:* Anyone with internet access can participate in the cryptocurrency ecosystem, promoting financial inclusion.
- **Low Transaction Costs—Minimal Fees:** Cryptocurrency transactions typically involve lower fees compared to traditional banking and payment systems, especially for cross-border transactions.

- **Speed—Quick Transactions:** Transactions can be processed in minutes, regardless of the participants' geographical locations. This is particularly advantageous for international transactions.
- **Security:**
  - *Cryptographic Security:* Cryptocurrencies use cryptographic techniques to secure transactions, reducing the risk of fraud and chargebacks.
  - *Immutable Ledger:* Transactions recorded on the blockchain are irreversible, ensuring transaction integrity.
- **Transparency—Public Ledger:** Blockchain technology provides a transparent ledger where all transactions are publicly verifiable, enhancing trust among users.

### 7.1.3 Challenges of Cryptocurrencies as a Medium of Exchange

- **Volatility—Price Fluctuations:** Cryptocurrencies are notorious for their volatility, which can undermine their effectiveness as a stable medium of exchange. Merchants and consumers may be reluctant to use or accept a currency that can significantly change in value within a short period.
- **Scalability—Transaction Limits:** Many cryptocurrencies face scalability issues, leading to slower transaction times and higher fees during periods of high demand. For example, Bitcoin's transaction throughput is limited compared to traditional payment networks like Visa.
- **Regulatory Uncertainty—Varying Regulations:** The regulatory environment for cryptocurrencies varies significantly across different countries, creating uncertainty and potential legal challenges for users and businesses.
- **Adoption Barriers—Merchant Acceptance:** Widespread adoption by merchants and consumers is still limited. Many businesses are hesitant to accept cryptocurrencies due to volatility, regulatory concerns, and a lack of understanding.
- **Technological Hurdles—User Experience:** The complexity of cryptocurrency wallets and transactions can be a barrier for non-technical users. Improved user interfaces and education are needed to enhance accessibility.

### 7.1.4 Notable Cryptocurrencies as a Medium of Exchange

**Bitcoin (BTC):**

- **Pioneer Cryptocurrency:** Bitcoin is the first and most well-known cryptocurrency, often referred to as digital gold. While it is widely accepted and recognized, its use as a medium of exchange is hindered by its volatility and scalability issues.

- **Merchant Adoption:** Some major companies, like Microsoft and Overstock, accept Bitcoin for payments, but its primary use has shifted towards being a store of value.

**Litecoin (LTC):**

- **Faster Transactions:** Created as a "lighter" version of Bitcoin, Litecoin offers faster transaction times and lower fees, making it more practical for everyday transactions.
- **Adoption:** Litecoin is accepted by a growing number of merchants and is often used for small and medium-sized transactions.

**Dash (DASH):**

- **Focus on Payments:** Dash is specifically designed to be a digital currency for everyday transactions. It offers features like InstantSend and PrivateSend for fast and private transactions.
- **Merchant Integration:** Dash has been integrated into various payment systems and merchant platforms, particularly in regions with high inflation and unstable currencies.

**Bitcoin Cash (BCH):**

- **Larger Block Size:** Bitcoin Cash was created as a fork of Bitcoin to address scalability issues by increasing the block size, allowing for more transactions per block.
- **Use Case:** It aims to be a peer-to-peer electronic cash system, making it more suitable for everyday transactions compared to Bitcoin.

**Stablecoins:**

- **Price Stability:** Stablecoins, such as Tether (USDT), USD Coin (USDC), and Dai (DAI), are designed to maintain a stable value by being pegged to a fiat currency or other assets.
- **Adoption:** Due to their stability, stablecoins are increasingly being used for transactions, remittances, and as a store of value within the crypto ecosystem.

### 7.1.5 Future Outlook for Cryptocurrencies as a Medium of Exchange

**Increased Adoption:**

- **Mainstream Integration:** As cryptocurrencies become more widely accepted by merchants and payment processors, their use as a medium of exchange will likely grow. Partnerships between cryptocurrency platforms and traditional financial institutions can facilitate this integration.

- **E-commerce:** The rise of e-commerce and digital payments presents a significant opportunity for cryptocurrencies to be used for online transactions.

**Regulatory Clarity:**

- **Framework Development:** Clear and consistent regulatory frameworks can provide the necessary legal certainty for businesses and consumers to adopt cryptocurrencies more confidently.
- **Consumer Protection:** Regulations can also help protect consumers and ensure the stability and integrity of the cryptocurrency market.

**Technological Advancements:**

- **Scalability Solutions:** Developments in blockchain technology, such as the implementation of Layer 2 solutions (e.g., Lightning Network for Bitcoin) and sharding (e.g., Ethereum 2.0), can address scalability issues and improve transaction speeds.
- **Interoperability:** Projects focused on interoperability, like Polkadot and Cosmos, can enable seamless transactions across different blockchain networks, enhancing the usability of cryptocurrencies.

**Financial Inclusion:**

- **Access to Banking:** Cryptocurrencies can provide financial services to the unbanked and underbanked populations, especially in regions with limited access to traditional banking infrastructure.
- **Remittances:** Cryptocurrencies can offer a cost-effective and efficient way to send remittances across borders, bypassing the high fees and slow processing times of traditional remittance services.

**Stablecoin Growth:**

- **Stable Payment Medium:** The increasing use of stablecoins can mitigate the volatility issue, making cryptocurrencies more practical for everyday transactions.
- **DeFi Integration:** Stablecoins play a crucial role in the growing decentralized finance (DeFi) ecosystem, providing liquidity and stability for various financial products and services.

## 7.2 SMART CONTRACTS IN INDUSTRIES

Smart contracts are self-executing contracts with the terms of the agreement directly written into code. They automatically enforce and execute the terms of the contract when predefined conditions are met. In the blockchain industry, smart contracts play a pivotal role in automating processes, reducing the need for intermediaries, enhancing security, and enabling innovative decentralized applications (DApps).

Smart contracts are a fundamental building block of blockchain technology, enabling automated, transparent, and secure execution of digital agreements and transactions. While they offer numerous benefits, including automation, transparency, security, and efficiency, smart contracts also face challenges related to code vulnerabilities, legal compliance, scalability, privacy, and interoperability. Despite these challenges, ongoing advancements in technology, legal frameworks, and industry collaboration are driving the widespread adoption and evolution of smart contracts across various blockchain industries.

### 7.2.1 Applications of Smart Contracts

**Decentralized Finance (DeFi):**

- **Lending and Borrowing:** Smart contracts enable peer-to-peer lending and borrowing platforms where users can collateralize assets and receive loans without the need for intermediaries.
- **Automated Market Making:** Decentralized exchanges (DEXs) use smart contracts to facilitate automated trading and liquidity provision without relying on centralized order books.

**Supply Chain Management:**

- **Traceability and Transparency:** Smart contracts facilitate transparent and traceable supply chain transactions by recording product movements, certifications, and payments on the blockchain.
- **Automated Payments:** Payment terms and conditions in supply chain contracts can be encoded into smart contracts, automating payments based on delivery milestones and quality assessments.

**Digital Identity:**

- **Self-Sovereign Identity:** Smart contracts enable individuals to manage their digital identities autonomously, granting or revoking access to personal information as needed without relying on centralized identity providers.
- **Authentication and Authorization:** Authentication and access control mechanisms can be enforced through smart contracts, ensuring secure and verifiable identity verification processes.

**Real Estate:**

- **Property Transactions:** Smart contracts streamline real estate transactions by automating processes such as title transfers, escrow services, and payment settlements, reducing the need for intermediaries and paperwork.
- **Tokenization:** Real estate assets can be tokenized and represented as digital tokens on the blockchain, with ownership rights enforced through smart contracts, enabling fractional ownership and increased liquidity.

**Gaming and Non-Fungible Tokens (NFTs):**

- **Digital Asset Ownership:** Smart contracts enable the creation and trading of unique digital assets, such as in-game items, collectibles, and artwork, represented as non-fungible tokens (NFTs) on blockchain platforms.
- **Royalty Payments:** NFT smart contracts can automate royalty payments to content creators and original owners whenever their digital assets are sold or traded in secondary markets.

### 7.2.2 Benefits of Smart Contracts

**Automation and Efficiency:**

- Smart contracts automate contract execution, reducing the need for manual intervention, paperwork, and administrative overhead.
- Processes such as payment settlements, asset transfers, and compliance checks can be executed automatically based on predefined conditions.

**Transparency and Immutability:**

- Transactions recorded on the blockchain through smart contracts are transparent, verifiable, and tamper-proof.
- Participants can trust the integrity of the data and transactions, as they are cryptographically secured and stored across multiple nodes in the network.

**Cost Reduction:**

- Smart contracts eliminate the need for intermediaries, such as lawyers, brokers, and escrow agents, reducing transaction costs and fees.
- Overheads associated with manual contract processing, reconciliation, and dispute resolution are minimized.

**Security and Trust:**

- Smart contracts are executed according to predefined rules and cryptographic protocols, reducing the risk of fraud, manipulation, and human error.

- The decentralized nature of blockchain networks ensures that no single party has control or authority over the execution of smart contracts.

**Global Accessibility:**

- Smart contracts can be deployed and accessed globally, enabling borderless transactions and interactions without the need for intermediaries or geographical restrictions.
- Anyone with internet access can interact with smart contracts, fostering financial inclusion and participation in the digital economy.

### 7.2.3 Challenges of Smart Contracts

**Code Vulnerabilities:**

- Smart contracts are susceptible to coding errors, bugs, and vulnerabilities that can lead to security breaches, exploits, and financial losses.
- Thorough code auditing, testing, and best practices for secure development are essential to mitigate these risks.

**Legal and Regulatory Compliance:**

- Legal enforceability and regulatory compliance of smart contracts may vary across jurisdictions, posing challenges for widespread adoption and acceptance.
- Hybrid approaches combining smart contracts with traditional legal frameworks may be necessary to address legal uncertainties and ensure enforceability.

**Scalability:**

- Scalability remains a challenge for blockchain platforms hosting smart contracts, as transaction throughput and processing speeds may be limited, especially during periods of high network congestion.
- Research and development efforts are underway to improve blockchain scalability through layer 2 solutions, sharding, and optimized consensus mechanisms.

**Privacy and Confidentiality:**

- Public blockchain networks may lack privacy features, exposing sensitive contract details, transaction history, and participant identities to the public.
- Privacy-enhancing technologies, such as zero-knowledge proofs and

private transactions, are being developed to address privacy concerns while maintaining transparency and integrity.

**Interoperability:**

- Interoperability between different blockchain platforms and smart contract languages is essential for seamless integration and collaboration across diverse ecosystems.
- Standardization efforts and interoperability protocols aim to facilitate communication and data exchange between disparate blockchain networks and applications.

### 7.2.4 Future Outlook and Trends

**Integration with Emerging Technologies:**

- Integration with emerging technologies such as artificial intelligence (AI), Internet of Things (IoT), and decentralized finance (DeFi) will enhance the capabilities and use cases of smart contracts.
- Smart contracts can automate decision-making processes, IoT device interactions, and complex financial transactions in decentralized ecosystems.

**Hybrid Smart Contracts:**

- Hybrid smart contracts that combine on-chain and off-chain components, known as "oracle" services, will bridge the gap between blockchain-based contracts and real-world events and data.
- Oracles provide external data feeds to smart contracts, enabling them to interact with off-chain systems, APIs, and external events, expanding their utility and functionality.

**Enterprise Adoption:**

- Increased adoption of smart contracts by enterprises and governments for a wide range of applications, including supply chain management, digital identity, regulatory compliance, and procurement.
- Integration with enterprise resource planning (ERP) systems and business process automation platforms will streamline enterprise workflows and operations.

**Legal and Regulatory Frameworks:**

- Development of legal and regulatory frameworks tailored to smart contracts, blockchain technology, and decentralized applications to provide clarity, certainty, and enforceability.

- Collaboration between policymakers, legal experts, and industry stakeholders to address legal challenges, promote innovation, and foster responsible adoption of smart contracts.

**Interoperability Standards:**

- Standardization of smart contract languages, protocols, and interoperability standards to enable seamless communication and collaboration between different blockchain networks, platforms, and ecosystems.
- Interoperability initiatives aim to create a unified and interoperable infrastructure for deploying and executing smart contracts across diverse blockchain environments.

## 7.3 SUPPLY CHAIN MANAGEMENT ON BLOCKCHAIN

Supply chain management (SCM) involves the coordination and integration of various processes, resources, and activities across the entire supply chain, from raw material sourcing to the delivery of finished products to customers. Blockchain technology offers unique capabilities that can revolutionize traditional supply chain management practices by providing transparency, traceability, efficiency, and security.

Blockchain technology holds immense promise for transforming supply chain management by providing transparency, traceability, efficiency, and security across the entire supply chain.

While there are challenges to overcome, including integration complexity, scalability concerns, and regulatory uncertainties, ongoing advancements in blockchain technology, interoperability solutions, and industry collaboration are paving the way for widespread adoption. As organizations continue to recognize the value of blockchain in optimizing supply chain operations and driving business value, the future outlook for blockchain-enabled supply chain management remains promising.

### Applications of Blockchain in Supply Chain Management

**Traceability and Provenance:**

- Blockchain enables the transparent tracking of products throughout the supply chain, allowing stakeholders to verify the origin, authenticity, and journey of goods from production to consumption.
- Each transaction recorded on the blockchain provides an immutable record of product movements, facilitating compliance with regulations and quality control standards.

**Inventory Management:**

- Blockchain can streamline inventory management by providing real-time visibility into inventory levels, locations, and movements across multiple parties.
- Smart contracts can automate inventory replenishment, trigger reorder points, and facilitate just-in-time inventory management, reducing stockouts and excess inventory.

**Supplier Management:**

- Blockchain enhances supplier management by creating a decentralized and tamper-proof database of supplier information, certifications, and performance metrics.
- Smart contracts can automate supplier onboarding, payments, and contract execution, reducing administrative overhead and ensuring compliance with contractual terms.

**Logistics and Transportation:**

- Blockchain improves logistics and transportation by optimizing route planning, load optimization, and delivery scheduling.
- Smart contracts can automate freight payments, customs clearance, and documentation processes, reducing delays and errors in cross-border trade.

**Quality Assurance and Compliance:**

- Blockchain provides a transparent and auditable record of product quality inspections, certifications, and compliance with regulatory requirements.
- Smart contracts can enforce compliance with quality standards, trigger alerts for non-compliant products, and facilitate recalls when necessary.

## Benefits of Blockchain in Supply Chain Management

**Transparency and Trust:**

- Blockchain creates a shared and immutable record of transactions, enhancing trust and transparency among supply chain participants.
- Stakeholders can access real-time data on product movements, transactions, and inventory levels, reducing disputes and discrepancies.

**Traceability and Accountability:**

- Blockchain enables end-to-end traceability of products, allowing stakeholders to identify the source of any issues or defects quickly.

- With transparent and tamper-proof records, accountability is improved, leading to better quality control and risk management.

**Efficiency and Cost Savings:**

- Blockchain streamlines supply chain processes by reducing manual paperwork, intermediaries, and delays.
- Automation through smart contracts eliminates the need for third-party intermediaries, reducing administrative costs and processing times.

**Enhanced Security:**

- Blockchain's cryptographic features ensure data integrity and security, protecting sensitive information from unauthorized access or tampering.
- Decentralization reduces the risk of a single point of failure or data breach, enhancing resilience and data protection.

**Compliance and Sustainability:**

- Blockchain facilitates compliance with regulatory requirements, industry standards, and sustainability initiatives by providing transparent and auditable records.
- With improved visibility into supply chain operations, organizations can better monitor and report on their environmental, social, and governance (ESG) practices.

## Challenges of Implementing Blockchain in Supply Chain Management

- **Integration with Legacy Systems:** Integrating blockchain with existing supply chain management systems and legacy technologies can be complex and require significant investment in infrastructure and training.
- **Data Standardization:** Achieving interoperability and data standardization across different blockchain networks and supply chain participants is a challenge, as each organization may use different data formats and protocols.
- **Scalability:** Scalability remains a concern for blockchain networks, particularly in supply chains with high transaction volumes and large numbers of participants. As the number of transactions increases, blockchain networks may face congestion and slower transaction processing times.

- **Regulatory Compliance:** Regulatory uncertainty and evolving legal frameworks pose challenges for implementing blockchain in supply chain management, especially in highly regulated industries and cross-border trade.
- **Privacy and Confidentiality:** Balancing the need for transparency with the protection of sensitive business information and intellectual property is a challenge in blockchain-based supply chains. Privacy-enhancing technologies, such as zero-knowledge proofs and private transactions, can address confidentiality concerns but may add complexity to the system.

### Future Outlook and Trends

- **Interoperability Solutions:** Efforts to develop interoperability protocols and standards will enable seamless data exchange and collaboration across different blockchain networks and supply chain ecosystems.
- **Scalability Improvements:** Research and development efforts focused on scalability solutions, such as sharding, layer 2 scaling solutions, and optimized consensus mechanisms, will enhance blockchain's capacity to handle large-scale supply chain transactions.
- **Regulatory Clarity:** Clearer regulatory frameworks and guidelines for blockchain-based supply chain applications will provide legal certainty and encourage broader adoption by enterprises and governments.
- **Emerging Technologies Integration:** Integration with emerging technologies such as Internet of Things (IoT), artificial intelligence (AI), and big data analytics will further enhance the capabilities of blockchain-based supply chain management systems.
- **Industry Collaboration:** Increased collaboration among industry stakeholders, technology providers, and regulatory bodies will drive innovation and best practices in blockchain-enabled supply chain management.

## 7.4 IDENTITY MANAGEMENT AND AUTHENTICATION

Identity management and authentication are critical components of various industries, ensuring secure access to systems, data, and services. In the context of blockchain technology, identity management and authentication solutions are undergoing significant innovation, leveraging the decentralized and cryptographic properties of blockchain networks.

Identity management and authentication are fundamental aspects of blockchain industries, enabling secure and trustworthy interactions in digital ecosystems. While blockchain-based identity solutions offer numerous benefits, including security, privacy, interoperability, and cost efficiency, they also face challenges related to usability, regulatory compliance, scalability, privacy, and security. Ongoing advancements in technology, regulatory frameworks, and industry collaboration are driving the evolution of identity management and authentication in blockchain industries. As the adoption of blockchain-based identity solutions continues to grow, their impact on security, privacy, and trust in digital transactions will be increasingly profound, shaping the future of digital identity management.

### 7.4.1 Applications of Identity Management and Authentication in Blockchain Industries

**Digital Identity:**

- Blockchain enables the creation of self-sovereign digital identities, allowing individuals to control and manage their personal information without reliance on centralized authorities.
- Digital identities on the blockchain can be used for accessing online services, participating in decentralized applications (DApps), and verifying credentials.

**Decentralized Authentication:**

- Blockchain-based authentication solutions replace traditional username-password authentication methods with cryptographic keys and digital signatures.
- Users can authenticate themselves securely using private keys stored in their wallets, eliminating the need for passwords and reducing the risk of unauthorized access.

**Supply Chain Management:**

- Identity management on the blockchain facilitates secure and transparent supply chain transactions by verifying the identity and authenticity of participants, such as suppliers, manufacturers, and distributors.
- Digital signatures and cryptographic proofs ensure the integrity and provenance of product information recorded on the blockchain.

**Healthcare:**

- Blockchain-based identity management solutions enable secure and interoperable sharing of patient health records among healthcare providers while maintaining patient privacy and consent.

- Patients can control access to their medical data, grant permissions to healthcare professionals, and track the usage of their health information on the blockchain.

**Government Services:**

- Governments can leverage blockchain for identity management and authentication in citizen services, such as voting, taxation, and social welfare programs.
- Blockchain-based identity systems enhance transparency, security, and trust in government processes, reducing fraud and corruption.

## 7.4.2 Benefits of Identity Management and Authentication in Blockchain Industries

**Security and Integrity:**

- Blockchain provides a secure and tamper-proof platform for identity management and authentication, reducing the risk of identity theft, fraud, and unauthorized access.
- Cryptographic techniques ensure the integrity and confidentiality of identity-related data stored on the blockchain.

**Privacy and Control:**

- Self-sovereign identity solutions empower individuals to control their personal information, granting and revoking access as needed without relying on centralized authorities.
- Users can maintain privacy while selectively sharing identity attributes with trusted parties, enhancing privacy and data protection.

**Interoperability:**

- Blockchain-based identity systems promote interoperability and data portability across different platforms, services, and applications.
- Standardized protocols and open-source frameworks enable seamless integration and communication between diverse identity management solutions.

**Transparency and Trust:**

- Identity management on the blockchain enhances transparency and trust in digital transactions by providing verifiable and auditable records of identity-related activities.
- Participants can verify the authenticity and validity of identities using cryptographic proofs and consensus mechanisms.

**Cost Efficiency:**

- Blockchain-based identity management solutions reduce administrative overhead, operational costs, and reliance on intermediaries for identity verification and authentication.
- Automated identity processes and decentralized infrastructure minimize the need for manual intervention and paperwork.

### 7.4.3 Challenges of Identity Management and Authentication in Blockchain Industries

**User Experience:**

- User-friendly interfaces and seamless integration with existing systems are essential for widespread adoption of blockchain-based identity solutions.
- Improving usability and accessibility while maintaining security and privacy remains a challenge for developers and designers.

**Regulatory Compliance:**

- Regulatory compliance requirements, such as Know Your Customer (KYC) and Anti-Money Laundering (AML) regulations, pose challenges for blockchain-based identity solutions.
- Balancing regulatory requirements with privacy and data protection principles is essential for legal compliance and acceptance.

**Scalability:**

- Scalability is a concern for blockchain networks processing identity transactions, especially during periods of high demand and network congestion.
- Optimizing blockchain protocols, consensus mechanisms, and network infrastructure is necessary to handle increasing volumes of identity-related transactions.

**Data Privacy:**

- Ensuring privacy and confidentiality of identity-related data on the blockchain while enabling selective disclosure and verification of identity attributes is a complex challenge.
- Privacy-enhancing technologies, such as zero-knowledge proofs and homomorphic encryption, can address privacy concerns but may add complexity to identity systems.

**Identity Theft and Fraud:**

- Despite the security features of blockchain, identity theft, spoofing, and social engineering attacks remain potential risks in blockchain-based identity systems.
- Implementing robust authentication mechanisms, multi-factor authentication, and continuous monitoring are essential to mitigate these risks.

### 7.4.4 Future Outlook and Trends

**Interoperable Identity Standards:**

- Adoption of interoperable identity standards and protocols, such as Decentralized Identifiers (DIDs) and Verifiable Credentials, will facilitate seamless integration and communication between diverse identity systems.
- Standardization efforts by industry consortia, standards bodies, and open-source communities will drive interoperability and innovation in identity management.

**Privacy-Preserving Technologies:**

- Continued development of privacy-preserving technologies, such as zero-knowledge proofs, secure multi-party computation (MPC), and homomorphic encryption, will address privacy concerns while enabling secure identity transactions.
- Integration of privacy-enhancing techniques into blockchain platforms and identity solutions will enhance privacy, confidentiality, and data protection.

**Regulatory Frameworks:**

- Regulatory frameworks and compliance guidelines specific to blockchain-based identity management will provide legal clarity and certainty for developers, organizations, and users.
- Collaboration between policymakers, regulators, and industry stakeholders is essential to develop flexible, risk-based regulatory approaches that balance innovation with consumer protection.

**User-Centric Design:**

- Focus on user-centric design principles and human-centered approaches to enhance the usability, accessibility, and inclusivity of blockchain-based identity solutions.

- User education and awareness programs will empower individuals to understand and manage their digital identities effectively, fostering trust and adoption.

**Decentralized Identity Ecosystem:**

- Emergence of a vibrant ecosystem of decentralized identity providers, service providers, and application developers collaborating to create innovative identity solutions.
- Decentralized identity platforms and consortia will enable cross-border identity verification, portable credentials, and seamless user experiences across different domains and industries.

# CHAPTER 8
# CHALLENGES AND RISKS

## 8.1 SECURITY CONCERNS IN BLOCKCHAIN

Blockchain technology has garnered significant attention and acclaim for its potential to revolutionize various industries, ranging from finance to supply chain management. Its decentralized and immutable nature promises enhanced transparency, efficiency, and trust in transactions. However, alongside its numerous advantages, blockchain also presents a myriad of security concerns that must be addressed to realize its full potential securely.

Security concerns pose significant challenges to the widespread adoption and implementation of blockchain technology. From external threats such as double spending and 51% attacks to internal vulnerabilities like smart contract bugs and privacy concerns, blockchain networks face a multitude of risks that must be addressed to realize their full potential securely. By implementing robust security measures, fostering decentralization, and promoting education and awareness, we can enhance the security and resilience of blockchain ecosystems, paving the way for a more secure and trusted digital future.

### 8.1.1 Understanding Blockchain Security

At its core, blockchain is a distributed ledger technology that maintains a continuously growing list of records, or blocks, linked together through cryptographic hashes. Each block contains a timestamp and a reference to the previous block, creating a chain of blocks that is resistant to tampering and revision. This immutability is one of blockchain's key security features, as it ensures the integrity of the data stored on the network. However, despite its inherent security mechanisms, blockchain is not impervious to threats. Various vulnerabilities and attack vectors pose risks to the security and stability of blockchain networks, threatening the trust and reliability that underpin their adoption.

### 8.1.2 Common Security Threats

One of the most well-known security threats in blockchain is the double-spending attack. Double spending occurs when a user maliciously spends the same cryptocurrency more than once, effectively creating counterfeit coins. This threat undermines the integrity of the blockchain and erodes trust in the system. While blockchain consensus mechanisms, such as proof-of-work and proof-of-stake, are designed to prevent double spending, they are not immune to exploitation under certain conditions.

Another significant security concern is the 51% attack, wherein a single entity or group gains control of the majority of the network's computing power, enabling them to manipulate transactions and disrupt the consensus process. This attack exploits the decentralized nature of blockchain, highlighting the importance of decentralization in ensuring network security.

Sybil attacks pose another threat to blockchain security, wherein an attacker creates multiple fake identities to gain control or influence over the network. By controlling a significant portion of the network's nodes, the attacker can manipulate transactions and compromise the integrity of the blockchain.

Smart contract vulnerabilities also present a significant security risk in blockchain ecosystems. Smart contracts are self-executing contracts with the terms of the agreement directly written into code. However, flaws or bugs in smart contract code can lead to vulnerabilities that are exploited by attackers to steal funds or disrupt operations.

### 8.1.3 Privacy Concerns

In addition to external threats, privacy concerns also loom large in blockchain technology. While blockchain transactions are pseudonymous, meaning they are not directly linked to real-world identities, they are still traceable and subject to analysis. This lack of privacy poses risks to user anonymity and can lead to deanonymization, wherein transaction patterns are used to identify individuals.

### 8.1.4 Regulatory Challenges

Regulatory uncertainty and compliance requirements further complicate the security landscape for blockchain technology. The decentralized and global nature of blockchain networks presents challenges for regulators seeking to enforce laws and regulations governing financial transactions, identity verification, and data privacy. Jurisdictional issues and conflicting regulatory frameworks further exacerbate these challenges, creating a fragmented landscape that hampers innovation and adoption.

### 8.1.5 Scalability and Performance

Scalability remains a significant obstacle to blockchain security and adoption. As blockchain networks grow in size and scope, they face challenges related to transaction throughput, latency, and resource consumption. Scalability solutions, such as sharding and layer 2 protocols, aim to address these issues without compromising security or decentralization. However, implementing these solutions effectively requires careful consideration and testing to ensure they do not introduce new security vulnerabilities.

### 8.1.6 Interoperability

Interoperability is another key consideration for blockchain security. As blockchain ecosystems expand and diversify, the ability to exchange value and data seamlessly between different networks becomes increasingly important. However, interoperability introduces security risks, as cross-chain transactions expose networks to potential vulnerabilities and attack vectors. Standardizing protocols and establishing secure communication channels are essential for ensuring interoperability without compromising security.

### 8.1.7 Centralization Risks

While decentralization is a foundational principle of blockchain technology, centralization risks persist in various forms. Centralized exchanges, mining pools, and governance structures introduce single points of failure and concentration of power, undermining the security and resilience of blockchain networks. Promoting decentralization and distributed governance models is essential for mitigating centralization risks and safeguarding the integrity of blockchain ecosystems.

### 8.1.8 Quantum Computing Threat

The emergence of quantum computing poses a significant threat to blockchain security. Quantum computers have the potential to break existing cryptographic algorithms, rendering blockchain networks vulnerable to attacks. Research efforts to develop quantum-resistant cryptographic algorithms are underway, but significant challenges remain in achieving robust and scalable solutions capable of withstanding quantum threats.

### 8.1.9 Social Engineering and Phishing Attacks

Social engineering and phishing attacks pose additional risks to blockchain security. By exploiting human psychology and trust relationships, attackers can deceive users into revealing sensitive information or executing malicious transactions. Educating users about common attack vectors and implementing security best practices are critical for mitigating the risk of social engineering and phishing attacks.

### 8.1.10 Education and Awareness

Ultimately, education and awareness are key to addressing security concerns in blockchain technology. By empowering users with knowledge about potential risks and best practices for mitigating them, we can enhance the security and resilience of blockchain networks. Industry stakeholders, regulatory bodies, and educational institutions all play a role in promoting blockchain security awareness and fostering a culture of cybersecurity within the blockchain community.

## 8.2 SCALABILITY ISSUES AND TRANSACTION SPEED

### 8.2.1 Scalability Issues

Blockchain technology has emerged as a transformative force, promising decentralization, transparency, and security in various industries. However, as blockchain networks continue to grow in size and scope, they face significant challenges related to scalability. Scalability refers to the ability of a system to handle increasing demands without sacrificing performance or efficiency. In the context of blockchain, scalability issues arise primarily due to limitations in transaction throughput, latency, and resource consumption.

Scalability issues pose significant challenges to the widespread adoption and scalability of blockchain technology. Transaction throughput, latency, and resource consumption are among the key scalability concerns facing blockchain networks, limiting their performance and efficiency in real-world applications.

However, through innovations such as sharding, layer 2 solutions, consensus mechanism optimization, and blockchain interoperability, scalability solutions offer promising avenues for improving network scalability and performance. By addressing scalability challenges in a collaborative and systematic manner, blockchain technology can unlock its full potential as a scalable, secure, and decentralized infrastructure for the future.

#### Understanding Scalability in Blockchain

At its core, blockchain is a distributed ledger technology that maintains a continuously growing list of records, or blocks, linked together through cryptographic hashes.

Each block contains a set of transactions and a reference to the previous block, creating a chain of blocks that is resistant to tampering and revision. However, as more transactions are added to the blockchain, the size of the ledger grows, leading to scalability challenges.

Scalability issues in blockchain manifest in several ways. One of the primary concerns is transaction throughput, which refers to the number of transactions that can be processed per unit of time. As blockchain networks become congested with transactions, the time it takes to validate and confirm new transactions increases, leading to delays and higher fees. This congestion can result in a poor user experience and limit the scalability of blockchain applications.

Another scalability challenge is latency, or the time it takes for a transaction to be confirmed and added to the blockchain. High latency can hinder real-time transaction processing and limit the applicability of blockchain technology in time-sensitive applications such as financial transactions and supply chain management.

Resource consumption is also a critical scalability consideration in blockchain networks. As the size of the blockchain grows, so too does the storage and computational resources required to maintain and validate the network. This poses challenges for nodes participating in the consensus process, as well as for users running blockchain applications on resource-constrained devices.

## Scalability Solutions

Addressing scalability issues in blockchain requires a multi-faceted approach that combines technical innovations, protocol upgrades, and community collaboration. Several scalability solutions have been proposed and implemented to improve the performance and efficiency of blockchain networks.

- **Sharding:** Sharding is a technique that involves partitioning the blockchain into smaller, more manageable segments called shards. Each shard is responsible for processing a subset of transactions, reducing the burden on individual nodes and improving overall network throughput. Sharding can significantly increase scalability by parallelizing transaction processing and reducing congestion on the blockchain.
- **Layer 2 Solutions:** Layer 2 solutions, such as payment channels and sidechains, aim to offload transaction processing from the main blockchain while retaining its security guarantees. By moving transactions off-chain and settling them periodically on the main blockchain, layer 2 solutions can increase transaction throughput and reduce latency without compromising security or decentralization.
- **Consensus Mechanism Optimization:** Consensus mechanisms play a crucial role in blockchain scalability, as they determine how transactions are validated and added to the blockchain. Optimizing consensus mechanisms for scalability, such as transitioning from proof-of-work to proof-of-stake, can improve network efficiency and reduce resource consumption.
- **Blockchain Interoperability:** Interoperability between different blockchain networks allows for seamless exchange of value and data, enhancing scalability by distributing transaction load across multiple chains. By enabling cross-chain interoperability, blockchain networks can leverage the strengths of each platform while mitigating scalability limitations.

- **Off-Chain Computation**: Off-chain computation involves performing computationally intensive tasks outside of the blockchain and then recording the results on-chain. By offloading computation from the main blockchain, off-chain solutions can improve scalability and reduce congestion, particularly for applications requiring complex computations or large datasets.
- **Data Compression and Pruning**: Data compression and pruning techniques aim to reduce the size of the blockchain by removing unnecessary or redundant data. By compressing transaction data and removing old or obsolete blocks, blockchain networks can reduce storage requirements and improve scalability without compromising data integrity.

### Challenges and Considerations

While scalability solutions offer promising avenues for addressing blockchain scalability, they also present challenges and considerations that must be carefully evaluated. For example, sharding introduces complexities related to shard coordination and cross-shard transactions, while layer 2 solutions require robust security mechanisms to prevent fraud and ensure trustless operation.

Furthermore, scalability improvements must be balanced with considerations for decentralization, security, and consensus. Changes to blockchain protocols and consensus mechanisms can impact network security and resilience, requiring thorough analysis and testing to ensure compatibility and stability.

Additionally, achieving scalability in blockchain requires collaboration and consensus among stakeholders, including developers, miners, node operators, and users. Community engagement and participation are essential for implementing scalability solutions effectively and ensuring the long-term success of blockchain networks.

## 8.2.2 Transaction Speed

Blockchain technology has gained widespread recognition for its potential to revolutionize various industries by providing decentralized, transparent, and secure transaction systems. However, one of the significant challenges facing blockchain networks is transaction speed. Transaction speed refers to the time it takes for a transaction to be processed, confirmed, and added to the blockchain.

Transaction speed is a critical consideration for the scalability and usability of blockchain networks. Factors such as network congestion, block size, consensus mechanism, and transaction fees influence transaction speed and scalability, impacting user experience, scalability, and decentralization. However, through innovations such as optimized consensus mechanisms, layer 2 scaling solutions, increased block size, transaction fee optimization, off-chain computation, and blockchain interoperability, blockchain networks can enhance transaction speed and scalability, unlocking their full potential as scalable, efficient, and decentralized transaction systems for the future.

### Factors Influencing Transaction Speed

Several factors contribute to the speed of transactions in blockchain networks:

- **Network Congestion**: High transaction volumes can lead to network congestion, causing delays in transaction processing and confirmation. As more transactions compete for limited block space, miners prioritize transactions with higher fees, resulting in slower confirmation times for transactions with lower fees.
- **Block Size**: The size of blocks in the blockchain determines the maximum number of transactions that can be included in each block. Larger block sizes can accommodate more transactions per block, increasing throughput and reducing congestion. However, larger blocks also require more computational resources to process, leading to scalability challenges.
- **Consensus Mechanism**: The consensus mechanism used by a blockchain network affects transaction speed and throughput. Proof-of-work (PoW) consensus mechanisms, such as those used by Bitcoin, require miners to solve complex mathematical puzzles to validate transactions and add them to the blockchain. This process can be time-consuming and resource-intensive, leading to slower transaction speeds. In contrast, proof-of-stake (PoS) and delegated proof-of-stake (DPoS) consensus mechanisms, such as those used by Ethereum 2.0 and EOS, respectively, aim to improve transaction speed and scalability by reducing the computational overhead associated with block validation.
- **Network Latency**: Network latency, or the time it takes for data to travel between nodes on the blockchain network, can impact transaction speed. Higher latency can lead to delays in transaction propagation and confirmation, particularly in geographically distributed networks.
- **Transaction Fee**: Transaction fees play a crucial role in determining transaction priority in blockchain networks. Miners prioritize transactions with higher fees, as they provide greater incentives for block validation. Consequently, transactions with lower fees may

experience longer confirmation times during periods of network congestion.

## Implications of Slow Transaction Speeds

Slow transaction speeds can have several implications for blockchain networks and their users:

- **Poor User Experience:** Long confirmation times and delays in transaction processing can result in a poor user experience, particularly for applications requiring real-time transactions, such as payments and gaming.
- **Scalability Limitations:** Slow transaction speeds limit the scalability of blockchain networks, as they restrict the maximum number of transactions that can be processed per unit of time. This scalability bottleneck hampers the adoption of blockchain technology for mainstream applications with high transaction throughput requirements.
- **Increased Transaction Costs:** High transaction fees and congestion-related delays can increase transaction costs for users, discouraging participation and limiting accessibility.
- **Network Centralization:** Inefficient consensus mechanisms and scalability limitations can lead to centralization pressures, as larger miners and validators gain disproportionate influence over transaction processing and block validation. This concentration of power undermines the decentralization and security of blockchain networks.

## Solutions to Enhance Transaction Speed and Scalability

Several solutions have been proposed to address the challenges of slow transaction speeds and scalability in blockchain networks:

- **Optimized Consensus Mechanisms:** Optimizing consensus mechanisms, such as transitioning from proof-of-work to proof-of-stake or implementing sharding techniques, can improve transaction speed and scalability by reducing the computational overhead and resource requirements associated with block validation.
- **Layer 2 Scaling Solutions:** Layer 2 scaling solutions, such as payment channels and sidechains, aim to offload transaction processing from the main blockchain while retaining its security guarantees. By moving transactions off-chain and settling them periodically on the main blockchain, layer 2 solutions can increase transaction throughput and reduce latency without compromising security or decentralization.

- **Increased Block Size**: Increasing the block size limit in blockchain networks can accommodate more transactions per block, improving throughput and reducing congestion. However, larger blocks also require more storage and bandwidth, leading to scalability challenges.
- **Transaction Fee Optimization**: Dynamic fee adjustment algorithms and fee market mechanisms can optimize transaction fees based on network congestion and demand, ensuring fair and efficient transaction processing while incentivizing miners to prioritize high-value transactions.
- **Off-Chain Computation**: Off-chain computation techniques involve performing computationally intensive tasks outside of the blockchain and then recording the results on-chain. By offloading computation from the main blockchain, off-chain solutions can improve scalability and reduce congestion, particularly for applications requiring complex computations or large datasets.

## 8.3 REGULATORY CHALLENGES AND LEGAL IMPLICATIONS

Blockchain technology has rapidly gained traction across various industries due to its decentralized, transparent, and immutable nature. However, as blockchain applications continue to proliferate, they encounter a complex web of regulatory challenges and legal implications.

Regulatory challenges and legal implications pose significant hurdles for blockchain projects seeking to innovate and operate in a compliant manner. The fragmented regulatory landscape, unclear legal frameworks, and compliance requirements create uncertainty and complexity for blockchain businesses, hindering adoption and investment in the sector. However, by understanding key legal considerations, engaging with regulators, implementing compliance by design principles, seeking legal counsel and compliance expertise, and participating in regulatory sandbox programs, blockchain projects can navigate regulatory challenges effectively and build trust and confidence among users, investors, and regulators. Despite the regulatory challenges, blockchain technology holds immense potential to transform industries and drive innovation, provided that regulatory barriers are addressed in a collaborative and proactive manner.

### 8.3.1 Understanding Regulatory Challenges

- **Fragmented Regulatory Landscape**: The regulatory environment for blockchain technology varies significantly from one jurisdiction to another. While some countries have embraced blockchain innovation and enacted supportive regulations, others have adopted a more cautious or hostile approach. This fragmented regulatory landscape creates uncertainty for blockchain businesses and inhibits global adoption and interoperability.

- **Unclear Legal Frameworks:** The legal frameworks governing blockchain technology are often ambiguous or outdated, failing to address the unique characteristics and challenges of decentralized systems. As a result, blockchain projects may face regulatory hurdles, compliance risks, and legal uncertainties, hindering innovation and investment in the sector.
- **Compliance Requirements:** Blockchain projects must navigate a myriad of compliance requirements, including anti-money laundering (AML), know-your-customer (KYC), securities regulations, tax obligations, and data protection laws. Ensuring compliance with these regulations is essential for mitigating legal risks and maintaining the trust and confidence of users, investors, and regulators.

### 8.3.2 Key Legal Considerations

- **Securities Regulation:** The classification of tokens and digital assets as securities has significant legal implications for blockchain projects. Securities regulations govern the issuance, trading, and sale of securities, imposing disclosure requirements, registration obligations, and investor protections. Failure to comply with securities regulations can result in regulatory enforcement actions, fines, and legal liabilities.
- **AML and KYC Compliance:** Blockchain projects that involve the transfer or exchange of digital assets are subject to anti-money laundering (AML) and know-your-customer (KYC) regulations. Implementing robust AML and KYC procedures is essential for preventing illicit activities, such as money laundering, terrorist financing, and fraud, and for maintaining regulatory compliance.
- **Data Protection and Privacy:** Blockchain technology raises significant data protection and privacy concerns due to its immutable and transparent nature. While blockchain offers enhanced security and transparency, it also poses challenges for data privacy and compliance with data protection laws, such as the General Data Protection Regulation (GDPR) in the European Union. Ensuring data privacy and compliance with data protection regulations is critical for building trust and maintaining regulatory compliance.
- **Smart Contract Legality:** Smart contracts, self-executing contracts with the terms of the agreement directly written into code, raise legal questions regarding their enforceability, validity, and compliance with

contract law. Legal issues related to smart contracts include contract interpretation, performance, enforceability, and dispute resolution. Clarifying the legal status of smart contracts and addressing legal uncertainties is essential for facilitating their widespread adoption and use.

### 8.3.3 Navigating Regulatory Challenges

- **Engagement with Regulators:** Engaging with regulators and policymakers is essential for shaping blockchain regulations and addressing regulatory concerns effectively. Blockchain projects should proactively engage with regulators, industry associations, and policymakers to educate them about blockchain technology, address regulatory concerns, and advocate for favorable regulatory frameworks.
- **Compliance by Design:** Implementing compliance by design principles involves integrating regulatory compliance requirements into the design and development of blockchain projects from the outset. By incorporating compliance mechanisms, such as AML and KYC procedures, data privacy safeguards, and legal compliance frameworks, blockchain projects can mitigate legal risks and ensure regulatory compliance throughout the project lifecycle.
- **Legal Counsel and Compliance Experts:** Seeking legal counsel and compliance expertise from professionals with experience in blockchain regulations and legal frameworks is essential for navigating regulatory challenges effectively. Legal advisors and compliance experts can provide guidance on regulatory compliance requirements, legal risks, and best practices for mitigating legal liabilities.
- **Regulatory Sandbox Programs:** Regulatory sandbox programs offer a controlled environment for blockchain projects to test innovative solutions and demonstrate compliance with regulatory requirements under the supervision of regulators. Participating in regulatory sandbox programs can provide blockchain projects with regulatory certainty, guidance, and support for navigating regulatory challenges.

## 8.4 ENVIRONMENTAL IMPACT AND ENERGY CONSUMPTION

### 8.4.1 Environmental Impact

Blockchain technology has emerged as a transformative force, promising decentralized, transparent, and secure transaction systems across various industries. However, the environmental impact of blockchain has become a growing concern, particularly due to the energy-intensive consensus mechanisms employed by some blockchain networks. The environmental impact of blockchain technology is a pressing concern that must be addressed to ensure its long-term sustainability and viability. The energy-intensive nature of blockchain mining operations, coupled with the carbon emissions and e-waste generated, highlights the need for proactive measures to mitigate its environmental impact. By transitioning to more energy-efficient consensus mechanisms, integrating renewable energy sources, adopting energy-efficient mining technologies, and implementing carbon offsetting initiatives, blockchain projects can reduce their carbon footprint and contribute to environmental sustainability. As blockchain technology continues to evolve and expand, it is essential to prioritize environmental considerations and embrace sustainable practices to minimize its environmental impact and foster a greener future.

### Understanding the Environmental Impact

- **Energy Consumption:** One of the primary environmental concerns associated with blockchain technology is its high energy consumption, particularly in proof-of-work (PoW) consensus mechanisms. PoW consensus mechanisms, such as those used by Bitcoin and Ethereum, require miners to solve complex mathematical puzzles to validate transactions and add them to the blockchain. This process consumes vast amounts of computational power and electricity, contributing to carbon emissions and environmental degradation.
- **Carbon Footprint:** The energy-intensive nature of blockchain mining operations has led to a significant carbon footprint for some blockchain networks. The carbon footprint of blockchain is calculated based on the energy consumption of mining operations and the carbon intensity of the electricity used. High carbon emissions associated with blockchain mining have raised concerns about its environmental sustainability and contribution to climate change.
- **E-Waste:** In addition to energy consumption and carbon emissions, blockchain mining also generates electronic waste (e-waste) due to the rapid turnover of mining hardware and equipment. As mining hardware becomes obsolete or inefficient, it is discarded and replaced with newer, more powerful hardware, leading to the accumulation of e-waste and environmental pollution.

### Factors Contributing to Environmental Impact

- **Proof-of-Work Consensus Mechanism:** Proof-of-work (PoW) consensus mechanisms, such as those used by Bitcoin and Ethereum, are the primary contributors to the environmental impact of blockchain.

PoW requires miners to solve complex mathematical puzzles through trial and error, consuming vast amounts of computational power and electricity. As blockchain networks grow and the difficulty of mining increases, so too does their energy consumption and carbon footprint.

- **Energy Sources:** The environmental impact of blockchain mining operations is influenced by the sources of energy used to power them. Mining operations powered by fossil fuels, such as coal and natural gas, have a higher carbon footprint compared to those powered by renewable energy sources, such as solar, wind, and hydroelectric power. The carbon intensity of electricity generation plays a significant role in determining the environmental sustainability of blockchain networks.
- **Hardware Efficiency:** The efficiency of mining hardware and equipment also affects the environmental impact of blockchain mining operations. More efficient hardware consumes less energy per hash and produces fewer carbon emissions per transaction. Improvements in hardware efficiency and the adoption of energy-efficient mining technologies can help reduce the environmental footprint of blockchain networks.

## Mitigating Environmental Impact

- **Transition to Proof-of-Stake:** Transitioning from proof-of-work (PoW) to proof-of-stake (PoS) consensus mechanisms can significantly reduce the energy consumption and environmental impact of blockchain networks. Unlike PoW, which relies on computational power and electricity consumption, PoS selects validators to create and validate new blocks based on their stake or ownership of cryptocurrency. PoS requires minimal energy consumption, making it a more environmentally sustainable alternative to PoW.
- **Renewable Energy Integration:** Increasing the use of renewable energy sources, such as solar, wind, and hydroelectric power, to power blockchain mining operations can reduce their carbon footprint and environmental impact. Integrating renewable energy into blockchain networks promotes sustainability and reduces reliance on fossil fuels, mitigating the environmental consequences of energy-intensive mining operations.
- **Energy-Efficient Mining Technologies:** Developing and deploying energy-efficient mining technologies and hardware can help reduce the energy consumption and environmental impact of blockchain mining operations. Innovations such as energy-efficient mining chips, cooling systems, and optimization algorithms can improve the efficiency of mining hardware and reduce energy waste.

- **Carbon Offsetting and Carbon Neutrality:** Implementing carbon offsetting initiatives and strategies can help blockchain projects mitigate their carbon footprint and environmental impact. Carbon offsetting involves investing in projects that reduce or offset greenhouse gas emissions, such as reforestation, renewable energy development, and energy efficiency initiatives. By offsetting their carbon emissions, blockchain projects can achieve carbon neutrality and contribute to global climate action efforts.

### 8.4.2 Energy Consumption

Blockchain technology has revolutionized various industries with its promise of decentralized, transparent, and secure transactions. However, one of the most significant challenges facing blockchain networks is their energy consumption. Energy consumption is a significant challenge facing blockchain technology, particularly due to the energy-intensive nature of proof-of-work (PoW) consensus mechanisms.

The growth of blockchain networks and the increasing demand for mining operations contribute to higher energy usage and carbon emissions. However, by transitioning to more energy-efficient consensus mechanisms, deploying energy-efficient mining technologies, integrating renewable energy sources, and optimizing resource allocation, blockchain networks can mitigate their environmental impact and promote sustainability. As blockchain technology continues to evolve, it is essential to prioritize energy efficiency and environmental sustainability to ensure its long-term viability and contribution to a greener future.

#### Understanding Energy Consumption

- **Proof-of-Work (PoW) Mechanism:** The primary driver of energy consumption in blockchain networks is the proof-of-work (PoW) consensus mechanism. PoW requires miners to solve complex mathematical puzzles to validate transactions and add them to the blockchain. This process involves vast amounts of computational power and electricity, leading to high energy consumption.
- **Mining Operations:** Mining operations, which involve running specialized hardware and software to solve PoW puzzles, consume significant amounts of energy. Miners compete to find the solution to the PoW puzzle, with the first miner to solve it earning the right to add a new block to the blockchain and receive a reward in the form of cryptocurrency. The energy-intensive nature of mining operations contributes to the overall energy consumption of blockchain networks.

- **Network Growth:** As blockchain networks grow in size and complexity, their energy consumption also increases. More miners join the network, competing for block rewards and contributing to higher energy usage. Additionally, as the difficulty of mining increases over time, miners require more powerful hardware and consume more energy to remain competitive.

## Factors Contributing to Energy Consumption

- **Hardware Efficiency:** The efficiency of mining hardware and equipment plays a significant role in determining energy consumption. More efficient hardware consumes less energy per hash and produces fewer carbon emissions per transaction. However, as blockchain networks become more competitive, miners may upgrade to newer, more powerful hardware to maintain their competitive edge, leading to higher energy consumption.
- **Electricity Costs:** The cost of electricity also influences energy consumption in blockchain mining operations. Mining operations located in regions with lower electricity costs may consume more energy to maximize profits. Conversely, miners operating in regions with higher electricity costs may seek to reduce energy consumption to minimize operating expenses.
- **Renewable Energy Usage:** The sources of energy used to power blockchain mining operations impact their environmental sustainability. Mining operations powered by renewable energy sources, such as solar, wind, and hydroelectric power, have a lower carbon footprint compared to those powered by fossil fuels, such as coal and natural gas. Integrating renewable energy into blockchain networks can reduce their environmental impact and promote sustainability.

## Mitigating Energy Consumption

- **Transition to Proof-of-Stake (PoS):** Transitioning from proof-of-work (PoW) to proof-of-stake (PoS) consensus mechanisms can significantly reduce energy consumption in blockchain networks. Unlike PoW, which requires miners to solve computationally intensive puzzles, PoS selects validators to create and validate new blocks based on their stake or ownership of cryptocurrency. PoS requires minimal energy consumption, making it a more environmentally sustainable alternative to PoW.
- **Energy-Efficient Mining Technologies:** Developing and deploying energy-efficient mining technologies and hardware can help reduce

energy consumption in blockchain mining operations. Innovations such as energy-efficient mining chips, cooling systems, and optimization algorithms can improve the efficiency of mining hardware and reduce energy waste.

- **Renewable Energy Integration:** Increasing the use of renewable energy sources, such as solar, wind, and hydroelectric power, to power blockchain mining operations can further reduce their energy consumption and environmental impact. Integrating renewable energy into blockchain networks promotes sustainability and reduces reliance on fossil fuels.
- **Efficient Resource Allocation:** Optimizing resource allocation and utilization in blockchain networks can help minimize energy consumption. By prioritizing energy-efficient mining operations and incentivizing renewable energy usage, blockchain networks can reduce their environmental footprint while maintaining network security and integrity.

# CHAPTER 9
# BLOCKCHAIN IN FINANCE AND BANKING

## 9.1 DECENTRALIZED FINANCE (DEFI)

Decentralized finance (often stylized as DeFi) offers financial instruments without relying on intermediaries such as brokerages, exchanges, or banks by using smart contracts on a blockchain, mainly Ethereum.

DeFi platforms allow people to lend or borrow funds from others, speculate on price movements on assets using derivatives, trade cryptocurrencies, insure against risks, and earn interest in savings-like accounts. DeFi uses a layered architecture and highly composable building blocks. Some applications promote high-interest rates but are subject to high risk. Coding errors and hacks have been common in DeFi.

### 9.1.1 History

Decentralized exchanges (abbreviated DEXs) are alternative payment ecosystems with new protocols for financial transactions that emerged within the framework of decentralized finance, which is part of blockchain technology and fintech.

CEXs (centralized exchanges), DEXs and DEX aggregators are all built on the multi-layered DeFi architecture or components, where each layer serves a well-defined purpose.

While they share common components of the first four layers, such as *the Settlement layer*, *Asset layer*, *Protocol layer* and *Application layer*, DEX aggregators have an additional component or *Aggregator layer*, which allows them to connect and interact with other DEXs via smart contracts.

The Ethereum blockchain popularized smart contracts, which are the basis of DeFi, in 2017. Other blockchains have since implemented smart contracts.

MakerDAO is a prominent lending DeFi platform based on a stablecoin that was established in 2017. It allows users to borrow DAI, a token pegged to the US dollar. Through a set of smart contracts that govern the loan, repayment, and liquidation processes, MakerDAO aims to maintain the stable value of DAI in a decentralized and autonomous manner.

In June 2020, Compound Finance, a decentralized finance protocol enabling users to lend or borrow cryptocurrency assets and which provides typical interest payments to lenders, started rewarding lenders and borrowers with a cryptocurrency called Comp. This token, which is used for running Compound, can also be traded on cryptocurrency exchanges. Other platforms followed suit, leading to stacked investment opportunities known as "yield farming" or "liquidity mining", where speculators shift cryptocurrency assets between pools in a platform and between platforms to maximize their total yield, which includes not only interest and fees but also the value of additional tokens received as rewards.

In July 2020, *The Washington Post* described decentralized finance techniques and the risks involved. In September 2020, Bloomberg said that DeFi made up two-thirds of the cryptocurrency market in terms of price changes and that DeFi collateral levels had reached $9 billion. Ethereum saw a rise in developers during 2020 due to the increased interest in DeFi.

DeFi has attracted venture capitalists such as Andreessen Horowitz and Michael Novogratz.

*The Economist* regarded the future of digital finance in 2022 as a "three-way fight" between: Big Tech, such as Facebook with its digital wallet; "big rich countries" that have been testing their own digital currencies; and software developers "building all sorts of applications" to decentralize finance. Handling the risks presented by crypto-assets already valued at $2.5 trillion was a particular challenge for US regulators.

### 9.1.2 Key Characteristics

DeFi revolves around decentralized applications, also known as DApps, that perform financial functions on distributed ledgers called blockchains, a technology that was made popular by Bitcoin and has since been adapted more broadly. Rather than transactions being made through a centralized intermediary such as a cryptocurrency exchange or a traditional securities exchange, transactions are directly made between participants, mediated by smart contract programs. These smart contracts, or DeFi protocols, typically run using open-source software that is built and maintained by a community of developers.

DApps are typically accessed through a browser extension or application. For example, MetaMask allows users to directly interact with Ethereum through a digital wallet. Many of these DApps can be linked to create complex financial services. For example, stablecoin holders can lend assets such as USD Coin or DAI to a liquidity pool in a borrow/lending protocol such as Aave Protocol, and allow others to borrow those digital assets by depositing their own collateral. The protocol automatically adjusts interest rates based on the demand for the asset.

Some DApps source external (off-chain) data, such as the price of an asset, through blockchain oracles.

Additionally, Aave Protocol introduced "flash loans", which are uncollateralized loans of an arbitrary amount that are taken out and paid back within a single blockchain transaction. Many exploits of DeFi platforms have used flash loans to manipulate cryptocurrency spot prices.

Another DeFi protocol is Uniswap, which is a decentralized exchange (DEX) set up to trade tokens issued on Ethereum. Rather than using a centralized exchange to fill orders, Uniswap pays users to form liquidity pools in exchange for a percentage of the fees collected from traders swapping tokens in and out of the liquidity pools. Because no centralized party runs Uniswap (the platform is governed by its users), and any development team can use the open-source software, there is no entity to check the identities of the people using the platform and meet KYC/AML regulations. As of 2020, it is not clear what position regulators will take on the legality of such platforms.

### 9.1.3 Decentralized Exchanges

Decentralized exchanges (DEX) are a type of cryptocurrency exchange, which allow for either direct peer-to-peer, or Automated Market Maker (AMM) liquidity pool cryptocurrency transactions to take place without the need for an intermediary. The lack of an intermediary differentiates them from centralized exchanges (CEX).

In transactions made through decentralized exchanges, the typical third party entities which would normally oversee the security and transfer of assets (e.g., banks, stockbrokers, online payment gateways, government institutions, etc.) are substituted by a blockchain or distributed ledger.

Some common methods of operation include the use of smart contracts or order book relaying – although many other variations are possible, with differing degrees of decentralization.

Because traders on a decentralized exchange often do not need to transfer their assets to the exchange before executing a trade, decentralized exchanges reduce the risk of theft from hacking of exchanges, but liquidity providers do need to transfer tokens to the decentralized exchange. Decentralized exchanges are also more anonymous than exchanges that implement know your customer (KYC) requirements.

There are some signs that decentralized exchanges have been suffering from low trading volumes and reduced market liquidity. The 0x project, a protocol for building decentralized exchanges with interchangeable liquidity, attempts to solve this issue.

## Disadvantages

Due to a lack of KYC processes, and no way to revert a transaction, users are at a loss if they are ever hacked for their passwords or private keys. Additionally, liquidity providers staking in DeFi protocols can suffer what is called an impermanent loss if, when withdrawn, the token pairs they have invested have altered in value ratio significantly.

Although liquidity pool DEX are the most widely used, they may have some drawbacks. The most common problems of liquidity pool DEXes are market price impact, slippage, and front running.

Price impact occurs because of the AMM (Automated Market Makers) nature itself — the larger the deal, the stronger impact it has on the price. For example, if the constant product AMM is in use, every deal must keep the product $xy = k$ constant, where x and y are quantities of two cryptocurrencies (or tokens) in the pool. Price impact is non-linear, so the larger is the input amount $\Delta x$, the lower is the final ratio $y/x$ that gives an exchange price. The problem is mostly significant for relatively large deals versus the liquidity pool size.

Front running is a special type of attack in public blockchains when some participant (usually a miner) seeing an upcoming trading transaction puts his own transaction ahead (playing with a transaction fee for example), making the initial transaction less profitable or even reverted. To provide some protection against front running attacks, many DeFi exchanges offer a slippage tolerance option for end-users. This option serves as a safeguard, allowing users to set a limit on the worst acceptable price they are willing to accept from the time of transaction signing.

## Degrees of Decentralization

A decentralized exchange can still have centralized components, whereby some control of the exchange is still in the hands of a central authority. The governance of a DeFi platform, typically as part of a Decentralized Autonomous Organization, is done through tokens that grant voting rights and are distributed amongst participants. However, the majority of these tokens are often held by few individuals and are rarely used to vote.

In July 2018, the decentralized exchange Bancor was reportedly hacked and suffered a loss of $13.5M in assets before freezing funds. In a Tweet, Charlie Lee, the creator of Litecoin spoke out and claimed an exchange cannot be decentralized if it can lose or freeze customer funds.

Operators of decentralized exchanges can face legal consequences from government regulators. One example is the founder of EtherDelta, who in November 2018 settled charges with the U.S. Securities and Exchange Commission over operating an unregistered securities exchange.

### 9.1.4 Errors and Hacking

Coding errors and hacks are common in DeFi. Blockchain transactions are irreversible, which means that an incorrect or fraudulent DeFi transaction cannot be corrected easily. The person or entity behind a DeFi protocol may be unknown and may disappear with investors' money. Investor Michael Novogratz has described some DeFi protocols as "Ponzi-like".

DeFi has been compared to the initial coin offering craze of 2017, part of a cryptocurrency bubble. Inexperienced investors are at particular risk of losing money because of the sophistication required to interact with DeFi platforms and the lack of any intermediary with customer support. On the other hand, as the code for DeFi smart contracts is generally open-source software that can be copied to set up competing platforms, experienced users and user-created bots might create instabilities as funds shift between platforms which share the same code. In addition, DeFi platforms might inadvertently provide incentives for cryptocurrency miners to destabilize the system.

In 2021, half of cryptocurrency crime was related to DeFi. This rise has been attributed to a combination of developer incompetence and non-existent or poorly enforced regulations. Theft from DeFi can come from either external hackers stealing from vulnerable projects, or "rug pulls", where the developers and influencers promote a project and then take the money, as a form of pump-and-dump.

### 9.1.5 Regulation

In October 2021, the FATF included DeFi in the guidance for crypto service providers, making the authority's aim to regulate this type of asset. They are expecting each individual country to determine if individuals involved in DeFi can be considered a virtual asset provider and be subjected to the FATF's guidelines.

## 9.2 CENTRAL BANK DIGITAL CURRENCIES (CBDCS)

A central bank digital currency (CBDC; also called digital fiat currency or digital base money) is a digital currency issued by a central bank, rather than by a commercial bank. It is also a liability of the central bank and denominated in the sovereign currency, as is the case with physical banknotes and coins.

The two primary categories of CBDCs are retail and wholesale. Retail CBDCs are designed for households and businesses to make payments for everyday transactions, whereas wholesale CBDCs are designed for financial institutions and operate similarly to central bank reserves.

Retail CBDCs can be distributed through various models. In the intermediated model, the central bank issues the CBDC and manages core infrastructures, while financial intermediaries offer customer services. The ECB and the Federal Reserve have proposed intermediated CBDCs. Alternatively, the central bank could either provide the full service or delegate responsibilities further.

The present concept of CBDCs differs from virtual currency and cryptocurrency in that a CBDC would be issued by a state. Most CBDC implementations will likely not use or need any sort of distributed ledger such as a blockchain.

In 2023, over 120 different jurisdictions, including major economies like the ECB, UK, and the US, were evaluating national digital currencies. As it currently stands, 9 countries and the 8 islands making up the Eastern Caribbean Currency Union have launched CBDCs; 38 countries and Hong Kong have CBDC pilot programs; and 67 countries and 2 currency unions are researching CBDCs. In the United States, some states have introduced legislation to ban state payments using CBDCs with Florida being the first state to pass such a law citing privacy concerns.

CBDCs have faced a plethora of criticisms among those being that a "centrally managed, centrally controlled, CBDC is a tool for coercion and control" and that it would "allow the government to spy on" the citizenry. Some critics of CBDCs say Bitcoin is a better currency alternative that is "global, immutable, and accessible digital cash open to all," as well as "decentralized, open, and permissionless," since it does not rely on a central bank such as the Federal Reserve.

### 9.2.1 History

Although the term "CBDC" did not become widely used until after 2019, central banks have researched and launched digital currency projects for decades. For example, Finland's central bank issued the Avant stored value e-money card in the 1990s.

In 2014, the Chinese central bank began researching the idea of issuing a CBDC. Elsewhere, the Ecuadorian central bank operated a mobile payment system from 2014 to 2018. In 2021, Australia's central bank conducted a proof of concept for a wholesale CBDC using Ethereum to tokenize syndicated loans, aiming to automate and secure high-value transactions in the banking sector.

### 9.2.2 Implementation

A central bank digital currency would likely be implemented using a database run by the central bank, government, or approved private-sector entities. The database would keep a record (with appropriate privacy and cryptographic protections) of the amount of money held by every entity, such as people and corporations.

In contrast to cryptocurrency, a central bank digital currency would be centrally controlled (even if it was on a distributed database), and so a blockchain or other distributed ledger would likely not be required or useful - even as they were the original inspiration for the concept.

By March 2024, the central banks of 134 countries accounting for 98% of the world's GDP were said to be in various stages of evaluating the launch of a national digital currency. These included the ECB, the UK, and the US. China's digital RMB was the first digital currency to be issued by a major economy. Six central banks have launched a CBDC: the Central Bank of The Bahamas (Sand Dollar), the Eastern Caribbean Central Bank (DCash), the Central Bank of Nigeria (e-Naira), the Bank of Jamaica (JamDex), People's Bank of China (Digital renminbi), the Reserve Bank of India (Digital Rupee), and Bank of Russia (Digital Ruble). The Central Bank of Brazil has been rolling out tests of a digital Brazilian currency (Drex) since March 2023. The ECB/Eurozone decided in October 2023 to move forward to the preparation phase for the potential issuance of a digital euro after a two-year study phase.

Some states have also issued, or have considered issuing, cryptocurrencies: these include Venezuela (Petro) and the Marshall Islands (Sovereign). These cryptocurrencies are often considered with the intent of increasing a state's independence from global financial systems, such as by reducing dependence on a foreign currency or by evading international sanctions.

Contrasting attitudes towards digital currencies were demonstrated by developments in the UK and Switzerland in February 2023. The UK Treasury and the Bank of England said a state-backed digital pound was likely to be launched some time after 2025. Two weeks later, a Swiss lobby group triggered a national vote on maintaining a "sufficient quantity" of cash in circulation over fears that electronic payments make it easier for the state to monitor its citizens' actions. In a comment on the British government's plans, the BBC's Faisal Islam said the issue was about access to the data attached to every spending transaction, and whether people might choose to trust a global company more than the state: "The eye here is on maintaining UK monetary sovereignty against upheaval from the likes of Big Tech."

A major problem with central bank digital currencies is deciding whether the currency should be easily trackable. If it's traceable, the government has more control than it currently does. Additionally, there's a technical aspect to consider: whether CBDCs should be based on tokens or accounts and how much anonymity users should have.

### 9.2.3 Characteristics

A CBDC is a digital counterpart to fiat money, issued by central banks. Like paper banknotes, it is a means of payment, a unit of account, and a store of value. And like paper currency, each unit is uniquely identifiable to prevent counterfeiting. CBDC will have implications for commercial banks, probably in the field of lowering banks' commissions, no big customer data-selling ability, accumulating the deposits and deposit policies and credit policies due to higher funding costs for banks.

Digital fiat currency is part of the base money supply, together with other forms of the currency. As such, DFC is a liability of the central bank just as physical currency is. It is a digital bearer instrument that can be stored, transferred and transmitted by all kinds of digital payment systems and services. The validity of the digital fiat currency is independent of the digital payment systems storing and transferring the digital fiat currency. Proposals for CBDC implementation often involve the provision of universal bank accounts at the central banks for all citizens.

### 9.2.4 Benefits and Impacts

Governments and central banks are studying CBDCs and their implications for financial inclusion, economic growth, technology innovation, and the efficiency of bank transactions. Potential advantages include:

#### Technological Efficiency

Instead of relying on intermediaries such as banks and clearing houses, money transfers and payments could be made in real time, directly from the payer to the payee. Being real time has some advantages:

- **Reduces Risk:** Payment for goods and services often needs to be done in a timely manner and when payment verification is slow, merchants usually accept the risk of some payments not succeeding in exchange for faster service to customers. When these risks are eliminated with instant payment verifications, merchants no longer need to use intermediaries to handle the risk or to absorb the risk cost themselves.
- **Reduces Complexity:** Merchants will not need to separately keep track of transactions that are slow (where the customer claims to have paid but the money has not arrived yet), therefore eliminate the waiting queue, which could simplify the transaction process from payment to rendition of goods/services.
- **Reduces (or Eliminates) Transaction Fees:** Current payment systems like Visa, Mastercard, American Express etc. have a fee attached to each transaction and lowering or eliminating these fees could lead to widespread price drops and increased adoption of digital payments.

#### Financial Inclusion

Safe money accounts at the central banks could constitute a strong instrument of financial inclusion, allowing any legal resident or citizen to be provided with a free or low-cost basic bank account.

## Preventing Illicit Activity

A CBDC makes it feasible for a central bank to keep track of the exact location of every unit of the currency (assuming the more probable centralized, database form):

- **Tax Collection:** It makes tax avoidance and tax evasion much more difficult, since it would become impossible to use methods such as offshore banking and unreported employment to hide financial activity from the central bank or government. However, cryptos like Bitcoin risk undermining effort to crack down on corporate tax avoidance.
- **Combating Crime:** It makes it much easier to spot criminal activity (by observing financial activity), and thus put an end to it. Furthermore, in cases where criminal activity has already occurred, tracking makes it much harder to successfully launder money, and it would often be straightforward to instantly reverse a transaction and return money to the victim of the crime.

## Proof of Transaction

A digital record exists to prove that money changed hands between two parties which avoids problems inherent to cash such as short-changing, cash theft and conflicting testimonies.

## Protection of Money as a Public Utility

Digital currencies issued by central banks would provide a modern alternative to physical cash – whose abolition is currently being envisaged.

## Safety of Payments Systems

A secure and standard interoperable digital payment instrument issued and governed by a Central Bank and used as the national digital payment instruments boosts confidence in privately controlled money systems and increases trust in the entire national payment system while also boosting competition in payment systems.

## Preservation of Seigniorage Income

Public digital currency issuance would avoid a predictable reduction of seigniorage income for governments in the event of a disappearance of physical cash.

## Banking Competition

The provision of free bank accounts at the central bank offering complete safety of money deposits could strengthen competition between banks to attract bank deposits, for example by offering once again remunerated sight deposits.

### Monetary Policy Transmission

The issuance of central bank base money through transfers to the public could constitute a new channel for monetary policy transmission (i.e., helicopter money), which would allow more direct control of the money supply than indirect tools such as quantitative easing and interest rates, and possibly lead the way towards a full reserve banking system. In digital Yuan trial in Shenzhen, the CBDC was programmed with an expiration date, which encouraged spending and discouraged money from sitting in a saving account. In the end, 90% of vouchers were spent in shops. Demurrage could be implemented, such as by shaving off fractions of the value on a scheduled basis, as a supplement to traditional inflation targets.

### Financial Safety

CBDC would provide an alternative to fractional reserve banking for daily uses, for those who want to avoid all risk of bank runs, despite the relative safety provided by deposit insurance.

## 9.2.5 Risks

Despite having potential advantages, CBDCs remain a controversial topic, and there are risks associated with their implementation.

### Banking System Disintermediation

With the ability to provide digital currency directly to its citizens, one concern is that depositors would shift out of the banking system. Customers may deem the safety, liquidity, solvibility, and publicity of CBDCs to be more attractive, weakening the balance sheet position of commercial banks. In the extreme, this could precipitate potential bank runs and thus make banks' funding positions weaker. However, the Bank of England found that if the introduction of CBDC follows a set of core principles, the risk of a system-wide run from bank deposits to CBDC is addressed. A central bank could also limit the demand of CBDCs by setting a ceiling on the amount of holdings.

### Centralization

Since most central bank digital currencies are centralized, rather than decentralized like most cryptocurrencies, the controllers of the issuance of CBDCs can add or remove money from anyone's account with a flip of a switch. In contrast, cryptocurrencies with a distributed ledger such as Bitcoin prevent this unless a group of users controlling more than 50% of mining power is in agreement.

### Digital Dollarization

A well-run foreign digital currency could become a replacement for a local currency for the same reasons as those described in dollarization. The announcement of

Facebook's Libra contributed to the increased attention to CBDCs by central bankers, as well as China's progress with DCEP to that of several Asian economies.

## Privacy

- "Governments have direct visibility of financial transactions", an "eagle-eyed view on the spending of everyone".
- Digital currency would give a country "broad new powers when it comes to surveillance and controlling its population."
- Data from tracing money routes could lead to losing financial privacy if the CBDC implementation does not have adequate privacy protections. This could lead to encouraging of self-censorship, deterioration of freedom of expression and association, and ultimately to stalling social developments.

## Government Social Manipulation

- **Digital Currency:** Digital currency "will simply become an extension of the surveillance state" and "it could see citizens fined in a split second for behaviors deemed undesirable. Dissidents and activists could see their wallets emptied or taken offline."
- **Limiting Individual Freedom:** "Digital currencies could also empower the state to make it impossible to donate to a vocal NGO"
- **Limiting or Prohibiting Purchases of Products:** Digital currency could prohibit a "purchase alcohol on a weekday. "
- **Digital Currency is also Programmable:** The government could theoretically give out money that expires within a certain period of time or money that could only be used on certain items, which could be used to induce behaviour that the government is seeking."
- **Direct Interaction with Individuals:** "In times of crisis, they enable governments to send aid and stimulus payments directly to the smartphones of affected citizens, regardless of whether the recipients have a bank account or not."
- **Forcing Consumer Behavior:** "Digital currencies can also be tailored to specific purposes. For example, in the Chinese pilot program, money has an expiration date of a few weeks because authorities are hoping to drive consumption"

## 9.3 CROSS-BORDER PAYMENTS AND REMITTANCES

### 9.3.1 Cross-Border Payments

Cross-border payments play a vital role in facilitating international trade, commerce, and remittances, enabling individuals and businesses to transfer funds across borders efficiently and securely. However, traditional cross-border payment systems are often slow, costly, and cumbersome, characterized by high fees, long settlement times, and limited accessibility.

Cross-border payments are essential for facilitating global trade, commerce, and remittances, but traditional payment systems are plagued by inefficiencies, high costs, and long settlement times. Blockchain technology offers promising solutions for improving cross-border payments by enabling faster, cheaper, and more transparent transactions. By leveraging blockchain-based payment networks, financial institutions and businesses can reduce costs, streamline settlement processes, and enhance the efficiency and accessibility of cross-border transactions. However, achieving widespread adoption of blockchain-based cross-border payment solutions requires addressing regulatory challenges, promoting interoperability and standardization, and fostering collaboration among stakeholders. As blockchain technology continues to evolve, it has the potential to revolutionize cross-border payments and transform the global financial landscape.

#### Challenges of Traditional Cross-Border Payments

- **High Fees and Costs:** Traditional cross-border payment systems are associated with high fees and costs, including currency conversion fees, transaction fees, and intermediary fees. These fees can significantly erode the value of cross-border transactions, especially for small-value transfers.
- **Long Settlement Times:** Settlement times for traditional cross-border payments are often lengthy, taking several days or even weeks to complete. Delays in settlement can disrupt business operations, increase counterparty risk, and hinder liquidity management.
- **Opaque and Complex Processes:** Traditional cross-border payment processes are opaque and complex, involving multiple intermediaries, correspondent banks, and clearing systems. Lack of transparency in the payment chain can lead to errors, disputes, and inefficiencies in cross-border transactions.

#### Role of Blockchain in Improving Cross-Border Payments

- **Decentralization and Transparency:** Blockchain technology offers decentralized and transparent platforms for cross-border payments, eliminating the need for intermediaries and providing a transparent and immutable record of transactions. By leveraging blockchain-based payment networks, participants can access real-time transaction information and track payments from initiation to settlement.

- **Cost Reduction**: Blockchain-based cross-border payment systems can reduce costs by eliminating intermediaries, streamlining settlement processes, and reducing transaction fees. Without the need for multiple intermediaries, blockchain payments can offer lower fees and more competitive exchange rates, especially for small-value transfers.
- **Faster Settlement**: Blockchain enables faster settlement of cross-border payments by automating transaction verification and settlement processes. With blockchain-based payment networks, transactions can be settled in real-time or within minutes, compared to days or weeks with traditional payment systems.

## Solutions for Enhancing Cross-Border Payments

- **Stablecoins and Digital Currencies**: Stablecoins and central bank digital currencies (CBDCs) offer promising solutions for improving cross-border payments by providing stable and efficient means of transferring value across borders. Stablecoins pegged to fiat currencies or commodities can reduce currency volatility and enhance the stability of cross-border transactions.
- **Interoperability and Standardization**: Interoperability and standardization of cross-border payment systems are essential for facilitating seamless and efficient transactions between different payment networks and financial institutions. Adopting common standards and protocols for cross-border payments can improve interoperability, reduce friction, and enhance the efficiency of global transactions.
- **Regulatory Harmonization**: Regulatory harmonization is critical for promoting innovation and adoption of blockchain-based cross-border payment solutions. Harmonized regulatory frameworks can provide clarity and certainty for market participants, encourage investment and innovation, and facilitate cross-border interoperability and collaboration.

## Case Studies: Blockchain-Based Cross-Border Payment Solutions

- **Ripple**: Ripple is a blockchain-based payment protocol and network designed to facilitate fast, low-cost cross-border payments for financial institutions and banks. Ripple's network enables real-time settlement of cross-border transactions using its native cryptocurrency, XRP, as a bridge currency.

- **Stellar:** Stellar is an open-source blockchain platform and payment protocol that facilitates cross-border transactions and remittances. Stellar's network enables fast and low-cost cross-border payments by connecting financial institutions, payment networks, and individual users through its decentralized platform.

### 9.3.2 Remittances

A remittance is a non-commercial transfer of money by a foreign worker, a member of a diaspora community, or a citizen with familial ties abroad, for household income in their home country or homeland. Money sent home by migrants competes with international aid as one of the largest financial inflows to developing countries. Workers' remittances are a significant part of international capital flows, especially with regard to labor-exporting countries. Due to its large diaspora, India consecutively remains the top receiver of remittances. In 2022, the top six recipient countries for remittances inflows in current U.S. dollars were India ($100 billion), Mexico ($60 billion), China ($51 billion), the Philippines ($38 billion), Egypt ($32 billion) and Pakistan ($29 billion).

#### History

Several European countries, for example Spain, Italy, and Ireland were heavily dependent on remittances received from their emigrants during the 19th and 20th centuries. In the case of Spain, remittances amounted to 21% of all of its current account income in 1946. All of those countries created policies on remittances developed after significant research efforts in the field. For instance, Italy was the first country in the world to enact a law to protect remittances in 1901 while Spain was the first country to sign an international treaty with Argentina in 1960 to lower the cost of the remittances received.

#### 21st Century

Since 2000, remittances have increased sharply worldwide, having almost tripled to $529 billion in 2012. In 2012, migrants from India and China alone sent more than $130 billion to their home countries. In 2004 the G8 met at the Sea Island Summit and decided to take action to lower the costs for migrant workers who send money back to their friends and families in their country of origin. In light of this, various G8 government developmental organizations, such as the UK government's Department for International Development (DFID) and USAID began to look into ways in which the cost of remitting money could be lowered.

In September 2008, the World Bank established the first international database of remittance prices. The Remittance Prices Worldwide Database provides data on sending and receiving remittances for over 200 "country corridors" worldwide. The "corridors" examined include remittance flows from 32 major sending countries to 89 receiving countries, which account for more than 60% of total remittances to developing countries. The resulting publication of the Remittance Prices Worldwide Database serves four major purposes: benchmarking improvements, allowing comparisons across countries, supporting consumers' choices, and putting pressure on service providers to improve their services.

At the July 2009 summit in L'Aquila, Italy, G8 heads of government and states endorsed the objective of reducing the cost of remittance services by five percentage points in five years. To drive down costs, the World Bank has begun certifying regional and national databases that use a consistent methodology to compare the cost of sending remittances.

At the G20 2011 Summit in Cannes, Bill Gates stated that, "If the transaction costs on remittances worldwide were cut from where they are today at around 10% to an average of 5% it would unlock $15bn a year in poor countries." A number of low-cost online services have emerged with the objective of lowering the cost of money transfers to developing and emerging economies. There are also a number of comparison sites when it comes to remittance which breaks down the costs of sending money overseas. According to the World Bank remittance to low- and middle-income countries reached $529 billion in 2018, which was a record high.

## Global Extent

Remittance has been defined by the World Bank as the part of the earnings which a migrant worker sends back to family members in the country of origin. Worldwide, the flow of remittance has increased from US$72.3 billion in 2001 to approximately US$483 billion in 2011. According to the World Bank, in 2018 overall global remittance grew 10% to US$689 billion, including US$528 billion in 2019 to developing countries. Overall global remittance is expected to grow 3.7% to US$715 billion in 2019, including US$549 billion to developing nations.

Economic research has focused on the motivation for remittance, suggesting that the key drivers for remittance are altruism, self-interest in exchange, and repayment of past expense. A mix of motivations may coexist, in scientific literature this state of mind is summarized as "tempered altruism and enlightened selfishness".

Remittances make up a significant portion of economies of developing countries. Many receive over 10% of their gross domestic product (GDP) in remittances each year, with some exceptional cases as high as a third of their GDP.

International remittances have a major impact on developing countries around the world because the majority of remittances, some $441 billion in 2015, goes to developing economies. This amount is nearly triple the $131 billion of global Official Development Assistance.

### Major Operators

The licensed money transmitter Western Union allows customers to designate a recipient who can pick up that money at any a Western Union agent. Western Union also operates as bureau de change with a fee ranging from eight to twelve percent. Western Union is the world's leading handler of remittance and the 170,000 Western Union agents handle about 25 percent of the total global remittance traffic.

Other companies such as MoneyGram have also been a key player for decades. Pure play money transfer providers may be owned by parent companies with more diverse interests. Two players dominate the international electronic funds transfer for interbank payments between two bank accounts. These are the Clearing House Interbank Payments System (CHIPS) and the Society for Worldwide Interbank Financial Telecommunication (SWIFT). Businesses as well as banks can subscribe to the international communications network Telex and initiate international financial transfers.

Although the remittance market share has diversified when fintech startups entered the market in the 2010s, Western Union continues to dominate the majority of the remittance market share. Since the advent of fintech, many digital remittances have emerged on the scene, leading to the rise of comparison platforms or aggregators such as FXcompared and Monito in Europe and Send4x in Southeast Asia. Blockchain-based remittances companies are also starting to be used and offer such advantages as fast transfer time and relatively low transaction costs.

## 2007–2008 Financial Crisis

The 2007–2008 financial crisis was triggered in the United States and rippled through the financial system in developed countries. Nevertheless, throughout the 2007–2008 financial crisis remittance was among the less volatile sources of foreign exchange for developing countries. In financial literature, remittance sent by migrant workers to households in the country of origin, is regarded as countercyclical when the economy is struck by hardship such as a financial crisis, natural disaster, or political instability. In 2009 remittance payments to developing countries declined globally for the first time in recorded history of the global financial system. But with a decline of only 5.2 percent in 2009, remittance was significantly less precarious than private capital flows including foreign direct investment.

## By Region

The United States has been the leading source of remittances globally every year since 1983. Russia, Saudi Arabia, and Switzerland have been the next largest senders of remittances since 2007. Between 9 million and 11 million workers send remittances from Russia each year.

### Asia

A majority of the remittances have been directed to Asian countries like India (approx. US$87.0 billion in 2021), China (approx. US$ 60.0 billion in 2021), the Philippines (approx. US$33.5 billion in 2020), Pakistan (US$26.0 billion in 2020), Bangladesh (US$21.5 billion in 2020) and more. Asian countries such as Tajikistan and Nepal are among the countries that rely the most on remittances, accounting for 35% and 25% of their GDP respectively. Most of the remittances happen by the conventional channel of agents. However, with the increasing relevance and reach of the Internet, online and mobile phone money transfers have grown significantly.

**Armenia:**

- Remittances are a major component of the Armenian economy. making up about 13% of Armenia's GDP in 2011. In 2013 around 40% of families of Armenia have received remittances. As a result, Armenia falls in the top 20 countries worldwide for receiving remittances. Total remittances to Armenia have reached their peak in 2013 being equal to $2.192 billion but plummeted after the 2014 Russian ruble devaluation and reached $1.528 billion in 2019.
- Armenia falls in the top 20 countries worldwide for receiving remittances. Armenia, being a country with one of the largest diasporas in the world, provides a case study of a developing economy that is dependent on remittances and the financial support they provide. Total remittances to Armenia reached $1.87 billion in 2013, a 10.8%. A study conducted in 2004 examined the impact of remittances from a micro perspective, and determined that households with average income were the most likely to have a family member abroad because poorer households lacked the financial ability to send family members out of the country and the most wealthy households did not have a reason to.
- In 2017, the majority of remittance flows to Armenia originated from Russia, about 60.5% of overall remittances. The figure amounted to nearly $945 million due to more than 2 million Armenians living in Russia. The next biggest inflows were recorded from the U.S. (with around 500,000-1,000,000 Armenians), at over $160 million, which is 10.25% of the overall figure. According to the IMF, starting from 2010

remittances in U.S. dollars, Armenian drams, and rubles, grew until they hit their peak in 2014 and started declining after that in a volatile fashion as a result of the Russian ruble devaluation. Remittances in drams and dollars declined to almost their 2010 levels.

**Bangladesh:**

- An estimated 10 million Bangladeshis, working abroad have sent $15 billion to home in 2018 and $18.32 billion in 2019. It is country's second-largest source of foreign earnings after its gigantic textile industry. Bangladesh is one of the top 10 countries in the world for migration and remittance according to World Bank. Most of the remittances come from gulf countries.

**Jordan:**

- The flow of remittances to Jordan experienced rapid growth during the 1970s and 1980s when Jordan started exporting skilled labor to the Persian Gulf. These remittances represent an important source of funding for many developing countries, including Jordan. According to the World Bank data on remittances, with about US$3 billion in 2010 Jordan ranked at 10th place among all developing countries. Jordan ranked among the top 20 recipients of remittances for the preceding decade. In addition, the Arab Monetary Fund (AMF) statistics in 2010 indicate that Jordan was the third biggest recipient of remittances among Arab countries after Egypt and Lebanon. The host countries that have absorbed most of the Jordanian expatriates are Saudi Arabia and the United Arab Emirates, where the available data indicate that about 90% of Jordanian migrants are working in the Persian Gulf.

**Philippines:**

- According to a World Bank Study, the Philippines is the second largest recipient for remittances in Asia. It was estimated in 1994 that migrants sent over US$2.6 billion back to the Philippines through formal banking systems. With the addition of money sent through private finance companies and return migrants, the 1994 total was closer to US$6 billion annually.
- The total is estimated to have grown by 7.8 percent annually to reach US$21.3 billion in 2010. Remittances are a reliable source of revenue for the Philippines, accounting for 8.9 per cent of the country's GDP.
- The Estrada administration in 2000 declared it "The Year of Overseas Filipino Worker in the Recognition of the Determination and Supreme Self-Sacrifice of Overseas Filipino Workers." This declaration connects

monetary remittances of overseas workers as the top foreign-exchange earnings in the Philippines.

**Turkey:**

- Since the 2000s remittances from Turkey has been increasing, reaching US$1.49 billion in 2021 according to the World Bank. Although remittances to Turkey had been a significant part of the economy in the past, since the 2000s they only represent a fraction of the Turkish economy with 0.1% of the total GDP.
- Since the Syrian civil war the foreign-born population of Turkey has been growing. It was reported that Syrians in Turkey were using the "hawala system" to send money to their country of origin. According to economist Gözde Güran remittances sent through hawala has become an integral part of the Syrian economy.

### Latin America and the Caribbean

In Latin America and the Caribbean, remittances play an important role in the economy of the region, totaling over US$66.5 billion in 2007, with about 75% originating in the United States. This total represents more than the sum of Foreign direct investment and official development aid combined. In seven Latin American and Caribbean countries, remittances even account for more than 10% of GDP and exceed the dollar flows of the largest export product in almost every country in the region. Percentages ranged from 2% in Mexico, to 18% in El Salvador, 21% in Honduras, and up to 30% in Haiti. The Inter American Development Bank's Multilateral Investment Fund (IDB-MIF) has been the leading agency on regional remittance research. Mexico received remittance inflows of almost US$24 billion in 2007, 95% of which originated in the US.

### In United States

- A 2004 study found that over 60% of the 16.5 million Latin American-born adults who resided in the United States at the time of the survey regularly sent money home. The remittances sent by these 10 million immigrants were transmitted via more than 100 million individual transactions per year and amounted to an estimated $30 billion during 2004. Each transaction averaged about $150–$250, and, because these migrants tended to send smaller amounts more frequently than others, their remittances had a higher percentage of costs due to transfer fees.
- Migrants sent approximately 10% of their household incomes; these remittances made up a corresponding 50–80% of the household incomes for the recipients. Significant amounts of remittances were sent from 37 U.S. states, but six states were identified as the "traditional sending"

states: New York (which led the group with 81% of its immigrants making regular remittances), California, Texas, Florida, Illinois, and New Jersey. According to the Mexican central bank, remittances grew just 0.6 during the first six months of 2007, as compared to 23% during the same period in 2006. Experts attribute the slowdown to a contraction in the U.S. construction industry, tighter border controls, and a crackdown in the U.S. on illegal immigration.

- Remittance culture in the United States has contributed to the formation of "micro-geographies", tightly knit networks that integrate U.S. communities with communities throughout Latin America, such as migrants from Oaxaca, Mexico, who have settled in Venice Beach, California. Oaxacans not only send money back to their communities, but they also travel back and forth extensively.
- After the Great Recession, remittances from the United States to Latin America have been on the decline. While there were US$69.2 billion worth of remittances sent in 2008, that figure has fallen to $58.9 billion for 2011. This trend is a result of many factors including the recession itself, more economic opportunity in Latin American countries, and rising fees charged by coyotes to smuggle immigrants across the border.
- The pattern of migration has changed from a circular flow, in which immigrants work in the United States for a few years before returning to their families in their home countries, to a one-way stream whereby migrants find themselves stuck in the United States. As a result, the new wave of migrants is both less likely to leave and more likely to stay in the United States for longer periods of time. Overall, this trend has contributed to falling levels of remittances sent to Latin American countries from the United States.

### Africa

Remittances to Africa play an important role in national economies. However, little data exists as many rely on informal channels to send money home. Immigrants from Africa today number approximately 20 to 30 million adults, who send around US$40 billion annually to their families and local communities back home. For the region as a whole, this represents 50 percent more than net official development assistance (ODA) from all sources, and, for most countries, the amount also exceeds foreign direct investment (FDI). In several fragile states, remittances are estimated to exceed 50 percent of GDP.

Most African countries restrict the payment of remittances to banks, which in turn, typically enter into exclusive arrangements with large money transfer companies, like Western Union or Money Gram, to operate on their behalf. This results in limited competition and limited access for consumers, which allows these Money Transfer Operators (MTOs) to charge the highest fees for remittances in the world. However, there are a number of new players aiming to disrupt this established MTO model, such as Xoom and Willstream, which leverage increasing mobile phone penetration in the region and provide different rate structures to Diaspora customers. Additionally, global initiative like the United Nations Sustainable Development Goal 10 has a target of reducing the transaction costs of migrant remittances to less than 3 percent by 2030.

According to a World Bank study, Nigeria is by far the top remittance recipient in Africa, accounting for $10 billion in 2010, a slight increase over the previous year ($9.6 billion). Other top recipients include Sudan ($3.2 billion), Kenya ($1.8 billion), Senegal ($1.2 billion), South Africa ($1.0 billion), Uganda ($0.8 billion), Lesotho ($0.5 billion), Ethiopia ($387 million), Mali ($385 million), and Togo ($302 million). As a share of Gross Domestic Product, the top recipients in 2009 were: Lesotho (25%), Togo (10%), Cape Verde (9%), Guinea-Bissau (9%), Senegal (9%), Gambia (8%), Liberia (6%), Sudan (6%), Nigeria (6%), and Kenya (5%).

**Nigeria:**

- A major source of foreign-exchange earnings for Nigeria are remittances sent home by Nigerians living abroad. In 2014, 17.5 million Nigerians lived in foreign countries, with the UK and the US having more than 2 million Nigerians each.
- According to the International Organization for Migration, Nigeria witnessed a dramatic increase in remittances sent home from overseas Nigerians, going from US$2.3 billion in 2004 to 17.9 billion in 2007, representing 6.7% of GDP. In 2016, remittances reached a new record of $35 billion. The United States accounts for the largest portion of official remittances, followed by the United Kingdom, Italy, Canada, Spain and France. On the African continent, Egypt, Equatorial Guinea, Chad, Libya, and South Africa are important source countries of remittance flows to Nigeria, while China is the biggest remittance-sending country in Asia.
- An August 2016 Nigerian Central Bank (NCB) decision to suspend the operations of all MTOs in the country, except those of Western Union, MoneyGram and Rio, was met with a strong backlash. It was argued that the decision was not appropriately justified, while also standing in contrast to the NCB's previous move to ban all exclusivity agreements with Western Union. The decision was considered to disproportionally strengthen the dominant position of Western Union, MoneyGram and

Rio. Under pressure, however, the Central Bank reversed the decision and granted new licenses to a number of competing MTOs.

**Somalia:**

- Somali expatriates often send remittances to their relatives in Greater Somalia through Dahabshiil and other Somali-owned money transfer companies. In order to ensure that these funds go to their intended recipients rather than Al-Shabaab and other militant groups, the governments of the United States, Australia, and a number of other Western countries tightened their banking requirements or stopped processing altogether the remittances. To address the concerns, the United States Congress passed the Money Remittances Improvement Act of 2014.
- In April 2015, the Federal Cabinet of Somalia also officially launched the Special Task Force on Remittances (STFR). The multi-agency initiative is mandated with facilitating the Federal Government of Somalia's new national policy pertaining to the money transfer industry. Its main priority is centered on establishing a comprehensive strategy and a consultative implementation plan for the formalization of the local financial sector. Additionally, the STFR is tasked with helping to foster a business environment and financial infrastructure conducive to growth. It is also empowered to coordinate and speed up the endorsement of financial governance instruments and transparency associated legislation, such as the laws on Anti-Money Laundering (AML) and Counter Financing of Terrorism (CFT). In accordance with the Financial Action Task Force (FATF)'s recommendations, the STFR is in turn slated to oversee the Somali federal government's campaign to ratify various international treaties. The Task Forces' membership is scheduled to be announced shortly, and will be drawn from government institutions, the remittance industry, banks, and other key private sector stakeholders.

## Dynamics

### Emergencies

During disasters or emergencies, remittances can be a vital source of income for people whose other forms of livelihood may have been destroyed by conflict or natural disaster.

According to the Overseas Development Institute, this is being increasingly recognized as important by aid actors who are considering better ways of supporting people in emergency responses. An illustrative example can be Armenia, that had experienced a devastating earthquake in Spitak on December 7, 1988, when the Karabakh conflict had already started. About 45,000 people have died, while 500,000 became homeless. Armenia got help from different countries, for example, the U.S. government immediately sent $10 million, which helped to more or less recover the economy. Refugees and other displaced populations also often remit to family members left behind in conflict areas.

### Potential Security Concerns

The recent internationally coordinated effort to stifle possible sources of money laundering and/or terrorist financing has increased the cost of sending remittances, directly increasing costs to the companies facilitating the sending, and indirectly increasing the costs to the person remitting. As in some corridors a sizable amount of remittances is sent through informal channels (family connections, traveling friends, local money lenders, etc.). According to the World Bank, some countries do not report remittances data.

Moreover, when data is available, the methodologies used by countries for remittance data compilation are not publicly available. A 2010 world survey of central banks found significant differences in the quality of remittance data collection across countries: some central banks only used remittances data reported from commercial banks, neglecting to account for remittance flows via money transfer operators and post offices.

Remittances can be difficult to track and potentially sensitive to money laundering (AML) and terror financing (CTF) concerns. Since 9/11 many governments and the Financial Action Task Force (FATF) have taken steps to address informal value transfer systems. This is done through nations' Financial Intelligence Units (FIUs). The principle legislative initiatives in this area are the USA PATRIOT Act, Title III in the United States and, in the EU, through a series of EU Money Laundering Directives. Though no serious terror risk should be associated with migrants sending money to their families, misuse of the financial system remains a serious government concern.

### Economic Benefits for Developing Countries

The extent to which remittances produce benefits for developing countries is argued. World Bank economists contend that remittance receivers' higher propensity to own a bank account means that remittances can promote access to financial services for the sender and recipient, claimed to be an essential aspect of leveraging remittances to promote economic development. For example, in Armenia, which has one of the highest remittance to GDP ratios, studies suggest that those households which receive remittances have a higher propensity to save, however, as opposed to some theoretic frameworks, these savings are not used to leverage borrowing more from the financial system as a way to grow their businesses.

Other studies suggest that another channel through which remittances can foster economic growth is a household investment. For instance, the study conducted in South Caucasus reveals that in Armenia having a migrant household member is associated with a higher probability of establishing a family business by that household.

Thus, the remittances sent by migrants can potentially encourage domestic investment, ensuring economic growth. However, new findings for Armenia suggest that remittances help potential migrants to ease the migration process, serving as a resource rather than as a contractual tool between migrants and non-migrants. It is concluded that remittances drastically shift emigration intentions upward. The need for remittances, and the ability and the strength of the migrant social capital (or the network) are factors which jointly determine emigration intentions. Meanwhile, critical migration scholars have expressed concern about the ability of remittances to address the structural causes of economic underdevelopment and see an increasing policy emphasis on finance as symptomatic of a paradigmatic shift towards a 'self-help development' that burdens the poor.

Remittances are generally thought to be counter-cyclical. The stability of remittance flows amidst financial crises and economic downturns make them a reliable source of foreign exchange earnings for developing countries. As migrant remittances are sent cumulatively over the years and not only by new migrants, remittances are able to be persistent over time. This is particularly true of remittances sent by circular migrants, migrant workers who move back and forth between their home and host countries in a temporary and repetitive manner. At the state level, countries with diversified migration destinations are likely to have more sustainable remittance flows.

From a macroeconomic perspective, there is no conclusive relationship between remittances and GDP growth. While remittances can boost aggregate demand and thereby spur economic activity, other research indicates that remittances may also have adverse macroeconomic impacts by increasing income inequality and reducing labour supply among recipient countries. The World Bank and the Bank for International Settlements have developed international standards for remittance services.

## 9.4 BLOCKCHAIN IN TRADITIONAL BANKING

Blockchain technology, renowned for its decentralized and transparent nature, has been increasingly explored for its potential application in traditional banking systems. Blockchain technology holds immense promise for transforming traditional banking systems by enhancing security, improving efficiency, and fostering transparency and trust in financial transactions. Despite regulatory challenges and scalability concerns, the integration of blockchain in traditional banking opens up new opportunities for innovation, collaboration, and competition in the financial industry. As banks continue to explore blockchain-based solutions, they must navigate regulatory complexities, address scalability issues, and prioritize data privacy and security to realize the full potential of blockchain technology in banking.

### 9.4.1 Understanding Blockchain in Banking

- **Enhanced Security:** One of the key benefits of integrating blockchain in traditional banking is enhanced security. The immutable and decentralized nature of blockchain ensures that transactions are securely recorded and tamper-proof, reducing the risk of fraud and unauthorized access.
- **Improved Efficiency:** Blockchain technology streamlines various banking processes by automating transaction verification and settlement. This leads to faster transaction speeds, reduced operational costs, and enhanced efficiency in banking operations.
- **Transparency and Trust:** Blockchain promotes transparency and trust in banking transactions by providing a transparent and auditable record of all transactions. This transparency fosters trust among stakeholders and reduces the need for intermediaries in the banking process.

### 9.4.2 Use Cases of Blockchain in Traditional Banking

- **Cross-Border Payments:** Blockchain facilitates faster and more cost-effective cross-border payments by eliminating intermediaries and reducing transaction fees. Banks can leverage blockchain-based payment networks to streamline cross-border transactions and enhance liquidity management.
- **Trade Finance:** Blockchain technology can streamline trade finance processes, such as letter of credit issuance and trade settlement, by providing a secure and transparent platform for recording and verifying trade transactions. This reduces paperwork, minimizes delays, and mitigates the risk of fraud in trade finance operations.
- **KYC and AML Compliance:** Blockchain-based identity verification solutions can streamline Know Your Customer (KYC) and Anti-Money Laundering (AML) compliance processes for banks. By securely storing customer identity information on the blockchain, banks can enhance regulatory compliance, reduce compliance costs, and improve customer onboarding experiences.

### 9.4.3 Challenges and Considerations

- **Regulatory Compliance:** Regulatory compliance is a significant challenge in integrating blockchain technology into traditional banking systems. Banks must navigate complex regulatory frameworks governing blockchain-based financial transactions, including AML, KYC, data privacy, and consumer protection regulations.
- **Scalability and Interoperability**: Scalability and interoperability issues pose challenges for blockchain adoption in traditional banking systems. Blockchain networks must scale to handle large transaction volumes while maintaining interoperability with existing banking infrastructure and legacy systems.
- **Data Privacy and Security**: Data privacy and security concerns arise in blockchain-based banking systems due to the immutable and transparent nature of blockchain. Banks must ensure the privacy and confidentiality of customer data while maintaining the integrity and security of blockchain transactions.

### 9.4.4 Implications for the Financial Industry

- **Disintermediation**: Blockchain technology has the potential to disrupt traditional banking models by eliminating intermediaries and reducing reliance on centralized financial institutions. This could democratize access to financial services and empower individuals and businesses to participate directly in the global economy.
- **Innovation and Collaboration**: Blockchain fosters innovation and collaboration in the financial industry by enabling banks to explore new business models and partnerships. Banks can collaborate with fintech startups and technology providers to develop innovative blockchain-based solutions for banking operations, such as digital identity, supply chain finance, and decentralized lending.
- **Competitive Landscape**: The integration of blockchain technology in traditional banking systems reshapes the competitive landscape of the financial industry. Banks that embrace blockchain innovation gain a competitive edge by offering faster, more efficient, and more secure banking services to customers.

# CHAPTER 10

# FUTURE TRENDS AND DEVELOPMENTS

## 10.1 INTEGRATION WITH INTERNET OF THINGS (IOT)

The integration of blockchain technology with the Internet of Things (IoT) holds immense promise for revolutionizing various industries, including supply chain management, healthcare, energy, and smart cities. The integration of blockchain technology with the Internet of Things (IoT) offers compelling opportunities for transforming various industries and applications, from supply chain management and healthcare to energy and smart cities.

By leveraging blockchain-enabled IoT solutions, organizations can enhance security, transparency, and efficiency in IoT networks, enabling real-time data exchange, automated transactions, and decentralized data management. However, implementing blockchain-enabled IoT solutions requires addressing scalability, interoperability, and data privacy and security challenges, as well as fostering collaboration among stakeholders to realize the full potential of blockchain and IoT integration. As blockchain technology continues to evolve and mature, it is poised to drive innovation and disruption across diverse sectors, shaping the future of interconnected and intelligent IoT ecosystems.

### 10.1.1 Understanding Blockchain-enabled IoT

- **Enhanced Security**: Blockchain technology provides a secure and immutable ledger for recording transactions and data exchanges between IoT devices. By encrypting data and storing it in tamper-proof blocks, blockchain enhances the security and integrity of IoT networks, protecting against data tampering, unauthorized access, and cyberattacks.
- **Decentralized Data Management**: Traditional IoT systems rely on centralized servers to store and manage data, creating single points of failure and vulnerability to cyber threats. In contrast, blockchain-enabled IoT networks leverage decentralized peer-to-peer architectures, distributing data across multiple nodes and ensuring redundancy, resilience, and fault tolerance.

- **Transparency and Trust**: Blockchain promotes transparency and trust in IoT networks by providing a transparent and auditable record of data transactions and interactions between devices. This transparency fosters trust among stakeholders, enhances data integrity, and enables greater accountability and traceability in IoT applications.

### 10.1.2 Use Cases of Blockchain-enabled IoT

- **Supply Chain Management**: Blockchain-enabled IoT solutions can streamline supply chain management by providing end-to-end visibility and traceability of goods and products throughout the supply chain. IoT devices, such as sensors and RFID tags, can collect real-time data on product movements, temperature, humidity, and other relevant parameters, which is then recorded on the blockchain, enabling stakeholders to track and verify the authenticity, provenance, and condition of products.
- **Smart Contracts and Automated Transactions:** Blockchain-enabled IoT networks can execute smart contracts and automated transactions based on predefined conditions and triggers. Smart contracts, self-executing contracts with the terms of the agreement directly written into code, enable automated and trustless transactions between IoT devices, such as automated payments for utility consumption, machine-to-machine transactions in autonomous vehicles, and self-executing agreements in smart homes.
- **Healthcare**: In the healthcare sector, blockchain-enabled IoT solutions can improve patient care, medical record management, and supply chain integrity. IoT devices, such as wearables and medical sensors, can collect real-time health data, which is securely recorded on the blockchain, enabling healthcare providers to access accurate and up-to-date patient information, facilitate remote monitoring and telemedicine services, and ensure the integrity and privacy of medical records.

### 10.1.3 Challenges and Considerations

- **Scalability**: Scalability is a significant challenge for blockchain-enabled IoT networks, particularly in large-scale deployments with millions of interconnected devices generating vast amounts of data. Scaling blockchain networks to accommodate the volume of transactions and data generated by IoT devices while maintaining performance, latency, and throughput requirements is a key consideration for implementing blockchain-enabled IoT solutions.

- **Interoperability**: Interoperability between different IoT devices, platforms, and blockchain networks is essential for ensuring seamless integration and communication in blockchain-enabled IoT ecosystems. Standardizing protocols, APIs, and data formats can promote interoperability and compatibility among heterogeneous IoT devices and blockchain platforms.
- **Data Privacy and Security**: Data privacy and security are critical considerations in blockchain-enabled IoT networks, as they involve sensitive and personal data collected from IoT devices. Ensuring data privacy, confidentiality, and compliance with data protection regulations, such as the General Data Protection Regulation (GDPR), is essential for building trust and maintaining the integrity of blockchain-enabled IoT ecosystems.

## 10.2 INTEROPERABILITY BETWEEN BLOCKCHAINS

Interoperability between blockchains has emerged as a crucial consideration in the blockchain ecosystem, enabling seamless communication, data exchange, and value transfer between different blockchain networks. Interoperability between blockchains is essential for realizing the full potential of blockchain technology and fostering collaboration, innovation, and adoption in the blockchain ecosystem. Interoperable blockchains enable seamless communication, cross-chain compatibility, and enhanced scalability and performance, driving liquidity, accessibility, and usability of blockchain assets and applications. However, achieving blockchain interoperability requires addressing technical, security, regulatory, and compliance challenges, as well as fostering collaboration and standardization among stakeholders. As blockchain technology continues to evolve, interoperability will play a crucial role in shaping the future of blockchain networks and driving the next wave of innovation and adoption in the decentralized digital economy.

### 10.2.1 Understanding Interoperability in Blockchain

- **Seamless Communication**: Interoperability enables different blockchain networks to communicate and interact with each other, facilitating the transfer of assets, data, and value across disparate blockchain platforms. Interoperable blockchains break down silos and barriers, fostering collaboration and interoperability in the broader blockchain ecosystem.
- **Cross-Chain Compatibility**: Interoperability allows for cross-chain compatibility, enabling assets and tokens to be transferred between different blockchain networks without the need for intermediaries or centralized exchanges. Cross-chain interoperability enhances liquidity,

accessibility, and usability of blockchain assets, promoting innovation and adoption in the blockchain space.

- **Scalability and Network Effect:** Interoperability enhances scalability by enabling transactions to be processed across multiple blockchain networks, distributing transaction load and improving throughput and performance. Moreover, interoperability creates network effects, where the value and utility of blockchain networks increase as they become interconnected and interoperable with each other.

### 10.2.2 Approaches to Achieving Blockchain Interoperability

- **Atomic Swaps:** Atomic swaps enable peer-to-peer exchange of assets between different blockchain networks without the need for intermediaries. Atomic swaps utilize smart contracts to ensure that transactions are executed atomically, meaning that either both transactions are completed successfully, or neither transaction occurs, preventing the risk of fraud or double-spending.
- **Interoperability Protocols:** Interoperability protocols such as Polkadot, Cosmos, and Aion provide frameworks and standards for achieving interoperability between different blockchain networks. These protocols utilize bridges, relays, and interoperability layers to facilitate cross-chain communication and asset transfer, enabling seamless interoperability across heterogeneous blockchain platforms.
- **Cross-Chain Bridges:** Cross-chain bridges establish connections and communication channels between different blockchain networks, allowing assets and data to be transferred securely and transparently between them. Cross-chain bridges use decentralized oracles, multi-signature wallets, and cryptographic proofs to ensure the integrity and validity of cross-chain transactions.

### 10.2.3 Benefits of Interoperable Blockchains

- **Enhanced Liquidity and Accessibility:** Interoperable blockchains improve liquidity and accessibility by enabling seamless transfer of assets and tokens between different blockchain networks. Users can access a wider range of assets and markets, trade across multiple platforms, and participate in diverse blockchain ecosystems.
- **Improved Scalability and Performance:** Interoperability enhances scalability and performance by enabling transactions to be processed across multiple blockchain networks, reducing congestion and improving throughput and transaction speeds. Interoperable

blockchains leverage network effects and synergies, enhancing the overall efficiency and scalability of the blockchain ecosystem.

- **Promotion of Innovation and Collaboration:** Interoperable blockchains foster innovation and collaboration by enabling developers, projects, and communities to leverage the strengths and features of different blockchain platforms. Developers can build interoperable applications and services that span multiple blockchain networks, driving innovation and interoperability in the blockchain space.

### 10.2.4 Challenges of Blockchain Interoperability

- **Technical Complexity:** Achieving interoperability between different blockchain networks involves technical challenges such as consensus mechanisms, data formats, and network protocols. Developing interoperable solutions requires coordination, standardization, and compatibility between heterogeneous blockchain platforms.
- **Security and Trust:** Interoperability introduces security and trust considerations, as cross-chain transactions involve multiple parties, networks, and protocols. Ensuring the security and integrity of cross-chain transactions, data exchanges, and asset transfers is essential for building trust and confidence in interoperable blockchain networks.
- **Regulatory and Compliance:** Regulatory and compliance considerations present challenges for blockchain interoperability, as cross-border transactions and asset transfers may be subject to different legal and regulatory frameworks. Ensuring compliance with regulatory requirements, such as anti-money laundering (AML) and know-your-customer (KYC) regulations, is essential for enabling cross-chain interoperability and adoption.

## 10.3 BLOCKCHAIN AND ARTIFICIAL INTELLIGENCE

Blockchain and artificial intelligence (AI) are two transformative technologies reshaping industries and driving innovation across various domains. The integration of blockchain and artificial intelligence holds tremendous potential for transforming industries, driving innovation, and addressing complex challenges in today's digital economy. By combining the security, transparency, and decentralized nature of blockchain with the analytical power and predictive capabilities of artificial intelligence, organizations can unlock new opportunities for data-driven insights, collaboration, and value creation. However, realizing the full potential of blockchain and AI integration requires addressing technical, regulatory, and ethical challenges, fostering collaboration among stakeholders, and promoting innovation in blockchain-based AI applications. As blockchain and AI technologies continue to evolve, their synergistic partnership is poised to shape the future of decentralized, intelligent, and trust-based systems in diverse domains.

### 10.3.1 Understanding Blockchain and Artificial Intelligence

- **Blockchain Technology**: Blockchain is a decentralized, distributed ledger technology that enables secure and transparent recording of transactions and data. It operates on a peer-to-peer network, where transactions are verified and recorded in blocks, forming an immutable chain. Blockchain ensures data integrity, transparency, and trust without the need for intermediaries.
- **Artificial Intelligence**: Artificial intelligence refers to the simulation of human intelligence in machines, enabling them to perform cognitive tasks, such as learning, reasoning, and problem-solving. AI algorithms analyze vast amounts of data, identify patterns, and make predictions or decisions based on learned insights. AI technologies include machine learning, deep learning, natural language processing, and computer vision.

### 10.3.2 Synergies Between Blockchain and Artificial Intelligence

- **Data Security and Privacy**: Blockchain provides a secure and tamper-proof platform for storing and sharing data, enhancing data security and privacy in AI applications. By leveraging blockchain's cryptographic algorithms and decentralized architecture, AI systems can access trusted, verified data sources while maintaining data integrity and confidentiality.
- **Data Sharing and Collaboration**: Blockchain enables secure and transparent sharing of data and AI models among multiple parties, fostering collaboration and knowledge sharing in AI research and development. Through blockchain-based data marketplaces and decentralized AI platforms, stakeholders can exchange data, models, and insights while retaining control over their assets and intellectual property.
- **Data Monetization and Incentives**: Blockchain facilitates data monetization and incentivization mechanisms, allowing individuals and organizations to monetize their data contributions and insights in AI applications. By tokenizing data assets and using smart contracts, blockchain enables transparent and fair compensation for data providers, incentivizing data sharing and participation in AI ecosystems.

### 10.3.3 Use Cases of Blockchain and AI Integration

- **Supply Chain Management:** Blockchain and AI integration can enhance transparency, traceability, and efficiency in supply chain management. AI algorithms analyze supply chain data to optimize inventory management, predict demand, and detect anomalies or fraudulent activities. Blockchain ensures the integrity and transparency of supply chain data, enabling stakeholders to track product provenance, authenticate products, and streamline logistics.
- **Healthcare:** In healthcare, blockchain and AI integration can improve patient care, medical research, and drug discovery. AI algorithms analyze electronic health records, medical images, and genomic data to diagnose diseases, predict patient outcomes, and personalize treatments. Blockchain ensures the security and privacy of patient data, facilitates data sharing among healthcare providers and researchers, and enables secure and auditable transactions in healthcare networks.
- **Financial Services:** Blockchain and AI integration have applications in financial services, such as fraud detection, risk management, and algorithmic trading. AI algorithms analyze financial data to detect fraudulent activities, assess credit risk, and optimize investment strategies. Blockchain enhances the security and transparency of financial transactions, facilitates cross-border payments, and enables decentralized finance (DeFi) applications, such as smart contracts and decentralized exchanges.

### 10.3.4 Challenges and Opportunities

- **Scalability and Performance:** Scalability and performance are key challenges in integrating blockchain and AI, as both technologies require processing and analyzing large volumes of data in real-time. Addressing scalability issues, such as transaction throughput and latency, is essential for deploying blockchain-based AI applications at scale.
- **Data Integration and Interoperability:** Integrating data from disparate sources and ensuring interoperability between blockchain and AI systems pose challenges in data integration and standardization. Developing data standards, protocols, and interoperability frameworks is critical for enabling seamless data exchange and collaboration in blockchain-based AI ecosystems.
- **Regulatory and Ethical Considerations:** Regulatory compliance, data privacy, and ethical considerations are important factors in deploying

blockchain-based AI applications, particularly in highly regulated industries, such as healthcare and finance. Ensuring compliance with data protection regulations, ethical guidelines, and industry standards is essential for building trust and confidence in blockchain-enabled AI solutions.

## 10.4 EVOLVING GOVERNANCE MODELS

Blockchain technology, known for its decentralized and transparent nature, has transformed various industries by enabling secure peer-to-peer transactions without the need for intermediaries. As blockchain ecosystems continue to expand and mature, the governance models governing these networks are also evolving.

The evolution of governance models in blockchain reflects the maturation and diversification of blockchain ecosystems, from emergent consensus to formalized on-chain governance mechanisms.

Blockchain governance emphasizes decentralized decision-making, community consensus, and transparency, enabling stakeholders to coordinate protocol upgrades and changes collaboratively. As blockchain governance continues to evolve, challenges such as governance coordination, regulatory uncertainty, and scalability must be addressed to realize the full potential of decentralized governance models. By fostering open discussions, inclusive participation, and transparent decision-making, blockchain governance can promote trust, resilience, and innovation in decentralized systems, shaping the future of blockchain technology and its impact on society.

### 10.4.1 Understanding Blockchain Governance

- **Decentralized Decision-Making**: Blockchain governance refers to the processes, mechanisms, and structures for making decisions and managing changes to blockchain protocols and networks. Unlike traditional centralized governance models, which rely on centralized authorities or governing bodies, blockchain governance emphasizes decentralized decision-making and community consensus.
- **Community Consensus**: Blockchain governance relies on community consensus to make decisions and implement changes to blockchain protocols. Participants in blockchain networks, including developers, miners, node operators, and users, contribute to governance decisions through open discussions, debates, and voting mechanisms.
- **Protocol Upgrades and Changes**: Blockchain governance is responsible for managing protocol upgrades, changes, and improvements to address technical issues, security vulnerabilities, and scalability challenges.

Governance mechanisms, such as soft forks, hard forks, and protocol proposals, enable stakeholders to coordinate and implement changes to blockchain protocols.

### 10.4.2 Evolution of Blockchain Governance Models

- **Bitcoin's Emergent Consensus:** Bitcoin, the first blockchain network, initially relied on an emergent consensus model for governance, where decisions were made based on the support and consensus of miners and node operators. Bitcoin Improvement Proposals (BIPs) were used to propose changes to the Bitcoin protocol, with community feedback and consensus determining their adoption.
- **Ethereum's On-Chain Governance:** Ethereum introduced on-chain governance mechanisms, such as Ethereum Improvement Proposals (EIPs) and decentralized autonomous organizations (DAOs), to enable more formalized and transparent governance processes. Ethereum's governance model combines on-chain voting and off-chain discussions to coordinate protocol upgrades and changes.
- **Tezos' Self-Amending Protocol:** Tezos introduced a self-amending protocol that enables automatic upgrades and changes to the Tezos blockchain through on-chain governance mechanisms. Tezos stakeholders can vote on proposed protocol amendments using a liquid democracy model, where token holders can vote directly or delegate their voting rights to others.

### 10.4.3 Approaches to Blockchain Governance

- **On-Chain Governance:** On-chain governance refers to governance mechanisms implemented directly on the blockchain, enabling stakeholders to propose, discuss, and vote on protocol changes and upgrades. On-chain governance models include token-based voting, governance tokens, and smart contracts for executing governance decisions.
- **Off-Chain Governance:** Off-chain governance involves governance mechanisms and processes conducted outside the blockchain, such as community forums, mailing lists, and developer meetings. Off-chain governance facilitates open discussions, debates, and collaboration among stakeholders, leading to informed governance decisions.
- **Hybrid Governance Models:** Hybrid governance models combine on-chain and off-chain governance mechanisms to achieve a balance between decentralization, transparency, and efficiency. Hybrid

governance models leverage both on-chain voting and off-chain discussions to coordinate protocol upgrades and changes while ensuring broad community participation and consensus.

### 10.4.4 Challenges and Opportunities

- **Governance Coordination:** Coordinating governance decisions and achieving consensus among diverse stakeholders pose challenges in blockchain governance. Ensuring effective communication, transparency, and inclusivity in governance processes is essential for fostering community participation and consensus.
- **Regulatory Uncertainty:** Regulatory uncertainty and legal challenges surrounding blockchain governance, such as securities regulation and governance token classification, pose risks and constraints on decentralized governance models. Addressing regulatory concerns and compliance requirements is crucial for ensuring the legality and legitimacy of blockchain governance.
- **Scalability and Efficiency:** Scalability and efficiency are key considerations in blockchain governance, particularly as blockchain networks grow and scale. Governance mechanisms must be scalable, efficient, and cost-effective to accommodate increasing network activity and participation while maintaining decentralization and security.

# CHAPTER 11

# SOCIAL AND ETHICAL CONSIDERATIONS

## 11.1 INCLUSIVITY AND ACCESS TO FINANCIAL SERVICES

Access to financial services is a fundamental aspect of economic empowerment and social inclusion. However, many individuals and communities worldwide lack access to basic financial services, such as banking, credit, and insurance.

Inclusivity and access to financial services are essential for promoting economic empowerment, social inclusion, and sustainable development. By addressing barriers to financial inclusion, such as geographical constraints, digital divide, and limited financial literacy, countries and organizations can unlock the potential of underserved populations and empower them to participate fully in the formal financial system. Innovative solutions and initiatives, such as mobile banking, agent banking, and fintech innovations, offer promising avenues for expanding financial inclusion and reaching marginalized communities. By promoting inclusivity and access to financial services, we can build a more equitable and inclusive society where everyone has the opportunity to thrive and prosper.

### 11.1.1 Understanding Financial Inclusion

- **Financial Inclusion Defined**: Financial inclusion refers to the availability and accessibility of financial services to all individuals and businesses, especially those historically underserved or excluded from the formal financial system. It encompasses access to banking, savings, credit, insurance, and payment services, as well as financial education and literacy.
- **Impact of Financial Inclusion**: Financial inclusion has far-reaching benefits for individuals, communities, and economies. It enables individuals to build assets, manage risks, and smooth consumption, leading to improved livelihoods, increased resilience, and poverty reduction. Moreover, financial inclusion promotes economic growth, job creation, and social stability, contributing to sustainable development and prosperity.

- **Barriers to Financial Inclusion:** Despite the importance of financial inclusion, numerous barriers and challenges hinder access to financial services for marginalized populations. These barriers include geographical constraints, lack of identification documents, limited financial literacy, discrimination, and exclusionary policies and practices by financial institutions.

### 11.1.2 Importance of Inclusivity and Access to Financial Services

- **Empowerment and Poverty Reduction:** Inclusivity and access to financial services empower individuals and communities to improve their economic well-being, build assets, and escape the cycle of poverty. Access to banking, credit, and savings accounts enables people to invest in education, healthcare, and entrepreneurship, leading to greater opportunities and upward mobility.
- **Resilience and Risk Management:** Financial inclusion enhances resilience and risk management by providing individuals with access to savings and insurance products. Savings accounts help individuals cope with financial emergencies and unexpected expenses, while insurance products protect against unforeseen risks, such as illness, disability, and natural disasters.
- **Social and Economic Development:** Inclusivity and access to financial services are essential drivers of social and economic development. By expanding financial inclusion, countries can promote economic growth, job creation, and income equality, as well as foster social cohesion, gender equality, and human rights.

### 11.1.3 Challenges to Financial Inclusion

- **Geographical Barriers:** Geographical barriers, such as remote rural areas, urban slums, and underserved regions, limit access to financial services for marginalized populations. Lack of physical infrastructure, banking branches, and internet connectivity exacerbates financial exclusion in these areas.
- **Digital Divide:** The digital divide, or the gap in access to digital technologies and internet connectivity, poses challenges to financial inclusion. Many underserved populations, including low-income individuals, elderly people, and rural communities, lack access to smartphones, computers, and reliable internet connections, hindering their participation in digital financial services.

- **Financial Literacy and Education:** Limited financial literacy and education among underserved populations contribute to financial exclusion and vulnerability. Many individuals lack basic knowledge and understanding of financial products, services, and concepts, such as interest rates, credit scores, and budgeting, making them susceptible to predatory practices and financial exploitation.

### 11.1.4 Innovative Solutions and Initiatives

- **Mobile Banking and Digital Wallets:** Mobile banking and digital wallets leverage mobile phones and digital technologies to provide access to financial services for underserved populations. Mobile money platforms, such as M-Pesa in Kenya and Paytm in India, enable people to send and receive money, pay bills, and access savings and credit services through their mobile devices.
- **Agent Banking and Branchless Banking:** Agent banking and branchless banking models extend the reach of financial services to remote and underserved areas through a network of agents, merchants, and community-based organizations. These models enable individuals to conduct banking transactions, such as deposits, withdrawals, and transfers, at convenient locations in their communities.
- **Fintech Innovations:** Fintech innovations, such as blockchain technology, artificial intelligence, and peer-to-peer lending platforms, are driving financial inclusion by offering innovative and affordable financial products and services. Blockchain-based platforms enable secure and transparent transactions, while AI-powered solutions provide personalized financial advice and credit scoring for underserved populations.

## 11.2 CRYPTOCURRENCY AND CRIMINAL ACTIVITY

Cryptocurrency and crime describe notable examples of cybercrime related to theft (or the otherwise illegal acquisition) of cryptocurrencies and some methods or security vulnerabilities commonly exploited.

Cryptojacking is a form of cybercrime specific to cryptocurrencies that have been used on websites to hijack a victim's resources and use them for hashing and mining cryptocurrency.

According to blockchain analysis company Chainalysis, around US$2.5 billion was laundered through Bitcoin between 2009 and 2018, and the fraction of cryptocurrency transactions linked to illicit activities has been on the rise since early 2019. In 2021, 0.15% of known cryptocurrency transactions conducted were involved in illicit activities like cybercrime, money laundering and terrorism financing, representing a total of $14 billion.

### 11.2.1 Background

There are various types of cryptocurrency wallets available, with different layers of security, including devices, software for different operating systems or browsers, and offline wallets. Novel exploits unique to blockchain transactions exist, and aim to generate unintended outcomes for those involved. One of the more well-known issues that open the possibility for exploits on Bitcoin is the transaction malleability problem. The Immunefi Crypto Losses 2022 Report lists industry losses from frauds and hacking as a combined total of US$3.9 billion for the year, and at US$8 billion for 2021.

### 11.2.2 Notable Thefts

In 2018, around US$1.7 billion in cryptocurrency was lost to scams, theft and fraud. In the first quarter of 2019, the amount of such losses rose to US$1.2 billion. 2022 was a record year for cryptocurrency theft, according to Chainalysis, with US$3.8 billion stolen worldwide during 125 system hacks, including US$1.7 billion stolen by "North Korea-linked hackers".

#### Exchanges

Notable cryptocurrency exchange compromises resulting in the loss of cryptocurrencies include:

- Between 2011 and 2014, US$350 million worth of bitcoin was stolen from Mt. Gox.
- In 2016, US$72 million was stolen through exploiting Bitfinex's exchange wallet, users were refunded.
- On December 7, 2017, Slovenian cryptocurrency exchange NiceHash reported that hackers had stolen over $70 million using a hijacked company computer.
- On December 19, 2017, Yapian, the owner of South Korean exchange Youbit, filed for bankruptcy after suffering two hacks that year. Customers were still granted access to 75% of their assets.
- In 2018, cryptocurrencies worth US$400 million were stolen from Coincheck.
- In May 2018, Bitcoin Gold had its transactions hijacked and abused by unknown hackers. Exchanges lost an estimated $18 m and Bitcoin Gold was delisted from Bittrex after it refused to pay its share of the damages.

- In June 2018, South Korean exchange Coinrail was hacked, losing over $37M worth of crypto. The hack worsened an already ongoing cryptocurrency selloff by an additional $42 billion.
- On July 9, 2018, the exchange Bancor, whose code and fundraising had been subjects of controversy, had $23.5 million in cryptocurrency stolen.
- Zaif US$60 million in Bitcoin, Bitcoin Cash and Monacoin was stolen in September 2018
- Binance In 2019 cryptocurrencies worth US$40 million were stolen.
- Africrypt founders are suspected of absconding in June 2021 with US$3.6 billion worth of Bitcoin
- PolyNetwork (DeFi) suffered the loss of US$611 million in a theft in August 2021.
- Japanese cryptocurrency exchange Liquid was compromised in August 2021 resulting in a loss of US$97 million worth of digital coins
- Cream Finance was subject to a US$29 million theft in August, 2021 and $130 million October 28, 2021.
- On December 2, 2021, users of the BadgerDAO DeFi lost around $118,500,000 worth of bitcoin and $679,000 worth of ethereum tokens in a front-end attack. A compromised API key of the Cloudflare content delivery network account allowed injecting a malicious script to the web interface. BadgerDAO "paused" all smart contracts due to user complaints.
- On December 6, 2021, the cryptocurrency exchange BitMart lost around $135M worth of Ethereum and an estimated $46 million in other cryptocurrencies due to a breach of two of its wallets. Although BitMart stated that it would reimburse its clients, many BitMart clients have not received any money from the exchange as of January 2022.
- On December 12, 2021, users of VulcanForge lost around $135M worth of PYR due to breaches of multiple wallets. Partnering centralized exchanges had been notified of the hack and they have pledged to seize any stolen funds upon deposit.
- On January 27, 2022, Qubit Finance (DeFi) lost around $80M worth of Binance Coin due to a flaw in the smart contract that enabled the withdrawal of the said amount in exchange for a deposit of 0 ETH.
- In March 2022, the largest cryptocurrency theft of the year, US$625 million in ether and USD coin was stolen from the Ronin Network. Hacked nodes were finally discovered when a user reported being

unable to withdraw funds. The heist was later linked to Lazarus Group, a North Korean state-backed hacking collective, by the U.S. Treasury Department.

- On September 20, 2022, Wintermute was hacked resulting in theft of US$160 million. The company attributed the vulnerability to a service used by the platform that generates vanity addresses for digital accounts.
- On September 25, 2023, it was reported that $200 million was stolen by hackers from crypto firm Mixin Network. The company stated that the database of its network's cloud service provider was attacked by hackers resulting in the loss of the assets.

## Wallets

The *Parity Wallet* has had two security incidents amounting to 666,773 ETH lost or stolen. In July 2017, due to a bug in the multisignature code, 153,037 ETH (approximately US$32 million at the time) were stolen. In November 2017, a subsequent multisignature flaw in *Parity* made 513,774 ETH (about US$150 million) unreachable; as of March 2019, the funds were still frozen.

## Energy

Notable cases of electricity theft to mine proof-of-work cryptocurrencies include:

- In February 2021 Malaysian police arrested six men involved in a Bitcoin mining operation which had stolen US$2 million in electricity.
- Ukraine authorities shut down an underground gaming and cryptocurrency farm in July, 2021, accused of stealing $259,300 of electricity each month.
- In July 2021 Malaysian authorities destroyed 1,069 cryptocurrency mining systems accused of stealing electricity from the grid.
- In May, 2021 UK authorities closed a suspected bitcoin mine after Western Power Distribution found an illegal connection to the electricity supply.

## Blockchains

### Bitcoin

There have been many cases of bitcoin theft. As of December 2017, around 980,000 bitcoins—over five percent of all bitcoin in circulation—had been lost on cryptocurrency exchanges.

One type of theft involves a third party accessing the private key to a victim's bitcoin address, or of an online wallet. If the private key is stolen, all the bitcoins from the compromised address can be transferred. In that case, the network does not have any provisions to identify the thief, block further transactions of those stolen bitcoins, or return them to the legitimate owner.

Theft also occurs at sites where bitcoins are used to purchase illicit goods. In late November 2013, an estimated US$100 million in bitcoins were allegedly stolen from the online illicit goods marketplace Sheep Marketplace, which immediately closed. Users tracked the coins as they were processed and converted to cash, but no funds were recovered and no culprits were identified. A different black market, Silk Road 2, stated that during a February 2014 hack, bitcoins valued at $2.7 million were taken from escrow accounts.

Sites where users exchange bitcoins for cash or store them in "wallets" are also targets for theft. Inputs.io, an Australian wallet service, was hacked twice in October 2013 and lost more than $1 million in bitcoins. GBL, a Chinese bitcoin trading platform, suddenly shut down on 26 October 2013; subscribers, unable to log in, lost up to $5 million worth of bitcoin. In late February 2014 Mt. Gox, one of the largest virtual currency exchanges, filed for bankruptcy in Tokyo amid reports that bitcoins worth US$350 million had been stolen. Flexcoin, a bitcoin storage specialist based in Alberta, Canada, shut down in March 2014 after saying it discovered a theft of about $650,000 in bitcoins. Poloniex, a digital currency exchange, reported in March 2014 that it lost bitcoins valued at around $50,000. In January 2015 UK-based bitstamp, the third busiest bitcoin exchange globally was hacked and US$5 million in bitcoins were stolen. February 2015 saw a Chinese exchange named BTER lose bitcoins worth nearly $2 million to hackers.

A major bitcoin exchange, Bitfinex, was compromised by the 2016 Bitfinex hack, when nearly 120,000 bitcoins (around US$71 million) was stolen in 2016. Bitfinex was forced to suspend its trading. The theft was the second-largest bitcoin heist ever, dwarfed only by the Mt. Gox theft in 2014. According to *Forbes*, "All of Bitfinex's customers... will stand to lose money. The company has announced a cut of 36.067% across the board." Following the hack the company failed to refund customers, though efforts are continuing. In 2022, the US government recovered 94,636 bitcoin (worth approximately $3.6 billion at the time of recovery) from the 2016 thefts of the Bitfinex exchange, reported as the "largest financial seizure" in U.S. history.

By February 2022, the amount of bitcoin stolen in 2016 had increased in value to $4.5 billion. Two people were arrested for the thefts in 2022; married couple Ilya "Dutch" Lichtenstein and rapper Heather "Razzlekhan" Morgan were charged with conspiracy to commit money laundering and conspiracy to defraud the United States.

On May 7, 2019, hackers stole over 7000 Bitcoins from the Binance Cryptocurrency Exchange, at a value of over 40 million US dollars. Binance CEO Zhao Changpeng stated: "The hackers used a variety of techniques, including phishing, viruses, and other attacks... The hackers had the patience to wait, and execute well-orchestrated actions through multiple seemingly independent accounts at the most opportune time."

Thefts have raised safety concerns. Charles Hayter, founder of the digital currency comparison website CryptoCompare said, "It's a reminder of the fragility of the infrastructure in such a nascent industry." According to the hearing of U.S. House of Representatives Committee on Small Business on April 2, 2014, "these vendors lack regulatory oversight, minimum capital standards and don't provide consumer protection against loss or theft."

**Ethereum**

- In June 2016, hackers exploited a vulnerability in The DAO to steal US$50 million. Subsequently, the currency was forked into Ethereum Classic, and Ethereum, with the latter continuing with the new blockchain without the exploited translations.
- On November 21, 2017, Tether announced that it had been hacked, losing $31 million in USDT from its core treasury wallet. The company has 'tagged' the stolen currency, hoping to 'lock' them in the hacker's wallet (making them unspendable).
- In 2022, hackers created a signature account on a blockchain bridge called "Wormhole" and stole more than $300 million worth of ether.

### 11.2.3 Fraud

#### Exit Scams and Ponzi Schemes through Initial Coin Offerings (ICOs)

Most exit scams (or *rugpulls*) as well as many ponzi schemes involving cryptocurrencies are performed through Initial Coin Offerings (ICOs). As an example, according to a report by Satis Group almost 80% of all projects launched through an ICO in 2017 were scams. These scams usually involve attracting investments from mostly retail investors, inflating the price and the perpetrators subsequently abandoning the project in question after selling off their own shares.

The novelty of ICOs accounts for the current lack of governmental regulation. This lack of regulatory measures as well as the pseudonymity of cryptocurrency transactions and their international nature across countless jurisdictions in many different countries can make it much more difficult to identify and take legal action against perpetrators involved in these scams. Since 2017 the SEC has been actively pursuing groups and individuals responsible for ICO-related scams.

### Examples of ICO-related Scams

- **AriseCoin (AriseBank):** *AriseBank* marketed itself as the world's first *decentralized bank*, falsely claiming to be able to offer FDIC-insured accounts, VISA-cards as well as services related to cryptocurrency and making other false statements. *AriseBank* promoted its *AriseCoin* through celebrity endorsement and social media in order to raise the US$1 billion the company was aiming for. Their ICO was halted by the SEC in early 2018 with their CEO and COO receiving a fine of US$2.7 million.
- **BitConnect:** Bitconnect was among the highest performing cryptocurrencies in 2017, promising investors enormous returns through a trading bot. At its height it reached a market capitalization of US$3.4 billion. In early 2018 the exchanged ceased to operate with investors losing millions of dollars, amounting to a total of US$14.5 million. It later turned out that the initial profits were generated through a ponzi scheme by paying earlier customers with money made through newer customers. Legal action against the perpetrators was taken on an international scale.
- **Centra:** Centra was a Miami-based company claiming to offer a cryptocurrency-based debit card backed by VISA and Mastercard. The company raised US$32 million by October 2017 through an ICO and few months later performing an exit-scam. In April 2018 two of the founders were arrested. It was soon revealed that neither Mastercard nor VISA backed the company in their alleged efforts.
- **Modern Tech (PinCoin/iFan):** Based in Vietnam, Modern Tech hosted two separate ICOs for *PinCoin* as well as *iFan* promising monthly returns of 48%. After the initial success the founders ran off with approximately US$660 million raised from 32,000 investors. The founders are still at large and none of the funds have been retrieved.
- **PlexCoin:** After Dominic Lacroix and Sabrina Paradis-Rogers (the founders of *PlexCoin*) had officially raised around US$15 million through a fraudulent ICO in August 2017 while promising a return of 1,354 % within a month, the SEC filed a civil complaint in December of the same year against them and sought an injunction to cease those sales, freeze the assets involved, pay civil penalties and prohibit the ones responsible behind the token launch from participating in any future offerings of cryptocurrency. Shortly after Lacroix was sentenced to two months in prison and fined CA$110,000 by the Quebec Superior Court. The SEC's proceedings lead to seven-figure fines for the defendants in 2019 and a retrieval of the investors' funds. During the proceedings the SEC was

able to prove that the success of the ICO was inflated by the founders who in fact had raised US$8.5 million instead of the US$15 million they had announced.

### Ponzi Schemes

Ponzi schemes are another common form of utilizing blockchainbased technologies to commit fraud. Most schemes of this sort use multi-level marketing schemes to encourage investors to conduct risky investments. Onecoin is one of the more notable examples of cryptocurrency-ponzi schemes: Founded in 2014 by Ruja Ignatova, OneCoin is estimated to have generated US$4 billion in income. While at least in China some of the investors' funds have been recovered and several members of the organisation arrested in the U.S., Ignatova herself is still at large.

### Money Laundering

Due to the inability of third parties to de-pseudonymize cryptotransactions criminal entities have often resorted to using cryptocurrency to conduct money laundering. Especially ICOs lacking KYC guidelines and anti-money laundering procedures are often used to launder illicit funds due to the pseudonymity offered by them. By using ICOs criminals launder these funds by buying tokens off of legitimate investors and selling them. This issue is intensified through the lack of measures against money laundering implemented by centralized cryptocurrency-exchanges.

A well-known early example of money laundering using cryptocurrencies is Silk Road. Shut down in 2013 with its founder Ross Ulbricht indicted for among other counts a money laundering conspiracy, the website was used for several illicit activities including money laundering solely using Bitcoin as a form of payment.

Apart from traditional cryptocurrencies, Non-Fungible Tokens (NFTs) are also commonly used in connection with money laundering activities. NFTs are often used to perform Wash Trading by creating several different wallets for one individual, generating several fictitious sales and consequently selling the respective NFT to a third party. According to a report by Chainalysis these types of wash trades are becoming increasingly popular among money launderers especially due to the largely anonymous nature of transactions on NFT marketplaces. Auction platforms for NFT sales may face regulatory pressure to comply with anti-money laundering legislation.

#### Regulatory Measures

Canada is generally regarded as the first state-actor implementing regulatory measures dealing with money laundering conducted by usage of cryptocurrencies. By 2013 the Financial Crimes Enforcement Network (FinCEN) — in direct reference to the centralized exchange Mt. Gox — issued regulations making it clear that all crypto-to-fiat exchangers had to apply KYC- as well as anti-money laundering methods. Any suspicious transactions have therefore to be reported to the authorities. Centralized exchanges have to register as money transmitters, with the exact definition of who and what constitutes a *money transmitter* in the cryptosphere being somewhat blurred and regulations differing between the different states of the U.S. An important exemption from these regulations are decentralized exchanges due to the fact that they do not hold any fiat-currency.

As part of the *Fourth Anti-Money Laundering Directive* of 2015 and in an effort to combat money laundering and the financing of terrorism, the European Union has issued a directive making all member-states to have to make sure that cryptoexchanges are licensed and registered. The EU is furthermore planning to take measures to ensure that all customers of cryptocurrency-exchanges are to verify their identity as part of the registration process.

**Regarding NFTs:**

- Auction platforms for NFT sales may face regulatory pressure to comply with anti-money laundering legislation. A February 2022 study from the United States Treasury assessed that there was "some evidence of money laundering risk in the high-value art market," including through "the emerging digital art market, such as the use of non-fungible tokens (NFTs)." The study considered how NFT transactions may be a simpler option for laundering money through art by avoiding the transportation or insurance complications in trading physical art. Several NFT exchanges were labeled as virtual asset service providers that may be subject to Financial Crimes Enforcement Network regulations.
- The European Union has yet to establish specific regulations to combat money laundering through NFTs. The European Commission announced in July 2022 that it is planning to draw regulations regarding that issue by 2024.

## Further Examples

Josh Garza, who founded the cryptocurrency startups GAW Miners and ZenMiner in 2014, acknowledged in a plea agreement that the companies were part of a pyramid scheme, and pleaded guilty to wire fraud in 2015. The U.S. Securities and Exchange Commission separately brought a civil enforcement action against Garza, who was eventually ordered to pay a judgment of US$9.1 million plus $700,000 in interest. The SEC's complaint stated that Garza, through his companies, had fraudulently sold "investment contracts representing shares in the profits they claimed would be generated" from mining. Garza was later found guilty of fraud and ordered to pay US$9 million and begin serving a 21-month sentence commencing January 2019 by the U.S. Attorney's Office District of Connecticut.

The cryptocurrency community refers to pre-mining, hidden launches, ICO or extreme rewards for the altcoin founders as deceptive practices. This is at times an inherent part of the cryptocurrency's design. Pre-mining refers to the practice of generating the currency before its released to the public.

FTX and Alameda Research founder and CEO Sam Bankman-Fried was indicted by the U.S. District Court for the Southern District of New York in December 2022 and charged with commodities and wire fraud, securities fraud and money laundering, as well as with violating campaign finance laws.

### 11.2.4 Malware

#### Malware Attacks

Some malware can steal private keys for bitcoin wallets allowing the bitcoins themselves to be stolen. The most common type searches computers for cryptocurrency wallets to upload to a remote server where they can be cracked and their coins were stolen. Many of these also log keystrokes to record passwords, often avoiding the need to crack the keys. A different approach detects when a bitcoin address is copied to a clipboard and quickly replaces it with a different address, tricking people into sending bitcoins to the wrong address. This method is effective because bitcoin transactions are irreversible.

One virus, spread through the Pony botnet, was reported in February 2014 to have stolen up to $220,000 in cryptocurrencies including bitcoins from 85 wallets. Security company Trustwave, which tracked the malware, reports that its latest version was able to steal 30 types of digital currency.

A type of Mac malware active in August 2013, Bitvanity posed as a vanity wallet address generator and stole addresses and private keys from other bitcoin client software. A different trojan for macOS, called CoinThief was reported in February 2014 to be responsible for multiple bitcoin thefts. The software was hidden in versions of some cryptocurrency apps on Download.com and MacUpdate.

#### Ransomware

Many types of ransomware demand payment in bitcoin. One program called CryptoLocker, typically spread through legitimate-looking email attachments, encrypts the hard drive of an infected computer, then displays a countdown timer and demands a ransom in bitcoin, to decrypt it. Massachusetts police said they paid a 2 bitcoin ransom in November 2013, worth more than $1,300 at the time, to decrypt one of their hard drives. Bitcoin was used as the ransom medium in the WannaCry ransomware. One ransomware variant disables internet access and demands credit card information to restore it, while secretly mining bitcoins. As of June 2018, most ransomware attackers preferred to use currencies other than bitcoin, with 44% of attacks in the first half of 2018 demanding Monero, which is highly private and difficult to trace, compared to 10% for bitcoin and 11% for Ether.

### Unauthorized Mining

Cryptojacking is the act of exploiting a computer to mine cryptocurrencies, often through websites, against the user's will or while the user is unaware. One notable piece of software used for cryptojacking was Coinhive, which was used in over two-thirds of cryptojacks before its March 2019 shutdown. The cryptocurrencies mined the most often are privacy coins—coins with hidden transaction histories—such as Monero and Zcash. Like most malicious attacks on the computing public, the motive is profit, but unlike other threats, it is designed to remain completely hidden from the user. Cryptojacking malware can lead to slowdowns and crashes due to straining of computational resources. Bitcoin mining by personal computers infected with malware is being challenged by dedicated hardware, such as FPGA and ASIC platforms, which are more efficient in terms of power consumption and thus may have lower costs than theft of computing resources.

## 11.2.5 Phishing

A phishing website to generate private IOTA wallet seed passphrases, and collected wallet keys, with estimates of up to US$4 million worth of MIOTA tokens stolen. The malicious website operated for an unknown amount of time and was discovered in January 2018.

## 11.2.6 Other Incidents

In 2015, two members of the Silk Road Task Force—a multi-agency federal task force that carried out the U.S. investigation of Silk Road—were convicted over charges pertaining to corruption. Former DEA agent, Carl Mark Force, had attempted to extort Silk Road founder Ross Ulbricht ("Dread Pirate Roberts") by faking the murder of an informant. He pleaded guilty to money laundering, obstruction of justice, and extortion under color of official right, and was sentenced to 6.5 years in federal prison.

Former U.S. Secret Service agent, Shaun Bridges, pleaded guilty to crimes relating to his diversion of $800,000 worth of bitcoins to his personal account during the investigation, and also separately pleaded guilty to money laundering in connection to another cryptocurrency theft. Bridges were sentenced to almost eight years in federal prison.

Gerald Cotten founded QuadrigaCX in 2013, after graduating from the Schulich School of Business in Toronto. Cotten was acting as the sole curator of the exchange. Quadriga had no official bank accounts since banks at the time had no method of managing cryptocurrency.

In late 2018, Canada's largest crypto exchange QuadrigaCX lost US$190 million in cryptocurrency when the owner died; he was the only one with knowledge of the password to a storage wallet. The exchange filed for bankruptcy in 2019.

Michael Terpin, the founder and chief executive officer of Transform Group, a San Juan, Puerto Rico-based company that advises blockchain businesses on public relations and communications, sued Ellis Pinsky in New York on May 7, 2020, for leading a "sophisticated cybercrime spree" that stole US$24 million in cryptocurrency by hacking into Terpin's phone in 2018. Terpin also sued Nicholas Truglia and won a $75.8 million judgment against Truglia in 2019 in California state court.

On July 15, 2020, Twitter accounts of prominent personalities and firms, including Joe Biden, Barack Obama, Bill Gates, Elon Musk, Jeff Bezos, Apple, Kanye West, Michael Bloomberg and Uber were hacked. Twitter confirmed that it was a coordinated social engineering attack on their own employees. Twitter released its statement six hours after the attack took place. Hackers posted the message to transfer the Bitcoin in a Bitcoin wallet, which would double the amount. The wallet's balance was expected to increase to more than $100,000 as the message spread among the Twitter followers.

In 2021, US Authorities carried out a raid on James Zhong's home in Gainesville, Georgia. Authorities found over 51,000 bitcoin that Zhong had stolen from Silk Road between 2012 and 2013. Through an error on Silk Road, Zhong was able to withdraw more bitcoin than what was initially deposited. He concealed his identity and was able to evade authorities for nearly a decade. Zhong ended up pleading guilty to wire fraud and was sentenced to 1 year and 1 day in prison along with a forfeiture of all bitcoin.

In 2022, the Federal Trade Commission reported that $139 million in cryptocurrency was stolen by romance scammers in 2020. Some scammers targeted dating apps with fake profiles.

In early 2022, the Beanstalk cryptocurrency was stripped of its reserves, which were valued at more than US$180 million, after attackers had managed to use borrowed US$80 million in cryptocurrency to buy enough voting rights to transfer the reserves to their own accounts outside the system. It was initially unclear if such an exploit of governance procedures was illegal.

## 11.3 ENVIRONMENTAL SUSTAINABILITY IN BLOCKCHAIN

Environmental sustainability has become a critical consideration in the development and adoption of blockchain technology. While blockchain offers numerous benefits in terms of decentralization, transparency, and security, its energy-intensive consensus mechanisms have raised concerns about its environmental impact. Addressing the environmental sustainability challenges associated with blockchain technology requires concerted efforts from industry stakeholders, policymakers, and environmental advocates. By transitioning to energy-efficient consensus mechanisms, adopting sustainable mining practices, and leveraging blockchain for environmental conservation efforts, the blockchain industry can mitigate its environmental impact and contribute to global efforts to combat climate change and promote environmental sustainability. With continued innovation, collaboration, and awareness, blockchain technology has the potential to be a powerful tool for environmental conservation and sustainability, driving positive social and environmental outcomes for future generations.

### 11.3.1 Understanding the Environmental Impact of Blockchain

- **Energy Consumption:** The most significant environmental concern associated with blockchain technology is its high energy consumption, particularly in proof-of-work (PoW) consensus mechanisms used in cryptocurrencies like Bitcoin and Ethereum. PoW consensus requires miners to solve complex mathematical puzzles to validate transactions and secure the network, consuming vast amounts of computational power and electricity.
- **Carbon Footprint:** The energy-intensive nature of blockchain mining operations contributes to significant carbon emissions, exacerbating concerns about climate change and global warming. Research has shown that Bitcoin mining alone consumes as much energy as entire countries, leading to substantial carbon footprints and environmental degradation.
- **E-Waste Generation:** In addition to energy consumption, blockchain technology also contributes to electronic waste (e-waste) generation through the production and disposal of mining hardware, such as ASICs (Application-Specific Integrated Circuits) and GPUs (Graphics Processing Units). The rapid turnover of mining equipment and the lack of recycling infrastructure further compound the environmental impact of blockchain mining.

### 11.3.2 Efforts to Mitigate the Environmental Impact

- **Transition to Proof-of-Stake (PoS):** One of the most promising solutions to reduce the environmental impact of blockchain is the transition from PoW to proof-of-stake (PoS) consensus mechanisms. PoS consensus requires validators to stake a certain amount of cryptocurrency as collateral to validate transactions and secure the network, eliminating the need for energy-intensive mining operations.

- **Energy-Efficient Mining Practices:** Blockchain mining operations are increasingly adopting energy-efficient mining practices, such as renewable energy sources (e.g., solar, wind, hydroelectric), energy-efficient hardware, and location-based optimization (e.g., siting mining facilities in regions with abundant renewable energy). These practices help reduce the carbon footprint of blockchain mining and promote environmental sustainability.
- **Carbon Offsetting and Compensation:** Some blockchain projects and cryptocurrency platforms have implemented carbon offsetting and compensation initiatives to mitigate their environmental impact. These initiatives involve investing in renewable energy projects, reforestation efforts, and carbon credits to offset the carbon emissions generated by blockchain operations.

### 11.3.3 Blockchain for Environmental Conservation

- **Supply Chain Traceability:** Blockchain technology can enhance supply chain traceability and transparency, enabling consumers to track the origins and environmental footprint of products throughout the supply chain. By recording and verifying environmental data, such as carbon emissions, water usage, and waste generation, on the blockchain, companies can improve accountability and sustainability in their supply chains.
- **Carbon Credits and Environmental Markets:** Blockchain-based platforms can facilitate the trading of carbon credits and participation in environmental markets, enabling individuals and organizations to buy, sell, and trade carbon offsets and environmental credits. These platforms leverage smart contracts and decentralized exchanges to automate transactions and ensure transparency and integrity in environmental markets.
- **Decentralized Conservation Initiatives:** Blockchain technology can support decentralized conservation initiatives, such as wildlife tracking, habitat restoration, and biodiversity monitoring. By recording wildlife sightings, habitat data, and conservation efforts on the blockchain, conservation organizations and researchers can collaborate, share data, and coordinate conservation efforts more effectively.

### 11.3.4 Challenges and Future Directions

- **Scalability and Efficiency:** While transitioning to PoS consensus can reduce the energy consumption of blockchain networks, scalability and efficiency remain significant challenges. Improving scalability and efficiency through protocol upgrades, layer 2 solutions, and optimization techniques is essential for promoting environmental sustainability in blockchain technology.

- **Regulatory and Policy Frameworks:** Developing regulatory and policy frameworks for environmental sustainability in blockchain requires collaboration among governments, industry stakeholders, and environmental organizations. Establishing standards, guidelines, and incentives for sustainable blockchain practices can foster innovation and adoption while ensuring environmental protection.
- **Public Awareness and Education:** Increasing public awareness and education about the environmental impact of blockchain technology is crucial for driving demand for sustainable solutions and encouraging responsible use of blockchain networks. Educational initiatives, awareness campaigns, and advocacy efforts can empower individuals and organizations to make informed decisions and take actions to reduce the environmental footprint of blockchain.

## 11.4 ETHICAL USE OF BLOCKCHAIN TECHNOLOGY

Blockchain technology holds immense potential to transform industries, empower individuals, and foster economic inclusion. However, like any powerful tool, its ethical use is paramount to ensuring positive social impact and preventing harm.

Ethical use of blockchain technology requires a commitment to transparency, privacy, security, inclusivity, and sustainability. By adhering to ethical principles and values, blockchain stakeholders can harness the transformative potential of blockchain technology to create positive social impact, empower individuals, and build trust in decentralized systems.

Addressing challenges, such as regulatory compliance, governance, and awareness, presents opportunities for collaboration and innovation in promoting ethical behavior within the blockchain ecosystem. Ultimately, by prioritizing ethics and social responsibility, blockchain technology can contribute to a more equitable, transparent, and sustainable future for all.

### 11.4.1 Understanding Ethical Considerations in Blockchain

- **Transparency and Trust:** Blockchain technology offers transparency and immutability, enabling trustless transactions and data integrity. Ethical use of blockchain involves maintaining transparency in blockchain networks, ensuring accurate and truthful representation of data, and fostering trust among stakeholders.

- **Data Privacy and Security**: Protecting data privacy and security is crucial in blockchain applications, particularly in decentralized systems where personal and sensitive information may be exposed to the public. Ethical use of blockchain involves implementing robust security measures, encryption techniques, and data protection protocols to safeguard user privacy and prevent unauthorized access or data breaches.
- **Inclusivity and Accessibility**: Blockchain technology has the potential to promote inclusivity and accessibility by providing financial services to underserved populations, enabling identity verification for marginalized communities, and facilitating cross-border transactions. Ethical use of blockchain involves ensuring equal access to blockchain-based services and opportunities for all individuals, regardless of their socioeconomic status, geographic location, or technical expertise.

### 11.4.2 Principles for Ethical Use of Blockchain

- **Transparency**: Transparency is a fundamental principle of ethical blockchain use, requiring open and transparent communication, disclosure of information, and accountability among stakeholders. Transparent governance mechanisms, public audits, and verifiable data sources promote trust and accountability in blockchain ecosystems.
- **Privacy**: Protecting user privacy and data confidentiality is essential for ethical blockchain use. Implementing privacy-enhancing technologies, such as zero-knowledge proofs and homomorphic encryption, and adhering to privacy regulations, such as the General Data Protection Regulation (GDPR), help preserve individual privacy rights and prevent misuse of personal data.
- **Security**: Ensuring the security and integrity of blockchain networks and applications is critical for ethical use. Implementing robust security measures, conducting regular security audits, and addressing vulnerabilities promptly help mitigate the risk of cyberattacks, data breaches, and fraud, safeguarding the interests of users and stakeholders.
- **Inclusivity**: Promoting inclusivity and accessibility is a key principle of ethical blockchain use, ensuring that blockchain-based services and opportunities are available to all individuals, regardless of their background or circumstances. Designing user-friendly interfaces, providing educational resources, and addressing barriers to entry help empower marginalized communities and promote equal participation in blockchain ecosystems.

- **Sustainability:** Environmental sustainability is an increasingly important consideration in blockchain use, given its energy-intensive consensus mechanisms and carbon footprint. Ethical blockchain use involves minimizing energy consumption, adopting renewable energy sources, and supporting sustainable mining practices to mitigate environmental impact and promote eco-friendly blockchain solutions.

### 11.4.3 Challenges and Opportunities

- **Regulatory Compliance:** Adhering to regulatory requirements and compliance standards presents challenges for ethical blockchain use, particularly in decentralized and borderless networks. Collaborating with regulators, policymakers, and industry stakeholders to develop clear and consistent regulatory frameworks helps ensure compliance with legal and ethical standards while fostering innovation and adoption.
- **Governance and Accountability:** Establishing transparent governance mechanisms and accountability structures is essential for promoting ethical behavior and resolving disputes within blockchain communities. Decentralized governance models, such as DAOs (Decentralized Autonomous Organizations) and token-based voting systems, enable stakeholders to participate in decision-making processes and hold platform operators accountable for their actions.
- **Education and Awareness:** Increasing awareness and understanding of ethical considerations in blockchain technology is crucial for promoting responsible use and preventing misuse. Educating developers, users, and policymakers about ethical principles, best practices, and potential risks helps foster a culture of ethical behavior and responsible innovation within the blockchain ecosystem.

# CHAPTER 12

# EDUCATIONAL RESOURCES AND FURTHER READING

## 12.1 ONLINE PLATFORMS AND COURSES

As interest in blockchain technology and cryptocurrency continues to grow, there is a growing demand for educational resources to help individuals and professionals deepen their understanding and expertise in this rapidly evolving field. Online platforms and courses offer a convenient and accessible way to learn about blockchain and cryptocurrency, covering topics ranging from fundamental concepts to advanced applications.

From introductory courses covering basic concepts to advanced tutorials on blockchain development and cryptocurrency trading, online platforms and courses offer a wealth of educational resources for learners interested in blockchain and cryptocurrency. Whether you're a beginner looking to understand the fundamentals or a professional seeking to deepen your expertise, there are plenty of options available to help you learn and grow in this exciting and rapidly evolving field. By leveraging online platforms and courses, individuals can acquire the knowledge and skills needed to navigate the world of blockchain and cryptocurrency with confidence and competence.

- **Coursera:** Coursera is a popular online learning platform that offers a wide range of courses and specializations in blockchain and cryptocurrency. From introductory courses covering basic concepts to specialized courses focusing on topics like smart contracts, decentralized finance (DeFi), and blockchain development, Coursera provides comprehensive learning resources for learners of all levels. Courses are taught by leading experts from top universities and institutions around the world.
- **Udemy:** Udemy is another popular online learning platform that offers a diverse selection of courses on blockchain and cryptocurrency. With courses ranging from beginner-friendly introductions to in-depth technical tutorials, Udemy caters to learners with varying levels of expertise and interests. Topics covered include blockchain fundamentals, cryptocurrency trading, blockchain development, and

more. Udemy courses are self-paced, allowing learners to study at their own convenience.

- **edX:** edX is an online learning platform that offers courses and programs from top universities and institutions worldwide. In collaboration with leading universities like MIT, Harvard, and UC Berkeley, edX offers a variety of courses and micro-credentials in blockchain and cryptocurrency. Learners can explore topics such as blockchain technology, cryptocurrency economics, digital currencies, and blockchain applications in different industries.
- **Blockchain Council:** Blockchain Council is a leading online platform dedicated to blockchain education and certification. Offering a wide range of courses, certifications, and training programs, Blockchain Council covers various aspects of blockchain technology and cryptocurrency. From introductory courses for beginners to advanced certifications for professionals, Blockchain Council provides comprehensive learning resources and certification exams to validate learners' skills and expertise.
- **Binance Academy:** Binance Academy is an educational platform operated by Binance, one of the world's largest cryptocurrency exchanges. Binance Academy offers a wealth of free educational content on blockchain, cryptocurrency, trading, and investing. With articles, tutorials, videos, and interactive quizzes, Binance Academy provides accessible and engaging learning resources for beginners and experienced enthusiasts alike.
- **CoinDesk Learn:** CoinDesk Learn is an educational platform offered by CoinDesk, a leading cryptocurrency news and information website. CoinDesk Learn provides free educational content on blockchain, cryptocurrency, and decentralized finance (DeFi). With beginner-friendly guides, articles, and video tutorials, CoinDesk Learn offers valuable insights and information for individuals looking to learn about the latest trends and developments in the cryptocurrency space.
- **CryptoZombies:** CryptoZombies is a unique online platform that offers interactive coding tutorials for learning blockchain development. Focusing on the Ethereum blockchain and Solidity programming language, CryptoZombies teaches learners how to build decentralized applications (DApps) and smart contracts. With hands-on coding exercises and gamified lessons, CryptoZombies provides an engaging learning experience for aspiring blockchain developers.

## 12.2 RESEARCH PAPERS AND JOURNALS

Research papers and journals are valuable resources for staying informed about the latest developments, advancements, and insights in the field of blockchain and cryptocurrency. These academic publications provide in-depth analysis, peer-reviewed research, and expert commentary on various aspects of blockchain technology, cryptocurrencies, decentralized finance (DeFi), and related topics.

Research papers and journals play a crucial role in advancing knowledge and understanding in the field of blockchain and cryptocurrency. By accessing reputable academic publications, researchers, practitioners, and enthusiasts can stay informed about the latest research findings, emerging trends, and best practices in blockchain technology, cryptocurrencies, and related areas. Whether you're seeking in-depth analysis, technical insights, or interdisciplinary perspectives, exploring research papers and journals can provide valuable insights and contribute to the ongoing discourse in the field.

- **IEEE Transactions on Blockchain:** IEEE Transactions on Blockchain is a peer-reviewed journal that publishes high-quality research papers, technical articles, and reviews on blockchain technology and its applications. Covering topics such as consensus mechanisms, smart contracts, privacy, security, scalability, and interoperability, IEEE Transactions on Blockchain provides valuable insights and analysis from leading researchers and experts in the field.
- **Journal of Cryptocurrency and Blockchain Technology Research:** The Journal of Cryptocurrency and Blockchain Technology Research is an academic journal dedicated to publishing original research papers, case studies, and literature reviews on cryptocurrency and blockchain technology. With a focus on interdisciplinary research and practical applications, the journal covers topics such as cryptographic protocols, distributed ledger technology, cryptocurrency economics, and regulatory issues.
- **International Journal of Blockchain and Cryptocurrency (IJBC):** The International Journal of Blockchain and Cryptocurrency (IJBC) is a scholarly journal that publishes research papers, technical reports, and theoretical articles on blockchain technology, cryptocurrencies, and decentralized systems. IJBC covers a wide range of topics, including blockchain security, consensus algorithms, digital asset management, and blockchain applications in various industries.
- **Blockchain Research Institute (BRI) Publications:** The Blockchain Research Institute (BRI) produces a wide range of research papers,

reports, and publications on blockchain technology and its impact on business, society, and government. Led by industry experts and thought leaders, BRI publications cover topics such as blockchain adoption, enterprise use cases, governance models, and regulatory frameworks.

- **CoinDesk Research:** CoinDesk Research is a leading provider of market insights, analysis, and research reports on cryptocurrency and blockchain technology. CoinDesk's research publications cover a range of topics, including market trends, investment analysis, industry developments, and regulatory updates. With contributions from industry analysts and experts, CoinDesk Research provides valuable intelligence for investors, businesses, and policymakers.
- **arXiv:** arXiv is a preprint repository that hosts research papers and academic articles in various disciplines, including computer science, mathematics, and physics. Researchers and scholars often submit preprints of their papers related to blockchain and cryptocurrency to arXiv for open access dissemination and peer review. Browsing arXiv's repository can uncover a wealth of cutting-edge research and emerging trends in the field.
- **Cryptology ePrint Archive:** The Cryptology ePrint Archive is an online repository of research papers, technical reports, and conference proceedings in the field of cryptography and cryptology. Researchers and practitioners often publish papers related to blockchain security, cryptographic protocols, and privacy-enhancing technologies in the Cryptology ePrint Archive, making it a valuable resource for staying updated on the latest developments in the field.

## 12.3 BOOKS AND PUBLICATIONS FOR DEEPER UNDERSTANDING

Books and publications are invaluable resources for gaining a deeper understanding of blockchain and cryptocurrency, covering a wide range of topics from technical concepts to business applications and investment strategies. These books and publications offer valuable insights and perspectives on blockchain and cryptocurrency, catering to readers with diverse interests and backgrounds. Whether you're a beginner looking to understand the basics or an experienced enthusiast seeking deeper knowledge, exploring these resources can provide a solid foundation for navigating the complex and dynamic world of blockchain and cryptocurrency.

- **"Mastering Bitcoin" by Andreas M. Antonopoulos:** "Mastering Bitcoin" is a comprehensive guide to understanding the technical intricacies of Bitcoin and blockchain technology. Written by renowned blockchain expert Andreas M. Antonopoulos, this book covers topics such as Bitcoin mining, transactions, wallets, and smart contracts, providing both beginner-friendly explanations and in-depth technical insights.

- **"Blockchain Basics:** A Non-Technical Introduction in 25 Steps" by Daniel Drescher: "Blockchain Basics" offers a non-technical introduction to blockchain technology, making it accessible to readers with varying levels of expertise. Author Daniel Drescher presents blockchain concepts through 25 simple steps, covering topics such as decentralized networks, consensus mechanisms, cryptographic principles, and blockchain applications in different industries.
- **"The Internet of Money" by Andreas M. Antonopoulos:** "The Internet of Money" is a collection of essays and talks by Andreas M. Antonopoulos, exploring the broader implications of blockchain technology and cryptocurrencies beyond Bitcoin. Antonopoulos discusses topics such as decentralized finance (DeFi), smart contracts, privacy, scalability, and the future of money in the digital age.
- **"Cryptocurrency:** How Bitcoin and Digital Money are Challenging the Global Economic Order" by Paul Vigna and Michael J. Casey: "Cryptocurrency" provides an in-depth exploration of the economic, political, and social implications of Bitcoin and other cryptocurrencies. Authors Paul Vigna and Michael J. Casey examine the history of money, the rise of cryptocurrencies, the evolution of blockchain technology, and the potential impact of digital currencies on the global financial system.
- **"The Age of Cryptocurrency:** How Bitcoin and Digital Money are Challenging the Global Economic Order" by Paul Vigna and Michael J. Casey: "The Age of Cryptocurrency" offers a comprehensive overview of Bitcoin and the broader cryptocurrency ecosystem, tracing their origins, development, and adoption. Vigna and Casey explore topics such as blockchain technology, cryptocurrency exchanges, regulatory challenges, and the potential transformative effects of digital currencies on finance and society.
- **"Blockchain Revolution:** How the Technology Behind Bitcoin and Other Cryptocurrencies is Changing the World" by Don Tapscott and Alex Tapscott: "Blockchain Revolution" explores the transformative potential of blockchain technology beyond cryptocurrencies. Authors Don Tapscott and Alex Tapscott discuss how blockchain can revolutionize industries such as finance, supply chain management, healthcare, and

government, leading to greater transparency, efficiency, and trust in decentralized systems.

- **"Digital Gold:** Bitcoin and the Inside Story of the Misfits and Millionaires Trying to Reinvent Money" by Nathaniel Popper: "Digital Gold" offers a compelling narrative of the early days of Bitcoin and the individuals and communities behind its creation and adoption. Author Nathaniel Popper delves into the personalities, conflicts, and events that shaped the rise of Bitcoin, providing a captivating account of the quest to reinvent money in the digital age.

# CHAPTER 13

# CONCLUSION

## 13.1 RECAPITULATION OF KEY CONCEPTS

Blockchain technology is a revolutionary concept that underpins cryptocurrencies like Bitcoin. It serves as a decentralized ledger, recording transactions across a network of computers in a secure and transparent manner. Unlike traditional centralized systems, blockchain enables peer-to-peer transactions without the need for intermediaries, providing increased security, transparency, and efficiency.

### 13.1.1 Cryptocurrencies: A Primer

Cryptocurrencies, such as Bitcoin and Ethereum, are digital assets designed to function as mediums of exchange, stores of value, and units of account. Built on blockchain technology, cryptocurrencies utilize cryptographic techniques to secure transactions, verify ownership, and control the creation of new units. This primer introduces the concept of cryptocurrencies, explaining their characteristics, functions, and role in the broader financial landscape. It explores key terms and concepts, such as wallets, addresses, and private keys, providing a foundational understanding of how cryptocurrencies operate.

### 13.1.2 Blockchain Architecture

Blockchain architecture refers to the structure and components of a blockchain network, including nodes, blocks, transactions, and consensus mechanisms. This summary outlines the basic architecture of blockchain networks, explaining how transactions are recorded, validated, and added to the blockchain. It explores different types of blockchain architectures, such as public, private, and consortium blockchains, highlighting their respective characteristics and use cases. Understanding blockchain architecture is essential for grasping the inner workings of blockchain technology and its applications across various industries.

### 13.1.3 Cryptography in Blockchain

Cryptography plays a crucial role in ensuring the security and integrity of blockchain networks. This summary explores the use of cryptographic techniques, such as hashing, digital signatures, and encryption, to protect data, authenticate users, and secure transactions on the blockchain. It explains how cryptographic algorithms are used to generate unique identifiers for transactions, verify the authenticity of digital signatures, and prevent tampering with blockchain data. Cryptography is a fundamental component of blockchain technology, providing the foundation for trust and security in decentralized systems.

### 13.1.4 Mining and Consensus Algorithms

Mining and consensus algorithms are essential mechanisms that enable blockchain networks to achieve agreement on the validity of transactions and the ordering of blocks in the blockchain.

This summary introduces the concept of mining, explaining how miners compete to solve complex mathematical puzzles to validate transactions and secure the network. It discusses various consensus algorithms, such as proof-of-work (PoW), proof-of-stake (PoS), and delegated proof-of-stake (DPoS), highlighting their respective strengths and weaknesses. Understanding mining and consensus algorithms is critical for grasping the scalability, security, and efficiency of blockchain networks.

### 13.1.5 Popular Cryptocurrencies

There are thousands of cryptocurrencies in existence, each with its unique features, use cases, and value propositions. This summary provides an overview of some of the most popular cryptocurrencies, such as Bitcoin, Ethereum, Ripple, and Litecoin. It explores their origins, functionalities, and market capitalizations, highlighting the factors that contribute to their popularity and adoption. Understanding popular cryptocurrencies helps investors, developers, and enthusiasts navigate the dynamic and competitive landscape of the cryptocurrency market.

### 13.1.6 Blockchain Use Cases

Blockchain technology has a wide range of potential applications beyond cryptocurrencies. This summary explores various blockchain use cases across industries such as supply chain management, healthcare, real estate, and voting systems. It discusses how blockchain technology can enhance transparency, traceability, and efficiency in business processes, leading to cost savings, risk mitigation, and innovation. Examining blockchain use cases provides insights into the diverse opportunities and challenges of implementing blockchain solutions in different sectors.

### 13.1.7 Challenges and Risks

While blockchain technology offers numerous benefits, it also poses challenges and risks that must be addressed. This summary highlights some of the key challenges and risks associated with blockchain adoption, such as scalability limitations, regulatory uncertainty, cybersecurity threats, and environmental concerns. It emphasizes the importance of addressing these challenges through research, innovation, and collaboration to realize the full potential of blockchain technology while mitigating its risks and drawbacks.

### 13.1.8 Blockchain in Finance and Banking

Blockchain technology has the potential to disrupt the traditional finance and banking industry by enabling faster, cheaper, and more secure financial transactions. This summary explores how blockchain is transforming various aspects of finance and banking, including payments, remittances, trade finance, and identity management. It discusses the benefits of blockchain adoption, such as improved efficiency, transparency, and financial inclusion, as well as the challenges and regulatory considerations facing the industry. Understanding blockchain in finance and banking is essential for stakeholders to navigate the evolving landscape of digital finance and capitalize on emerging opportunities.

## 13.2 FUTURE OUTLOOK FOR BLOCKCHAIN AND CRYPTOCURRENCIES

The future outlook for blockchain and cryptocurrencies is filled with both promise and uncertainty. While blockchain technology continues to disrupt traditional industries and revolutionize business processes, cryptocurrencies face regulatory challenges, market volatility, and scalability limitations.

The future outlook for blockchain and cryptocurrencies is characterized by rapid innovation, regulatory evolution, and increasing adoption across industries. Technological advancements in scalability, interoperability, and privacy are driving the development of more robust and versatile blockchain networks, paving the way for mainstream adoption and new use cases. Regulatory developments are providing greater clarity and legitimacy for blockchain and digital assets, encouraging institutional and enterprise adoption. Meanwhile, industry innovation in sectors such as DeFi and NFTs is pushing the boundaries of what is possible with blockchain technology, unlocking new opportunities for financial innovation, digital ownership, and decentralized applications. While challenges and uncertainties remain, the overall trajectory of blockchain and cryptocurrencies points towards continued growth, innovation, and transformation in the years to come.

### 13.2.1 Technological Advancements

- **Scalability Solutions:** Scalability remains a significant challenge for blockchain networks, limiting their ability to handle large transaction volumes and support widespread adoption. However, ongoing research and development efforts are focused on improving scalability through solutions such as sharding, layer 2 protocols, and off-chain scaling techniques. As scalability solutions mature and become more widely adopted, blockchain networks may be able to support mainstream use cases, such as global payments and decentralized applications (DApps).

- **Interoperability:** Interoperability between different blockchain networks is essential for realizing the full potential of blockchain technology. Projects and protocols are emerging to enable seamless interoperability, allowing data and assets to flow freely between disparate blockchain ecosystems. Interoperability solutions facilitate cross-chain transactions, interoperable smart contracts, and seamless integration with existing systems, fostering greater collaboration and innovation in the blockchain space.
- **Privacy and Confidentiality:** Privacy and confidentiality are critical considerations for blockchain applications, particularly in industries such as finance, healthcare, and supply chain management. Advances in privacy-preserving technologies, such as zero-knowledge proofs, ring signatures, and secure multi-party computation, are enhancing the privacy features of blockchain networks. By enabling confidential transactions and data sharing, privacy-enhancing technologies are paving the way for blockchain adoption in sensitive and regulated environments.

### 13.2.2 Regulatory Developments

- **Regulatory Clarity:** Regulatory uncertainty has been a major obstacle to blockchain and cryptocurrency adoption, with governments and regulatory agencies grappling with how to classify and regulate digital assets. However, there is growing recognition of the potential benefits of blockchain technology, leading to efforts to establish clear regulatory frameworks and guidelines. Regulatory clarity can provide greater certainty for businesses and investors, encouraging innovation and investment in the blockchain space.
- **Digital Asset Regulation:** The regulation of cryptocurrencies and digital assets is a complex and evolving landscape, with different jurisdictions taking varying approaches to oversight and enforcement. Some countries have embraced cryptocurrencies as legitimate financial instruments, while others have implemented strict regulations or outright bans. The future of digital asset regulation will likely involve a balance between consumer protection, financial stability, and innovation, with regulators seeking to foster responsible innovation while mitigating risks.

### 13.2.3 Market Adoption

- **Institutional Adoption:** Institutional adoption of blockchain and cryptocurrencies is gaining momentum, with traditional financial institutions, corporations, and governments exploring blockchain-based solutions and digital asset investments. Institutional investors are increasingly viewing cryptocurrencies as a hedge against inflation and portfolio diversification, driving demand for cryptocurrency custody services, derivatives markets, and exchange-traded products (ETPs).
- **Enterprise Adoption:** Enterprises across industries are leveraging blockchain technology to streamline business processes, enhance transparency, and reduce costs. From supply chain management and logistics to identity verification and intellectual property rights management, blockchain applications are being deployed to address a wide range of business challenges. As blockchain solutions mature and demonstrate real-world value, enterprise adoption is expected to accelerate, driving further innovation and investment in the space.

### 13.2.4 Industry Innovation

- **Decentralized Finance (DeFi):** Decentralized finance (DeFi) is one of the most exciting and rapidly growing sectors in the blockchain space. DeFi platforms and protocols enable peer-to-peer lending, borrowing, trading, and asset management without the need for traditional financial intermediaries. As DeFi continues to innovate and expand, it has the potential to disrupt traditional finance, democratize access to financial services, and unlock new opportunities for financial inclusion and economic empowerment.
- **Non-Fungible Tokens (NFTs):** Non-fungible tokens (NFTs) have emerged as a novel application of blockchain technology, enabling the tokenization of unique digital assets such as artwork, collectibles, and virtual real estate. NFTs are revolutionizing the way digital content is created, owned, and traded, opening up new revenue streams for creators and enabling new forms of digital ownership and expression. As the NFT market continues to grow, it is driving innovation in the creative industries and reshaping the digital economy.

# GLOSSARY

**Blockchain:** A distributed ledger technology that records transactions across a network of computers in a secure, transparent, and immutable manner. Each transaction is cryptographically linked to previous transactions, forming a chain of blocks.

**Cryptocurrency:** A digital or virtual currency that uses cryptographic techniques to secure transactions, control the creation of new units, and verify the transfer of assets. Cryptocurrencies operate on decentralized blockchain networks and are not controlled by any central authority.

**Bitcoin:** The first and most well-known cryptocurrency, created by an anonymous person or group of people using the pseudonym Satoshi Nakamoto in 2008. Bitcoin operates on a decentralized peer-to-peer network and is used for peer-to-peer transactions and store of value.

**Ethereum:** A decentralized platform that enables the creation and execution of smart contracts and decentralized applications (DApps). Ethereum introduced the concept of programmable blockchain, allowing developers to build and deploy applications on its blockchain.

**Smart Contract:** Self-executing contracts with the terms of the agreement directly written into code. Smart contracts automatically execute and enforce the terms of the agreement when predefined conditions are met, without the need for intermediaries.

**Decentralized Finance (DeFi):** A financial ecosystem built on blockchain technology that aims to democratize access to financial services, such as lending, borrowing, trading, and asset management, without the need for traditional financial intermediaries.

**Token:** A digital representation of an asset or utility on a blockchain. Tokens can represent cryptocurrencies, digital assets, rights, or ownership in a decentralized network. Examples include ERC-20 tokens on the Ethereum blockchain and non-fungible tokens (NFTs).

**Consensus Mechanism:** A protocol used to achieve agreement on the validity of transactions and the ordering of blocks in a blockchain network. Common consensus mechanisms include proof-of-work (PoW), proof-of-stake (PoS), delegated proof-of-stake (DPoS), and proof-of-authority (PoA).

**Mining:** The process of validating transactions and adding them to the blockchain through cryptographic calculations. Miners compete to solve complex mathematical puzzles, with the first miner to solve the puzzle receiving a reward in the form of newly created cryptocurrency and transaction fees.

**Wallet:** Software or hardware that stores cryptographic keys used to access and manage cryptocurrencies. Wallets can be hot (online) or cold (offline) and may support multiple cryptocurrencies.

**Fork:** A split or divergence in the blockchain's protocol, resulting in two separate versions of the blockchain. Forks can be classified as soft forks (backward-compatible) or hard forks (not backward-compatible), depending on whether old nodes can still validate new transactions.

**Node:** A computer connected to a blockchain network that maintains a copy of the blockchain and participates in transaction validation and consensus. Nodes can be full nodes (stores a complete copy of the blockchain) or light nodes (syncs with the network without storing the entire blockchain).

**Immutable:** In the context of blockchain, immutability refers to the inability to alter or delete past transactions recorded on the blockchain. Once a transaction is added to the blockchain, it becomes immutable and tamper-resistant.

**Cryptography:** The practice of securing communication and information through the use of mathematical algorithms. Cryptography is a fundamental component of blockchain technology, providing security, privacy, and authentication mechanisms.

**Hash Function:** A cryptographic algorithm that generates a fixed-size output (hash) from an input data of arbitrary size. Hash functions are used to create unique identifiers for blocks and transactions on the blockchain, ensuring data integrity and security.

**Private Key:** A cryptographic key that grants access to cryptocurrency holdings and allows users to sign transactions and prove ownership of digital assets. Private keys must be kept secure and confidential to prevent unauthorized access to funds.

**Public Key:** A cryptographic key that is derived from a private key and used to receive cryptocurrency transactions. Public keys are mathematically linked to private keys and can be shared publicly without compromising security.

**ICO (Initial Coin Offering):** A fundraising method used by cryptocurrency projects to raise capital by selling digital tokens to investors in exchange for cryptocurrencies or fiat currency. ICOs are similar to IPOs (Initial Public Offerings) but are conducted in the cryptocurrency market.

**DApp (Decentralized Application):** An application that runs on a decentralized blockchain network and is not controlled by any single entity. DApps are designed to be transparent, censorship-resistant, and autonomous, leveraging blockchain technology for trustless transactions and data integrity.

**Non-Fungible Token (NFT):** A unique digital asset that represents ownership or proof of authenticity of a specific item or piece of content on the blockchain. NFTs are indivisible, non-interchangeable, and cannot be replicated, making them ideal for representing digital collectibles, artwork, and digital ownership rights.

# REFERENCES


Bitcoin and Cryptocurrency Technologies: A Comprehensive Introduction by Arvind Narayanan, Joseph Bonneau, Edward Felten, Andrew Miller, and Steven Goldfeder, Princeton University Press, 2016.

Bitcoin and Cryptocurrency Technologies: Blockchain book, Cryptocurrency investing, Cryptocurrency trading, Bitcoin book (Become an Expert in Crypto by Understanding Blockchain, Bitcoin, Cryptocurrency) by Keizer Söze, CreateSpace Independent Publishing Platform, 2018.

Bitcoin and Cryptocurrency Technologies: Everything You Need to Know to Get Started with Bitcoin by Christopher Nygaard, CreateSpace Independent Publishing Platform, 2018.

Bitcoin Billionaires: A True Story of Genius, Betrayal, and Redemption by Ben Mezrich, Flatiron Books, 2019.

Bitcoin Explained Simply: An Easy Guide to the Basics That Anyone Can Understand by Mark Jeffrey, CreateSpace Independent Publishing Platform, 2013.

Bitcoin for Dummies by Prypto, Wiley, 2016.

Bitcoin: A Peer-to-Peer Electronic Cash System by Satoshi Nakamoto, CreateSpace Independent Publishing Platform, 2008.

Bitcoin: The Future of Money? by Dominic Frisby, Unbound, 2014.

Bitcoin: The Ultimate Guide from Beginner to Expert: Bitcoin and Cryptocurrency Technologies, Mining, Investing and Trading - Bitcoin Book 1, Blockchain, Wallet, Business by Mark Smith, CreateSpace Independent Publishing Platform, 2017.

Bitcoin: The Ultimate Guide to the World of Bitcoin, Bitcoin Mining, Bitcoin Investing, Blockchain Technology, Cryptocurrency by Ikuya Takashima, CreateSpace Independent Publishing Platform, 2017.

Blockchain Basics: A Non-Technical Introduction in 25 Steps by Daniel Drescher, Apress, 2017.

Blockchain Basics: A Primer on Cryptocurrency and Blockchain Technology by Lee Sebastian, Independently published, 2018.

Blockchain For Dummies (For Dummies (Computer/Tech)) by Tiana Laurence, For Dummies, 2017.

Blockchain For Dummies by Tiana Laurence, Wiley, 2017.

Blockchain for Everyone: How I Learned the Secrets of the New Millionaire Class (And You Can, Too) by Sir John Hargrave, Gallery Books, 2019.

Blockchain Revolution: How the Technology Behind Bitcoin and Other Cryptocurrencies is Changing the World by Don Tapscott and Alex Tapscott, Portfolio, 2016.

Blockchain Revolution: How the Technology Behind Bitcoin Is Changing Money, Business, and the World by Don Tapscott and Alex Tapscott, Portfolio, 2016.

Blockchain Revolution: Understanding the Future of Business by Alex Tapscott and Don Tapscott, Portfolio, 2018.

Blockchain: A Practical Guide to Developing Business, Law, and Technology Solutions by Joseph J. Bambara and Paul R. Allen, McGraw-Hill Education, 2018.

Blockchain: Blueprint for a New Economy by Melanie Swan, O'Reilly Media, 2015.

Blockchain: The Beginners Guide to Understanding the Technology Behind Bitcoin & Cryptocurrency (The Future of Money) by Artemis Caro, CreateSpace Independent Publishing Platform, 2016.

Blockchain: The Insights You Need from Harvard Business Review by Harvard Business Review, Harvard Business Review Press, 2019.

Blockchain: The Ultimate Guide To Mastering Bitcoin, Ethereum & Other Cryptocurrencies. (Smart Contracts, Dapps, Investing, Mining, Litecoin, Ripple, Putincoin etc.) by Mark Gates, CreateSpace Independent Publishing Platform, 2018.

Blockchain: The Ultimate Guide to Understanding the Hidden Economy by Oscar Flynt, CreateSpace Independent Publishing Platform, 2018.

Blockchain: Transforming Your Business and Our World by Mark Van Rijmenam, CreateSpace Independent Publishing Platform, 2019.

Blockchain: Ultimate guide to understanding blockchain, bitcoin, cryptocurrencies, smart contracts and the future of money by Mark Gates, CreateSpace Independent Publishing Platform, 2018.

Cryptoassets: The Innovative Investor's Guide to Bitcoin and Beyond by Chris Burniske and Jack Tatar, McGraw-Hill Education, 2017.

Cryptocurrency Investing Bible: The Ultimate Guide About Blockchain, Mining, Trading, ICO, Ethereum Platform, Exchanges, Top Cryptocurrencies for

Investing and Perfect Strategies to Make Money by Alan T. Norman, CreateSpace Independent Publishing Platform, 2017.

Cryptocurrency: How Bitcoin and Digital Money are Challenging the Global Economic Order by Paul Vigna and Michael J. Casey, Picador, 2016.

Cryptocurrency: How Bitcoin and Digital Money are Challenging the Global Economic Order by Paul Vigna and Michael J. Casey, St. Martin's Press, 2016.

Digital Gold: Bitcoin and the Inside Story of the Misfits and Millionaires Trying to Reinvent Money by Nathaniel Popper, Harper, 2015.

Mastering Bitcoin: Unlocking Digital Cryptocurrencies by Andreas M. Antonopoulos, O'Reilly Media, 2014.

The Age of Cryptocurrency: How Bitcoin and the Blockchain Are Challenging the Global Economic Order by Paul Vigna and Michael J. Casey, St. Martin's Press, 2016.

The Basics of Bitcoins and Blockchains by Antony Lewis, O'Reilly Media, 2018.

The Bitcoin Guidebook: How to Obtain, Invest, and Spend the World's First Decentralized Cryptocurrency by Ian DeMartino, Skyhorse Publishing, 2016.

The Bitcoin Standard: The Decentralized Alternative to Central Banking by Saifedean Ammous, Wiley, 2018.

The Business Blockchain: Promise, Practice, and Application of the Next Internet Technology by William Mougayar, Wiley, 2016.

The Internet of Money: A Collection of Talks by Andreas M. Antonopoulos by Andreas M. Antonopoulos, Merkle Bloom LLC, 2016.

# INDEX

www.ingramcontent.com/pod-product-compliance
Lightning Source LLC
LaVergne TN
LVHW062116200926
848484LV00007B/1686